FALLING THROUGH THE SAFETY NET

Falling through the Safety Net

Insurance Status and Access to Health Care

JOEL S. WEISSMAN, PH.D.

Department of Health Care Policy, Harvard Medical School; and
Department of Medicine, Brigham and Women's Hospital
Boston, Massachusetts

AND

ARNOLD M. EPSTEIN, M.D., M.A.

Department of Medicine, Brigham and Women's Hospital; Department
of Health Care Policy, Harvard Medical School; and Department of
Health Policy and Management, Harvard School of Public Health
Boston, Massachusetts

THE JOHNS HOPKINS UNIVERSITY PRESS

Baltimore and London

© 1994 The Johns Hopkins University Press
All rights reserved
Printed in the United States of America on acid-free paper

The Johns Hopkins University Press
2715 North Charles Street
Baltimore, Maryland 21218-4319
The Johns Hopkins Press Ltd., London

Library of Congress Cataloging-in-Publication Data

Weissman, Joel S.
    Falling through the safety net : insurance status and access to
health care / Joel S. Weissman and Arnold M. Epstein,
        p.   cm.
    Includes bibliographical references and index.
    ISBN 0-8018-4865-2. – ISBN 0-8018-4917-9 (pbk.)
    1. Insurance, Health–United States.   2. Medical care–United
States.   3. Health care reform–United States.   I. Epstein, Arnold
M.   II. Title.
HD7102.U4W44   1994
368.3'82'00973–dc20   94-9049
                                                                       CIP

A catalog record for this book is available from the British Library.

To our families,

who withstood many late hours and days and nights without us,

and to the millions of people without health insurance,

who are waiting for health care reform.

CONTENTS

Foreword, by Hillary Rodham Clinton   ix

Preface   xi

List of Abbreviations and Statistical Terms   xiii

1. Introduction: A Framework for Thinking about Insurance Status and Access to Care   1

2. Who Are the Uninsured and How Did They Get That Way?   17

3. Health Status   49

4. Intermediate Process Indicators   55

5. The Quantity and Quality of Care   63

6. Outcomes of Care   99

7. Special Cases: Cost-Sharing, Changes in or Loss of Insurance, and Medicaid Managed Care   113

8. Insurance, Access, and Health Care Reform: Summary and Policy Implications   133

Appendix A. National Surveys and Major Studies on Access Included in This Book   155

Appendix B. Methods Used in Chapters 3–7   159

Notes   161

References   165

Index   185

FOREWORD

As I have traveled across our country to participate in our great national debate about health care, I have discovered much that is good about American medicine. I have seen committed doctors and nurses in inner-city emergency rooms battling to save lives hour after hour, day after day, sometimes under the worst of circumstances. I have seen talented young physicians donate their services to people in rural areas who cannot afford to pay for them. I have seen technological wonders used to work magic for those who are most ill, and I have seen medical scientists who are on the cutting edge of tomorrow's cures.

But in speaking to and reading letters from people all across America—farm families, small business owners, older Americans, and medical professionals—I hear the same message loud and clear: our health system is broken and it needs to be fixed. Today millions of hardworking people live on the edge. For those who lose their jobs, for those who change jobs, for those who get sick, loss of coverage can too often be a frightening reality.

Some in Washington have argued that there is no health care crisis. But the facts say otherwise. In this book, Joel Weissman and Arnold Epstein describe how people get and lose health insurance, and how they get, or fail to get, medical care for their illnesses. Their overwhelming conclusion: when it comes to health care, what you get depends on how you pay.

Persons without insurance are less likely to see the doctor than those with insurance. When they do seek care, it is more likely to be in a clinic or emergency ward. They are likely to be kept waiting for longer periods of time and do not always receive important preventive services. People who lack insurance delay care and come to the hospital more severely ill. They are hospitalized more frequently for conditions that could have been treated on an outpatient basis. Perhaps most disturbing, even after they are admitted to the hospital for a serious medical condition, their care is different; the use of the full range of hospital services is limited and sometimes the quality of their care is compromised.

These differences in medical care are not merely cosmetic; they have a measurable impact on people's health, longevity, and dignity—not to mention their pocketbooks. Drs. Weissman and Epstein point out, for example, that uninsured hospital patients have higher mortality, pregnant uninsured women have worse birth outcomes, and uninsured women with breast cancer have shorter life expectancies. Taken together, these findings put to rest the old myth that those without insurance somehow manage to receive all the care they truly need.

This book should provoke researchers and policy makers to think in a broad context about ways we can make health care more accessible and seek ways we can eliminate the problem of people being uninsured. This book puts into numbers and figures many of the things I have learned during the past year talking to hundreds of people across the country.

President Clinton has made clear his vision of the principles that underlie reform. The most important one is his insistence that there be guaranteed health insurance coverage for all Americans that can never be taken away. This book provides timely evidence that we must not delay.

Hillary Rodham Clinton

PREFACE

This book was inspired by our continued fascination with a uniquely American problem that just won't go away—the large numbers of persons without health insurance and the difficulties they have in obtaining the health care they need. Because this issue has received such widespread attention in recent years among the general public as well as the academic and policy worlds, we have attempted to address both of these communities. One might therefore think of the book as having two parts. One part is oriented toward readers comfortable with and interested in health services research, although anyone with a basic knowledge of statistics will be able to understand the content. The seed work for this part evolved from a report we prepared for the U.S. Office of Technology Assessment in 1992. We reviewed the relevant academic and governmental literature and summarized what it had to say about how access to health care was related to people's insurance status. The report was part of a larger effort on the part of OTA to gather a comprehensive set of background materials and policy options for the impending debate over health care reform. The original review was expanded, updated, and reorganized for this book, and comprises the bulk of Chapters 3 through 7.

The remaining chapters in this volume (1, 2, and 8) had a different origin, and serve different purposes. Their substance was derived largely from a series of lectures we gave over the years at the Harvard Medical School and the Harvard School of Public Health as part of special programs designed to give medical students and post-doctoral fellows insights into important questions of national health policy. Each chapter is a building block that provides information fundamental to understanding the "uninsured problem"; as such, this part is less technical and is oriented toward a more general readership or for introductory courses in health policy.

Chapter 1 begins by presenting some startling international statistics that provide part of the impetus for health care reform, and then describes a conceptual model for thinking about access. The model can be applied to any situation where someone wishes to compare access gaps among groups of persons, not just insured and uninsured. It may be particularly helpful for thinking critically about what the literature can and cannot say about these issues.

Readers seeking to become knowledgeable about health insurance and health system reform without getting steeped in theoretical models and research might wish to limit their attention to Chapters 2 and 8. Chapter 2 begins with a solid background on health insurance, its history and structure, and ends with a description of the uninsured population, focusing on characteristics that have relevance to the design of health reform and benefits. Chapter 8, the final chapter, is a primer on health reform as it affects the uninsured and underinsured. It summarizes the key conclusions from the literature, places our current national dialogue in historical perspective, and outlines major alternatives that health reform could take. It closes with a series of questions that zero in on the impact of health care reform on access to care, questions that should be important for all Americans to consider.

To complete this work required the input and assistance of many individuals, and we are indebted to those who helped transform our efforts into a finished product. We specifically acknowledge the leadership and guidance of Denise Dougherty, the project officer for the OTA report. Her expert advice guided us in the formulation of the ideas, the structure of the presentation, and the sources of the content. In addition to the very helpful anonymous reviewers who critiqued the OTA report, we received insightful comments that improved the clarity, crispness, and above all, relevance of the information from Lu Ann Aday, Bob Brook, Paula Diehr, Richard Frank, William Glaser, Harold Luft, James Hunt, and Nicole Lurie.

Any commitment of this magnitude always requires direction and backing from other sources. In our case, we wish to recognize a number of people who served as role models, mentors, and sources of institutional support for us, including Eugene Braunwald, Tony Komaroff, Howard Frazier, Barbara McNeil, and William Riker. Joe Newhouse read portions of selected chapters from later versions and offered valuable comments. Jaylyn Olivo helped us eliminate errors and avoid potential confusion with her careful copy editing. Once the manuscript was handed over to the Johns Hopkins University Press, the publishers and editors expedited the process so that the book could be released in a timely way. Finally, the support and encouragement we received from our life mates, Wendy Landman and Patricia O'Malley, got us through the days and nights; and of course we could not escape without mentioning our other major products, Gideon and Aaron Weissman, and Katie, Rebecca, and Elicia Epstein.

LIST OF ABBREVIATIONS AND STATISTICAL TERMS

ABBREVIATIONS

AALL, American Association for Labor Legislation
AFDC, Aid to Families with Dependent Children
AHCs, Avoidable Hospital Conditions
AHCCCS, Arizona Health Care Cost-Containment System
AHCPR, Agency for Health Care Policy and Research
CHAMPVA, Civilian Health and Medical Programs of the VA
CHAMPUS, Civilian Health and Medical Programs of the Uniformed Services
CHIP, Comprehensive Health Insurance Plan
COBRA, Consolidated Omnibus Budget Reconciliation Act
CPS, Current Population Survey
DEFRA, Deficit Reduction Act
DHEW, Department of Health, Education, and Welfare
DRG, Diagnosis-related group
EBRI, Employee Benefit Research Institute
EPSDT, Early and Periodic Screening, Diagnosis, and Treatment
ESRD, End-Stage Renal Disease
FHIP, Family Health Insurance Plan
FFS, Fee-for-Service
GAO, Government Accounting Office
HIE, Health Insurance Experiment
HIOs, Health Insuring Organizations
HMOs, Health Maintenance Organizations
HSA, Health Security Act
IPAs, Independent Practice Associations
MIA, Medically Indigent Adult
MOS-SF, Medical Outcomes Study Short Form
NCHS, National Center for Health Statistics
NCHSR, National Center for Health Services Research
NHI, National Health Insurance
NHIS, National Health Interview Survey
NHS, National Health Service
NMCES, National Medical Care Expenditure Survey
NMCUES, National Medical Care Utilization Expenditure Survey
NMES, National Medical Expenditure Survey
OBRA, Omnibus Budget Reconciliation Act

RWJF, Robert Wood Johnson Foundation
SIPP, Survey of Income and Program Participation
SSI, Supplemental Security Income
VA, Veterans Administration
VBACs, Vaginal Births after Cesarean
WIC, Women and Infant Children

STATISTICAL TERMS

CI   Confidence Interval—This is one way of thinking about statistical significance (see "p-value"). A 95% confidence interval says that there is a 95% chance that the true result is between the upper and lower limits of the confidence interval.

OR   Odds Ratio: See RR—Relative Risk

p   The "p-value"—The idea of a p-value or of statistical significance refers to the probability that the result or difference found by the researchers could have been due to chance. Thus, if a difference between insured and uninsured persons has p<.05 as the p-value, this says that the probability that the difference was due purely to chance was less than 5%, or one in twenty. Usually something is considered to be "statistically significant" with a p-value less than .05, but there is no concrete rule.

RR   Relative Risk—The Relative Risk and the Odds Ratio are two terms that are used to describe differences in rates of usage between two groups. In this book, the RR is simply the rate at which services (e.g., admissions to hospitals) are used in one group divided by the rate at which the same services are used in a second group. If the RR is equal to one, then there is no difference between the two groups; otherwise, one group has a higher rate than the other. The odds ratio is a good approximation of the relative risk when the event in question is rare.

FALLING THROUGH THE SAFETY NET

1

INTRODUCTION: A FRAMEWORK FOR THINKING ABOUT INSURANCE STATUS AND ACCESS TO CARE

The health system of the United States is broken, or at the very least, is not performing up to expectations. In a recent poll, more than 80 percent of Americans said that the U.S. health care system needed either "fundamental changes" or "to be completely rebuilt" (Kohut, Toth and Bowman, 1993). Among Western nations, we rank first in nearly all measures of health spending and increases in health spending, including total health expenditures, per capita health spending, and excess health inflation (a measure of the rate of growth of medical prices relative to overall prices) (Schieber, Poullier, and Greenwald, 1993) (Table 1-1). We are apparently not getting a good return on our spending. We have fewer contacts with medical providers than do other comparable countries. Our poor performance on indicators of health status is especially troubling. We rank in the bottom half of twenty-four countries in life expectancy at birth, and only three countries (Turkey, Portugal, and Greece) have higher infant mortality rates.

The United States is the only fully industrialized Western nation that does not assure all citizens a basic level of health care.[1] Instead, this country has attempted to weave a welfare safety net—a collection of programs and facilities loosely strung together with the purpose of caring for those most in need. There is little question that the safety net has had an impact. The use of health services by poor and sick people has increased substantially since the advent of Medicaid, community health centers, the National Health Service Corps, and other programs.

Despite this progress, evidence of access problems has accumulated over several decades. Since the 1960s, numerous national surveys of health care utilization and expenditure have documented gaps in the

Table 1-1. The Rank of the United States among Twenty-four OECD Countries on Selected Indicators of Health Expenditure, Utilization, and Outcome

Measure	Rank
EXPENDITURE	
Total health expenditures as a percentage of GDP, 1991	1
Per capita health spending in U.S. dollars, 1985–1991	1
Excess health care inflation (ranking out of 5 selected countries), 1985–1991	1
UTILIZATION	
Beds per 1,000 population, 1990	21
Admission rate (% population), 1989	18
Average length of stay (days), 1990	20
Physicians per 1,000, 1990	14
Physician contacts per capita, 1990	15
OUTCOME	
Infant mortality (deaths per 1,000 live births), 1990	4[a]
Life expectancy at birth, males (years), 1990	18
Life expectancy at birth, females (years), 1990	15

Source: Data from Schieber, Poullier, and Greenwald, 1993.
OECD = Organization for Economic Cooperation and Development; GDP = Gross domestic product.
[a] The low number indicates poor health status outcome.

amount, location, and type of health care consumed. From these data we know that barriers to care persist among disadvantaged groups including African Americans and other minorities, poor people, and those who live in rural areas (Rowland and Lyons, 1989).

During the last decade, interest in the plight of the uninsured has exploded, in part due to the rapid increase in the number of persons without health insurance. Between 1979 and 1986 the number of uninsured persons grew from approximately 28.4 million (14.6 percent of the U.S. population below age sixty-five) to 36.8 million (17.5 percent of the population below sixty-five) (Congressional Research Service, 1988a).[2] The impact on access by those who have inadequate insurance or who are covered by Medicaid has also come to the fore of state and national debates, due in large part to concerns over expenses for the Medicaid program and their impact on the budget process. Individual states have responded by restricting eligibility for Medicaid or by experimenting with alternative systems of delivering health care (Johns and Adler, 1989). Many Americans now perceive the health care system to be in crisis with costs that are out of control. It is not surprising that calls for major reforms, including some form of universal health insurance, now emanate from broad coalitions of consumer groups, major corporations, unions, professional organizations, and former U.S. presidents (Boston *Globe,* November 17, 1991).

The primary purpose of this book is to review and assess what is known about the link between insurance status and access to health care, and to put this knowledge in a policy context. We begin in this chapter by presenting a theoretical framework that defines access, and we suggest ways to measure its association with insurance status. The framework is based on economic and organizational theory. In essence, several actors or decision makers maximize their own goals within social constraints (such as resource limitations). As a result of this activity, variations in the utilization of health care may occur that are in some instances unrelated to medical need. Following the description of the framework, we introduce the key comparison groups: the uninsured, Medicaid beneficiaries, and the privately insured under age 65. We also describe some of the inevitable limitations in the research literature and the specific methodology used in this review.

In Chapter 2 we describe the types of insurance available and the factors that account for transitions. We also profile the uninsured population. In Chapters 3–6 we examine the evidence on differences in patients' health status, utilization of health care, and health outcome by payment status. Each chapter covers the key comparison groups. An additional chapter covers these same topics for selected special cases, including cost-sharing, loss of insurance, and managed care. In the final chapter, we summarize the history of legislative attempts to develop national health insurance. We also present a taxonomy of different approaches to bring about health reform and discuss criteria by which one might judge the access components of any health plan.

A CONCEPTUAL FRAMEWORK FOR THE STUDY OF HEALTH INSURANCE AND ACCESS

Assuring access, cost control, and quality—the triumvirate of health care goals—drives the thinking of health care system architects. The road through major health policy developments of the past thirty years is littered with attempts at achieving these goals via financial incentives, regulatory mandates, organizational change, or all three. While no country relies on just one strategy, the use of economics is certainly at the fore.[3] It makes sense to talk about economic theory in the study of insurance, which is, after all, a method of spreading financial risk. The study of access, however, involves social forces that may best be gauged by using tools from a number of theoretical disciplines.

ECONOMIC MODELS AND THEIR LIMITATIONS

Most economists view the demand for health care as a downward-sloping line, implying that as the price falls, the demand for services rises.

A considerable debate exists over the steepness of the slope and its shape, and how the line might change in different situations. For example, the line that describes the demand for preventive care, defined as services offered to healthy people with no apparent medical problem, may be fairly flat. Thus even small out-of-pocket costs are likely to deter use. However, most agree that someone with a severely broken leg would pay almost anything for necessary treatment, and thus the demand line would be nearly vertical.

Health insurance reduces the price of care to individuals at the time of demand and thus allows them to move along the demand curve. Total welfare is enhanced to the extent that consumers benefit by trading a fixed premium (in advance) for uncertain and potentially devastating expenditures on huge medical bills. In addition, society may benefit if, for example, the gain due to increased worker productivity outweighs the cost of care, or if illness is prevented when people receive vaccinations or treatment for communicable diseases that they would not have procured without insurance.

Insurance companies worry when insurance encourages persons to purchase more than they would have without insurance. *Moral hazard* is a term from the world of property and casualty insurance that describes this phenomenon. It refers to the tendency of people to consume more of an insured good than they would have if they had to pay the full cost (Newhouse, 1978). Of course, most people do not arrange to have serious automobile accidents or burn down their houses just because they are insured (although they may be less likely to install antitheft devices or sprinkler systems). The assumption is that health care is different from other insured goods—that persons require some health care on a continuing basis for minor illnesses or preventive services—not just when there has been a major traumatic event beyond their control. Insurers and policy-makers worry particularly about the use of health services with uncertain benefit or, worse yet, services that may be unnecessary or even deleterious.

The economic model of consumer demand goes only part way in explaining the utilization of health care. The departures of health care from conventional competitive models have been described elsewhere (see, for example, Pauly, 1978; or, for a more recent handling, Aaron, 1991), so we will review only a few of the important limitations here. One problem for analysts is that the demand for health care is complicated by the supply. For example, physicians who are the suppliers of medical care may also have an unusual ability to influence the demand. Since much of medical care is technical in nature, and since consumption is often uncertain or infrequent, there is a severe imbalance of information, most of it residing with the provider of care. The idea that a frail, sick patient can rationally debate the costs and benefits of his or her care with a physician does not seem to hold much weight (Reinhardt, 1989). While this may be an extreme example, most agree that physicians may induce demand (Rice and Labelle, 1989), although there has been debate (Feldman and Sloan, 1988).

Information problems do not stop with consumers; providers face them, too. All physicians face uncertainty over the benefits and adverse effects of certain medical procedures. The existence of uncertainty undoubtedly leads to large variations in practice patterns.

Organizational and structural factors also are helpful in understanding patterns of care-giving, when it is difficult to determine whose utility is being maximized or even how to define utility. For example, nonprofit hospitals may lack the overriding profit incentive or a single entrepreneurial decision maker so critical to the thinking of many economists. Nevertheless, the interests of physicians, administrators, and even uninsured patients themselves (who wish to reduce out-of-pocket expenses) might converge to limit the services that are consumed (Weissman, 1987). On the other hand, many physicians and hospitals provide free or subsidized care to uninsured patients even though it is not in their financial interest to do so. They may be moved by a belief in charity or a perception that subsidized care will diminish collection costs, or they may simply be trying to build up their practice volume in the face of increasing competition from a growing supply of physicians (Blumenthal and Rizzo, 1991).

Finally, economic models fail to consider adequately the influence of nonfinancial barriers to access. Race, ethnicity, social class, religion, geographic isolation, culture, education, professional codes of conduct, and psychosocial and organizational factors have all been linked to health and health care (see, generally, Mechanic, 1979; Bunker, Gomby, and Kehrer, 1989). Studies in Canada (Siemetiyacki, 1980; Roos, 1982), England (McKinlay, 1972; LeGrand, 1978; DHHS [The Black Report], 1980; Blane, 1985), and the United States (Dutton, 1978) have demonstrated that even after economic barriers are removed, inequities in the utilization of health care persist among socioeconomic classes. For example, patients with less education may not perceive the need for preventive or primary care or may not understand and be able to follow through on doctors' orders (Bullough, 1972). Differences in utilization by race persist even after control for insurance status and income (see, especially, Wenneker, Weissman, and Epstein, 1990; other studies of racial differences in utilization with various levels of control include: Wilson, Griffith, and Tedeschi, 1985; Held et al., 1988; Kjellstrand, 1988; Diehr et al., 1989; Ford et al., 1989; Mayer and McWhorter, 1989; Gittelsohn et al., 1991; Mort et al., 1994). Geographic location may be important, since physicians are more likely to locate in suburban locations where density and median incomes are reasonably high and professional peers are abundant. For patients in lower socioeconomic positions, the social distance between physicians and patients has been shown to affect utilization (Eisenberg, 1979).

It is clear, therefore, that economics alone cannot explain problems in access. Municipal hospitals, after all, offer free care to anyone who needs it, yet their presence alone does not assure universal access. Multiple perspectives are valuable in identifying barriers to care. Lack of insurance is only one of many. In the proposed framework that follows, we identify a number of factors that ought to be considered in concert with the financial ones, as well as a hierarchy of indicators of access.

DEFINING AND MEASURING ACCESS

Access cannot be defined absolutely. There is no set of specified services or characteristics, and no single index can summarize completely the overall access to health care for a particular group. Andersen et al. 1983 defined access as "those dimensions which describe potential and actual entry of a given population to the health care delivery system." They further defined "equity of access" as "services [that] are distributed on the basis of people's need for them. Inequity exists when one's race, income . . . or insurance coverage . . . are important predictors of realized access."

Based on more than a decade of work, Aday, Andersen, and others developed a conceptual approach to the study of access (Aday and Andersen, 1975; Andersen et al., 1983, 1987). In general, the authors claimed that a number of variables must be measured to assess access, and that these can generally be divided into two groups. One group consists of those characteristics that influence the utilization and outcomes of health care. This group is usually broken down into three categories of variables: predisposing (the "propensity" to seek or need care), enabling (individual resources such as income or insurance that provide the means to using the system), and illness (or need). The other group consists of realized indicators of access and includes those measures that reflect actual utilization (e.g., physician visits) or outcomes of care (confined by Andersen et al. to patient satisfaction). Some of the early work by these researchers attempted to relate the rates of service use directly to need by constructing indexes that looked at utilization with respect to the level of sickness or disability in the population (e.g., a use–disability ratio).

Much of the work in developing the analytic framework took place before the modern movement toward measuring the quality, appropriateness, and outcomes of care. We prefer a definition of access that reflects the shift toward outcomes, and which takes us beyond measuring mere volume of services. *Access is the attainment of timely, sufficient, and appropriate health care of adequate quality such that health outcomes are maximized.*[4] Table 1-2 presents a framework that builds on this foundation.

The top section of Table 1-2 lists characteristics of the health system. We separate these aspects from others because they are malleable by governmental intervention and are therefore directly affected by policies of a health care system. Insurance coverage falls into this category, as do physician and bed supply, reimbursement methods such as capitation or fee-for-service, and management techniques such as preadmission certification and concurrent review. Policy-makers, advocates, and some researchers naturally train their attention on these policy variables. There is a certain amount of overlap between *policy* characteristics as they are used in this book and previous authors' use of the term *enabling* characteristics, but the latter term is too broad. The "enabling" category absorbs patient characteristics that are subject to much more basic social change (e.g., affordability, racism), and as such is not as helpful in getting us to focus on the changes that can be made within the context of medical care.[5]

Gaining a fundamental sense of access *problems* will naturally shape health policies. The bottom two-thirds of Table 1-2 are therefore concerned with measurement issues. The patient variables in the middle of the table include those "predisposing" and "need" characteristics that might influence the demand for utilization and outcomes. Good studies usually control for one or more of these variables even though the main characteristic of interest may shift from insurance coverage to, say, gender or race. Patient attributes like income, education, and, of course, race and gender are distinct from the health policy variables in the top third because they are unlikely to be affected by the health care system, yet population groups *defined* by these characteristics may be particularly vulnerable to health system policies.[6] A person's health status is obviously linked to the need for services, and we list several options for its measurement. It is worth mentioning, however, that patients may perceive a health problem but not necessarily believe that medical care is needed or could provide effective treatment. Thus, health status can never be perfectly correlated with use.

The bottom third of Table 1-2 lists indicators for measuring access and is itself divided into thirds. Intermediate process indicators are those attributes of the process of care that may be desirable in terms of how patients interact with the system, yet might not be considered definitive indicators of access. These variables include having a regular provider, the convenience of use, and the location of care. Indicators of ultimate access to care include the process (quantity, quality) and outcomes of health care. *Process* in this sense encompasses what providers do to or for patients, while *outcomes* refers to the end result in terms of physical, mental, or emotional health status. Health care outcomes other than satisfaction were not included in early analytic frameworks of other authors. Health care outcomes are measures of health status that, if different among groups, may indicate differences

Table 1-2. An Analytic Model for Assessing Access to Care

HEALTH SYSTEM CHARACTERISTICS
Insurance coverage
Supply/availability of medical services
Organizational characteristics[a]

PATIENT (CONTROL) VARIABLES
Predisposing
  Age
  Gender
  Education
  Occupation
  Race
  Ethnicity
  Income
  Residency (urban/rural)
  Health behaviors
Need
  Perceived health
  Restricted activity
  Chronic conditions
  Other health status measures

ACCESS INDICATORS
Intermediate Indicators
  Regular source of care
  Location of care
  Convenience/acceptability
  Use of Public Facilities
Process Indicators (Quantity and Quality of Utilization)
  Expenditures
  Number and intensity of visits, procedures, drugs, etc.
  Appropriateness/sufficiency (e.g., timeliness, preventive care, care for serious
    problems)
  Technical quality
  Negligent adverse events
  Patient-doctor communication
Outcome Indicators
  Satisfaction
  Mortality/health status
  Preventable disease conditions

Source: Weissman and Epstein, 1993, p. 245. © 1993 by Annual Reviews, Inc.

[a] Organizational characteristics include ownership of facilities, methods of payment (e.g., capitation versus fee for service), and management techniques used by organizations, such as preadmission certification and concurrent review.

in access to care or its quality even after initial access is achieved. The quantity and quality of care patients receive (i.e., process) as well as the outcomes are the dependent variables in research on access.

Three points follow from this framework:

1. The purpose of the framework is to measure access problems within the context of health system policies, not other social policies (such as housing or income support), even though the latter may possess equal or greater potential for health enhancement than changes to the health care system. Moreover, health system characteristics are teased out because they are often mutable through changes in health policy.
2. Health status appears twice in the model: first as a measure of "need," and again as an outcome indicator.
3. Both process and outcome may be necessary to characterize access fully.

It is important to appreciate the interdependence of elements in this model. For example, measuring utilization and outcomes without controlling for confounding variables like age or prior health status may give biased or even untrue results. In this book we summarize unadjusted (uncontrolled) analyses as well as ones that control for confounding variables, although we attempt to keep the distinction clear. The relatively few multivariate studies usually confirm the findings of numerous unadjusted studies that are often merely reports of survey data.

Much of the past research on access considers variations in the use of medical services or other related processes of care to be prima facie evidence of a problem. Of course, there are methodologic difficulties with this assumption, since inequities may reflect overuse as well as underuse, and the impact on health of differential use of certain services may be minimal. Nevertheless, few would argue with the assertion that differences in process are *potentially* evidence of problems in access.

Finally, outcomes are important. Many use the term *access* to refer to the process of care; however, if differences in outcomes persist despite controls for other patient variables, outcome measures may serve as access "indicators" much as process measures do. One must be particularly cautious in interpreting outcome data because many factors other than access to health services can have an important impact, and because the link between patient characteristics and outcomes is not well understood. As information on the use of services and other processes of care is relatively easy to collect, a substantial literature is available. Less research is available on the existence of access problems as assessed through health care outcomes.

KEY COMPARISONS

The study of inequalities in health care naturally concerns numerous disadvantaged groups, including racial and ethnic minorities, the elderly, and the poor. We focus our attention on persons who would most likely be affected by systemwide insurance reform, specifically, those persons who are uninsured under age 65, are beneficiaries of Medicaid, or are privately insured. Persons over age 65 are almost universally insured by Medicare, and their vastly different health status on average makes it difficult to compare them to younger persons. In addition to these key comparisons, three special cases are considered where the influence of payment may be associated with access: (1) cost-sharing and underinsurance, (2) loss of or changes in insurance, and (3) prepaid managed care.

PATIENTS WITH MEDICAID, WITH PRIVATE INSURANCE COVERAGE, OR WHO ARE UNINSURED

To understand the potential for access barriers and the size of the problem, it is necessary to understand the make-up of the comparison groups. According to a recent analysis of the Current Population Survey (CPS) (see Appendix A), about 160 million Americans under age 65 had some private insurance in 1989, 24 million had coverage by Medicaid, and 36 million were uninsured (Foley, 1993). Slightly less than one-third of the uninsured are poor, according to federal poverty status, but more than three-quarters are poor or near-poor (Congressional Research Service, 1988a, p. 102; Needleman et al., 1990).[7] Persons who live in nonmetropolitan areas are more likely to be uninsured and are less likely to be covered by Medicaid than are those living in metropolitan areas (Wilensky and Berk, 1982).[8] A detailed description of the size, location, and sociodemographic characteristics of the uninsured population is provided in Chapter 2.

The initiation of Medicaid in 1966 (established in 1965 through Title XIX of the Social Security Act) carried with it two broadly stated goals: to increase access to medical care and to reduce the burden of out-of-pocket expenses for exceedingly poor people.[9] Eligibility for Medicaid is based on a variety of financial and demographic (categorical) factors. There is considerable variation by state in the income cut-off, in the make-up of eligible families (e.g., single parents versus married with unemployed spouse), and in whether the state covers medically needy persons. Under provisions for covering the medically needy, states may provide coverage to individuals whose income is above the state poverty cut-off if their medical expenses are so large that their income net of medical expenses qualifies them. Thus, some recipients of Medicaid may have incomes that would not be classified as "poor" or "below poverty" in national surveys. In 1986, 24 percent of

Medicaid recipients had incomes above the poverty level (Congressional Research Service, 1988b).

Most states set their income cut-off well *below* the federal poverty level.[10] As a result of this and other restrictions in categorical eligibility, many of the poor are not covered by this public program (Kasper, 1986). For example, Wilensky and Berk (1985) estimated that only 35 percent of persons with low income (less than 150 percent of poverty) were covered by Medicaid at least part of the year in 1977. Although Medicaid is the chief source of insurance for low-income children, it covered less than half of them during all or part of 1980, according to a special analysis of the National Medical Care Utilization Expenditure Survey (NMCUES) (Rosenbach, 1985). By 1986, those figures had improved: 41 percent of all persons below the poverty level were covered by Medicaid, while the figure for children was 52 percent (from the March 1987 CPS, compiled by the Congressional Research Service, 1988b).

SPECIAL CASES: COST-SHARING, LOSS OF INSURANCE, MANAGED CARE

The task of comparing access to health care by payment source would be simpler if people either did or did not have insurance—an either/or proposition like being male or female; however, it is not that simple. Insurance status in the United States is dynamic and uneven. It is dynamic because persons can change their status over time by gaining or losing insurance or by switching insurance carriers. Some people do not have insurance until entering the hospital, when their medical expenses and low incomes make them eligible for Medicaid. It is uneven because insurance plans differ in many ways, including the manner by which they pay providers, the magnitude of payments, the range of benefits covered, the size of premiums, the levels of coinsurance and/or deductibles, and the degree to which care is subject to third-party oversight. Therefore, in addition to the principal comparisons, we will examine access issues with respect to three other payment effects: cost-sharing; loss of insurance; and managed care.

Cost-Sharing. *Cost-sharing* refers to the portion of costs that insured people are expected to pay. Cost-sharing is comprised of the deductible, which is the amount of money the insured must pay before coverage "kicks in"; coinsurance, a percentage of covered services that the patient must pay; and copayments, a fixed payment per visit of service (Aaron, 1991). Deductibles are often several hundred dollars, while coinsurance is often around 20 percent (Sullivan and Rice, 1991). Some insurance plans set a maximal amount that beneficiaries can be expected to pay out-of-pocket. Health maintenance organizations (HMOs) often do not impose deductibles, or coinsurance but they may charge a fixed, small fee per medical visit. Cost-sharing represents an out-of-pocket cost to the insured person. In extreme cases of high deductibles and coinsurance or copayments, insured persons may face substantial financial barriers to health care, much as do uninsured persons.

Cost-sharing occurs whenever benefits are not covered in full. Insurance plans tend to encompass a multitude of specific categories of service, including hospital services, home health care, vision care, and even hospice care (Table 1-3). These services, however, are rarely covered in full. Of course, the cost and frequency of the service needed will determine its impact on out-of-pocket expenditures.

Like the concept of quality, the concept of *adequacy* of insurance can be terribly nebulous. Three definitions are in common use. Underinsurance can be defined as the lack of coverage of certain benefits, such as preventive care or primary care, or unduly restrictive limits on coverage, such as the number of hospital days or provider visits, as is often the case with mental health care. Second, a person is underinsured if he or she is insured only some of the time and is uninsured for an extended period of time.[11] Third, during the course of a year, a person is considered to be underinsured if the chance of incurring burdensome, or catastrophic, health care expenses is particularly high. Although the levels defining the underinsured person under this last definition are arbitrary, an example of such a case is one in which the chances are greater than 5 percent that a person or family will have to spend more than 10 percent of their income on health care (Farley, 1985). People who expect to have high health care expenses can avoid underinsurance by purchasing more comprehensive coverage (assuming they can afford the premiums). Such adverse selection, of course, is precisely what insurance carriers fear.

Many individuals with very low income and with private insurance are clearly likely to be underinsured. They are in a double bind. Their low incomes make them less able to afford the high premiums charged for a comprehensive insurance plan with low cost-sharing provisions. They are also more likely to have plans that "underinsure" them because they are less able to afford the cost-sharing bills that arrive when illness occurs.

The adequacy of insurance is naturally a product of a person's health status as well as the cost of necessary medical care relative to income or assets. Sick people are more likely to be underinsured because their expenses are higher. One's medical diagnosis may be the key determinant of whether one's insurance is adequate, especially for policies that do not cover preexisting chronic conditions. In studies of the financial burden of health care, family income and the "completeness" of health insurance were the strongest predictors, although health status affected burdens for the very old and the very poor (Dicker and Sunshine, 1988).

Table 1-3. The Percentage of Full-time Participants in Medium and Large Firms, by Insurance Coverage, for Selected Categories of Health Care Benefit, 1989

Category of Medical Care	Provided (%)	Covered in Full (%)
Hospital room and board	98	19
Hospitalization-miscellaneous services	98	19
Extended care facility	80	7
Home health care	75	20
Inpatient surgery	98	33
Outpatient surgery	98	38
Physician visits, in hospital	98	23
Physician visits, office	97	9
Diagnostic x-ray and laboratory	98	28
Prescription drugs, nonhospital	95	3
Private duty nursing	86	16
Mental health care	97	—
In-hospital	96	3
Outpatient	92	—
Vision	35	5
Alcohol abuse treatment	97	1
Drug abuse treatment	96	1
Hospice	42	9

Source: Adapted from U.S. Congress, Office of Technology Assessment, 1992, Table D-1, p. 52; data from, U.S. Department of Labor, Bureau of Labor Statistics, 1990.

Studies on the effects of coinsurance are not numerous, but some, such as the RAND Health Insurance Experiment, provide substantial evidence on the topic. We could find no studies that compare the utilization of health care or outcomes of persons with inadequate versus adequate insurance.[12]

Loss of Insurance. Loss of insurance, especially if it is involuntary, provides another perspective on access problems. The bulk of research on access to care by payment source consists of cross-sectional studies examining variations in utilization among patients in different insurance classes. A more compelling story sometimes emerges from natural experiments that occur when people lose their insurance unwillingly. This unfortunate event may occur, for example, when someone loses a job or a spouse and then loses the employment-related insurance, or when the eligibility for a public insurance program changes. The last situation has been studied more closely.

Managed Care. The traditional form of managed care is the staff or group model HMO. An HMO may be defined as "an organized group of physicians, working together full time, [who] agree to provide comprehensive services for a per capita payment fixed in advance, to a defined population of voluntarily enrolled members" (Enthoven 1980, p.

58). There are also a number of closely related variants, including network model HMOs and independent practice associations (IPAs). While the structures of these organizations vary somewhat, all of them share a common feature—they do not require direct fee-for-service payment between patient and provider (although they may require a small copayment). In 1992 there were approximately 550 HMOs covering nearly 42 million persons in the United States (GHAA, 1993).

There are at least three important limitations to studying the effect of managed care on access. The first is definitional. In the last ten years, it has become increasingly difficult to distinguish managed care programs (or alternative delivery systems, as they are sometimes called) from conventional fee-for-service systems. Fee-for-service insurance plans have gradually incorporated many of the principles from managed care, while many HMOs are offering increased flexibility that is usually associated with conventional insurance. Today, for example, a substantial proportion of those with fee-for-service coverage have policies that incorporate managed utilization review, such as preadmission certification, second opinion programs, and concurrent review (Luft and Morrison, 1991). At the same time an increasing but unknown number of HMOs have developed offerings known as point-of-service plans that permit out-of-plan use subject to varying deductibles and coinsurance.

The second limitation is that the organizational structure is often confounded by the financial incentives associated with prepayment and capitation (Hurley, Paul, and Freund, 1989). This is most obvious in HMOs referred to as having "closed panels." Let us say a researcher finds a reduction in emergency room use or hospital admissions in an HMO (in which physicians as a group receive capitated payment) versus a fee-for-service plan. How do we know whether these effects emanate from the gate-keeping role played by the family physician, the restrictions placed on referrals to specialists, or the financial incentives to the physician to avoid costly care?

The third limitation is that it is difficult to separate out evidence of cost control from problems of access (i.e., knowing whether lower rates of utilization reflect access problems or just more efficient care). This difficulty is not unique to the study of managed care programs; however, unlike comparisons within the fee-for-service system, the interest in managed care programs, especially for Medicaid recipients, lies chiefly in the expressed goal of cost savings (Spitz, 1987). In evaluating managed care, therefore, it is important to measure utilization for preventive care or other specific problems. This may provide a better yardstick to gauge access than merely measuring overall utilization.

Because managed care programs have been such an important policy option in the United States during the last 20 years, there is a substantial body of knowledge concerning the behavior of the prototypes—staff and group model HMOs, networks, and IPAs. The evidence on the association between these sorts of managed care and health care utilization, quality of care, and outcomes has been addressed in detail elsewhere and will be omitted from this review (see Luft, 1981, 1978; Manning et al., 1984; Ware et al., 1986; Luft and Morrison, 1991). Consistent with our focus on financial access, we will instead review a special case of particular relevance—the use of managed care in Medicaid.[13]

LIMITATIONS IN RESEARCH ON ACCESS TO CARE

The preceding sections highlight some of the problems in fitting economic and organizational models to health care. The ability to test rigorously the association of insurance status with use and outcomes is similarly compromised. One major problem is due to a phenomenon called *biased selection*. Biased selection describes what happens when groups of people that are fundamentally different are allowed to choose among insurance options, including the choice of no insurance. Biased selection can be favorable or adverse from the insurer's perspective. For example, insurance companies often attempt to ensure favorable selection by enrolling patients who are healthier than average and whose use of services is likely to be low. At the same time, insurance companies know less about individuals' predilection to consume services than the individuals themselves. Persons who expect to consume substantial amounts of services are more likely to buy extensive insurance, thereby creating adverse selection. It is a lot like a situation where someone tries to insure a house that is already burning. To prevent this individual "gaming," insurance companies prefer to insure groups rather than individuals. In addition, most insurance companies now practice "experience rating," where the premium levels reflect the predicted expenditures of the group, most often on the basis of past health care experience. Of course, some adverse selection is intentional—the Medicaid program was designed to care for the poorest, sickest citizens.

The effect of biased selection on research is apparent. Medicaid recipients have poorer health status both as a result of access to care, and partly because eligibility requirements mean they are sicker to begin with. At least some uninsured people may use less medical care because they are a self-selected group with a lower preference for health care consumption, not because they face access barriers. In addition, underutilization is a relative term, complicated by the tendency of insured groups to overutilize care. The difficulty in sorting out the effects of insurance on access certainly carries over to the effect of coinsurance. Persons may choose different levels of deductible and copayment to fit with their tastes and preferences for health care consumption.

It is important to remember that the effect of payment source on access focuses on just one aspect of demand—the financial one. Other factors, however, such as race and income and those noted previously are important and may confound observed relationships. Mechanic (1979) argued that organizational and psychosocial variables have real impacts on utilization. He claimed that they are often overlooked due to problems in defining variables and collecting and analyzing the data. Moreover, it may be difficult to isolate the effects of demand from those of supply, such as the influence of physicians on utilization (Ginsburg and Manheim, 1973). There are important regional variations in practice patterns as well.

Finally, there will be additional difficulties as we review the impact of managed care on Medicaid. It is nearly impossible to separate out the effects of capitated payment from the organizational aspects of managed care: Where some see lower utilization leading to access problems, others perceive efficient cost management. Medicaid recipients who voluntarily enroll in HMOs may be healthier because persons who switch doctors to join a plan are less likely to have a chronic illness than are those who choose to remain with their own doctors. Persons who join HMOs also may do so because they are more willing to accept restricted services. Understanding Medicaid and the behavior of its beneficiaries or its providers is complicated by the stigma attached to eligibility, to commonly slow payment rates and other red tape, and to philosophical notions about public welfare. Most health services research examines only the narrow band of economic behavior.

In summary, existing research on access to health care includes an abundance of data and studies comparing indicators of access by payment source, but there are numerous potential biases. Almost all of the data available are from studies that are quasi-experimental or nonexperimental.[14] Only a few studies control extensively for health status and other correlates of utilization. Particular caution is required in interpreting the results of studies that lump Medicaid with privately insured patients. Although Medicaid beneficiaries are a small proportion of the insured, they are more likely to be in substantially poorer health because of categorical qualification. Because of methodologic limitations, results from individual studies will rarely be conclusive. Rather, we will be forced to draw conclusions inferred from the overall pattern of results. The task is not easy. As will be evident in the chapters that follow, assessing the evidence on access to care is not unlike using a metal detector to search for coins and jewelry on the beach. It is necessary to search through tons of raw material to locate a few valuable items.

2

WHO ARE THE UNINSURED AND HOW DID THEY GET THAT WAY?

Until recently, we have known little about the uninsured—who they are, how they got that way, or even how many they number. Yet this knowledge is vital for health reform and related policy formation.

Most Americans obtain insurance through their jobs, elderly people have Medicare, and some poor people are covered by Medicaid. Nevertheless, approximately 37 million Americans of all ages are uninsured, which suggests large breaches in coverage. Where are these breaches and how do they occur? This chapter begins with a description of the sources and limitations of health insurance and how Americans obtain and lose coverage. Next, we describe how the size of the uninsured population is estimated, and then summarize the existing data on their current numbers, where they live and work, their age, gender, and other important characteristics. The chapter concludes with a similar description of the underinsured.

SOURCES OF INSURANCE AND PROBLEMS WITH COVERAGE

SOURCES OF INSURANCE COVERAGE

Persons may obtain health insurance through either public or private insurers.[1] There are three principal types of public insurance: Medicare serves the elderly and disabled with work histories and persons with end-stage renal disease (ESRD); Medicaid is directed at low-income women and children and those with certain disabilities; and the Civilian Health and Medical Programs of the Uniformed Services (CHAMPUS), the Department of Veterans Affairs, and other military programs cover active and retired members of the uniformed services and their dependents. Private insurance also takes several forms. It may be obtained through employer-based coverage at the work place or via purchase of individual policies from any of the Blue Cross/Blue Shield companies, commercial insurers, or HMOs.

In 1991 36.3 million Americans, or about 16.6 percent of the nonelderly population, had no private or public insurance (Foley, 1993). An estimated 14.5 percent of Americans under 65 received insurance coverage through public plans: 11.0 percent from Medicaid; 1.6 percent from Medicare; and 2.7 percent through CHAMPUS or the Department of Veterans Affairs (Foley, 1993). (Because of double coverage, the subtotals in this paragraph exceed the totals.) An estimated 64.1 percent of nonelderly Americans acquired coverage through employment-related private plans, and 8.2 percent received coverage through other private insurance including individual or nongroup policies. During the last decade, a growth in the number of uninsured has coincided with a drop in the proportion of Americans with private insurance (Levit, Olin, and Letsch, 1992). More detail on how the numbers of uninsured are estimated and the change over time is provided shortly in the section on Counting the Uninsured.

PRIVATE HEALTH INSURANCE

History. Understanding the birth and development of health insurance in this country can help to explain why certain forms predominate today and why gaps in coverage evolved. Despite efforts in the early part of this century to pass universal health insurance (see Chapter 8), the arrangements for coverage that existed were scarce. Before the 1930s, 90 percent of medical expenses were paid out-of-pocket. Early health insurance plans were private and were provided by a few employers or other collective organizations for their members. The impetus for broad private health insurance coverage came from hospitals seeking to bolster their revenues, and the idea was nurtured by the advent of the Depression when patients' ability to pay declined. The first Blue Cross plan is usually attributed to the efforts of Dr. Justin Ford Kimball, executive vice president of Baylor University, in Dallas, Texas (Law, 1976). Unpaid bills at the university's hospital were traced to school teachers who could not afford catastrophic expenses, so Baylor instituted a plan in 1929 whereby teachers could prepay fifty cents a month for twenty-one days of hospital coverage. A number of small, voluntary, mostly single-hospital plans blossomed in the next few years.

In 1932 the first multiple-hospital, nonprofit Blue Cross plan was established, in Sacramento, California. The new arrangement offered communitywide premiums (i.e., offered community rates based on average costs for large groups of people) and guaranteed payments to participating hospitals. Blue Cross plans were also distinguished by their unique regulatory arrangements, set up by state enabling legislation. These regulations exempted them from state insurance legislation and allowed control of the plans to be vested in representatives of hospitals and physicians. The laws also required that the financial viability and rate structure of the plans be subject to public oversight.

During the 1930s and 1940s a number of private alternatives to Blue Cross emerged. The commercial insurers were for-profit, taxable entities that offered group rates tailored to each group's claims experience. Commercial insurers also offered indemnity coverage. Under indemnity benefits, insurance companies make direct payments to subscribers. Contrast this with Blue Cross's service benefit, which is paid directly to the hospital. The commercial insurers were also the first to include benefits covering physician fees and other nonhospital medical costs. The first Blue Shield plans for physician bills were established beginning in the late 1930s in reaction to these developments. Despite competition from Blue Cross and Blue Shield, commercial insurers had captured half of the health insurance business by the middle of the 1950s. Seeing the writing on the wall, the Blues also began to provide a mix of service and indemnity benefits. They usually include cost-sharing as part of their plans, and have moved almost entirely away from community rates.

Until the last twenty years, the role of HMOs in the health insurance business went virtually unnoticed, but in fact their roots took hold at about the same time as the Blues and the commercial insurers. Most students of health policy are familiar with the Kaiser Permanente program in California. In the late 1930s Henry Kaiser was concerned with the ability of his workers to obtain care in remote company areas of California and Oregon and so arranged for an insurance company to pay a fixed fee per enrollee to local providers who agreed to provide care. The plan was opened to other members of the community in 1942. Kaiser was not alone in the early business of capitation for health care, however. The Group Health Association of Washington, D.C., began in 1937 as a consumer-owned cooperative; ten years later Mayor LaGuardia established The Health Insurance Plan of Greater New York, mostly to serve New York City employees. These three organizations remained the small giants of the HMO industry until 1973, when the Nixon administration passed the HMO Act. The purpose of the act was to encourage HMO growth by overriding restrictive state laws and offering incentives for investment of capital in fledgling plans. By 1992, approximately 550 HMOs representing 42 million subscribers had established themselves in the American health landscape (GHAA, 1993).

The Role of Employers.   The tradition of employer-based health insurance as a standard worker benefit in U.S. companies took form after World War II. When wages began to stagnate under the stabilization controls, bargaining over increases in tax-free benefits, including health insurance, began in earnest.

Today, the majority of Americans under age 65 receive health insurance through some attachment to the work force, as either workers or their dependents. A special analysis of the Current Population Survey by Lewin/ICF provides some insight into how coverage was obtained in 1987 (Needleman et al., 1990). The analysis was limited to workers (estimated at 114 million persons), their nonworking dependent spouses (19 million), and their children (58 million). Of these estimated 191 million persons, 142 million (74 percent) were covered by employer plans. An additional 26 million (14 percent) were able to obtain health insurance from other sources: 15 million from nongroup insurance policies and 11 million from public sources. The remaining 23 million persons (12 percent of all workers and their dependent spouses and children) were uninsured.

Problems with Employer-Based Insurance. Workers do not obtain health insurance through their employers for one of two conspicuous reasons: The employer does not offer a plan or the employee chooses not to purchase a plan that is offered.

In 1987, 44 percent of all firms did not offer health benefits; these firms tended to be small. For example, in 1986 54 percent of firms with 10 or fewer employees did not offer health benefits, whereas only 2 percent of firms with 100–499 employees did not do so (Table 2-1). Why do some employers not offer coverage? Why might smaller firms be at a disadvantage? A national survey for the Small Business Administration was conducted by Lewin/ICF to answer these questions. The number of firms surveyed was not cited in the report, but the authors noted that many of their results paralleled those of smaller single-state studies. The principal reasons cited for not offering health insurance as a benefit were: insufficient profits (67 percent); the high cost of insurance (62 percent); job turnover among the work force (19 percent); and the unavailability of group insurance (16 percent).

Small employers pay 10–15 percent more on average than do larger groups for equivalent insurance plans (Pepper Commission, 1990). Proportionately higher administrative costs account for much of this difference. Administrative expenses of the smallest plans (one to four employees) constitute on average 40 percent of claims. This amount falls to 35 percent for groups of five to nine employees, 30 percent for groups of ten to nineteen employees, and 25 percent for groups of twenty to forty-nine employees. The total administrative expenses of the largest conventional insurance plans, for groups of 10,000 or more employees, constitute only 5.5 percent of all claims. In addition to paying proportionately greater administrative fees, smaller employers pay proportionately greater commissions to the insurance agent or broker. Commissions to the broker average 8.4 percent of all claims for groups of five or fewer and less than 1 percent for groups of 1,000 or more (Pepper Commission, 1990).

Higher "risk and profit" charges (profits plus protection against unexpectedly high claims expenses) are also associated with smaller

Table 2-1. Firms that Did Not Offer Health Coverage, 1986

Number of Employees	Percentage of Firms Not Offering Health Coverage
1–9	54
10–24	22
25–99	8
100–499	2
500+	0
Average all firms	44

Sources: Needleman et al., 1990; data from Lewin/ICF Analysis, Health Benefits Data Base, 1986.

groups. These charges average 8.5 percent for groups of less than five compared with 3.5 percent for groups of more than 500 employees (Pepper Commission, 1990). These charges can be explained by the practice of experience rating (i.e., setting premiums based on the claims experience of the group in the previous year). Contrast this with community rating, defined earlier, which establishes single rates for large classes of people in the region. Under experience rating, groups that incur higher-than-average medical expenditures will be charged proportionately higher rates over time. Small employers cannot be experience-rated because the low numbers make it difficult to project future expenditures accurately; thus, they present increased financial risk for the insurer, who in turn charges higher premiums (the risk charge). In a small firm, one or two very sick employees can have a huge effect on the total claims experience for the group, thus raising the premium in the following year to an unaffordable level. In a very large group, one or two expensive cases would go unnoticed.

As alternatives to pure experience rating, insurers may refuse to write a policy, discontinue existing coverage, or disallow coverage for selected individuals with preexisting conditions. As a consequence, employers may exclude certain groups of employees a priori from health benefits to obtain coverage for the rest of the firm or to cut costs. In 1986, 68 percent of all employers excluded part-time workers from health insurance plans. Insurance plans also practice *medical underwriting,* that is, they use information on the demographic and clinical characteristics of applicants to estimate their health expenditure and to determine "whether or not, and under what conditions, to accept an applicant for insurance" (Congressional Research Service, 1988a). Workers with preexisting medical conditions like diabetes and heart disease may be singled out, or new enrollees may be subject to a waiting period.

Entire industries are sometimes singled out as being ineligible for coverage or at least poor risks. Insurance companies consider industry-

specific characteristics such as seasonal employment or high-hazard oc-
cupations when determining eligibility. This means that obtaining
health insurance can be a challenge for people who work in aviation,
bars and taverns, construction, logging, restaurants, roofing companies, security guard firms, and others.

Some employees choose not to buy insurance even though most employers pay part of the health insurance premiums for their employees
as a benefit. About 13 percent of employees do not buy insurance
through their employers even when it is offered (Needleman et al.,
1990). One reason given is that the premium is too expensive. While
affordability is certainly a function of personal income, it is also apparent that the cost of premiums facing individual workers varies tremen-
dously.

In 1987 employers paid about 86 percent of the total plan premium
for workers with individual coverage and about 79 percent of the total
premium for workers with family coverage. The proportion of premium paid by employers ranged from 100 percent of coverage for 40
percent of workers to 0 percent (i.e., no subsidies) for 7 percent of
workers (Needleman et al., 1990). The generosity of coverage tends to
mirror the salary level of the worker. The percentage of workers for
whom *employers* paid the full amount of the premium was 35 percent in
firms with average earnings of less than $150.00 per week and 44 per-
cent in firms where the average wage was $800.00 or more weekly. The
percentage of *workers* paying the full amount of the premium was as
high as 12 percent in the same low-wage firms and only 5 percent in
the high-wage firms.

Rising insurance premiums during the last decade have exacerbated
the problem. Some employers have begun to require employees to pay
greater shares. Lewin/ICF found that the percentage of workers with
coverage financed by the employer has been decreasing, and cost-sharing requirements have been growing more burdensome (Needleman
et al., 1990).

NONGROUP INSURANCE

Persons who do not receive employer provided health insurance may
obtain coverage by purchasing a private nongroup plan. About 15 million persons under age 65 purchased nongroup insurance in 1987.
The majority of these policies were provided by commercial insurers,
about one-fourth by Blue Cross/Blue Shield, and a small number
(about 2 million) by HMOs (Congressional Research Service, 1988a).

As with the small-employer market, the individual market is plagued
by medical underwriting and high costs. High premiums are a particular problem since lower-income workers are more likely than higher-
income workers to be without employer health benefits. Also, persons

with preexisting medical conditions, such as diabetes, asthma, and AIDS, may either be rejected as uninsurable or be offered only partial coverage when they apply for nongroup policies. The extent of denial of insurance due to preexisting conditions has been difficult to document because private insurance companies are not eager to disclose this information. Strangely, denials of coverage appear to be only rarely a reason for people being completely without insurance. On the basis of findings from the NMES survey, Beauregard (1991) estimated that in 1987 889,000 persons (2.5 percent of the uninsured) had been denied private health insurance or offered limited coverage because of preexisting conditions. The rate of denial varied widely according to the specific type of health problem. More than 16 percent of uninsured persons reporting poor health had tried unsuccessfully to obtain coverage, a rate 12 times that for persons in excellent health. Still, these figures include only those who were uninsured and were denied coverage. The estimates do not include the number of privately insured whose policies excluded preexisting conditions, nor do they account for uninsured individuals who were too discouraged to seek insurance, formally. Thus, they are lower-bound estimates of the extent to which coverage is denied or limited because of preexisting conditions.

MEDICAID

Those unable to obtain any or sufficient coverage through private insurance may still attempt to obtain coverage through public programs such as Medicaid. Medicaid is a health insurance program for the poor, covering preventive, acute, and chronic care for about 28 million people (all ages). Medicaid is jointly financed by the federal and state governments. The federal share averages 55 percent but ranges from 50 to about 80 percent, with larger shares going to poorer states.

In 1991 Medicaid accounted for 13 percent of all health care spending in the United States (all ages) and had been growing rapidly during the previous two years; the total federal, state, and local expenditure in 1991 was nearly $100 billion, an increase of nearly 34 percent from the previous year, which in turn was 21 percent greater than the year before (Letsch et al., 1992). These rates represent the highest growth in the program's history. Much of the increase can be traced to expansions in enrollment, whether through new eligibility mandates legislated by Congress (e.g., to cover poor pregnant women and their children), increased outreach by states, or the natural growth in the Medicaid rolls that comes with a recession (see Waid, 1990, for a summary of Medicaid and expanded eligibility rules).

To receive the federal match, states are required to enroll persons eligible for federally assisted income maintenance programs, including

Aid to Families with Dependent Children (AFDC) or Supplemental Security Income (SSI). The elderly, blind, or disabled, pregnant women and children, certain Medicare beneficiaries, and others are also covered if they are poor. States have the option to have a program for the medically needy to cover persons who, except for their incomes and assets, would qualify for one of the covered categories. With this option, medically needy individuals may "spend down" to Medicaid eligibility if they get sick and incur medical expenses.

As a result of restrictions on eligibility and other limitations, only about 41 percent of persons living in poverty were eligible for Medicaid in 1986 (Congressional Research Service, 1988b). Why is it that Medicaid covers only a fraction of the low-income population? Either individuals do not fall into one of the covered categories or their incomes, although low, are still too high to meet the eligibility criteria. For example, persons under age sixty-five who are single or childless and who are not disabled are not eligible for the federally subsidized Medicaid program no matter how poor they are. Furthermore, states have great flexibility in setting their income limits and might also consider such factors as whether a family member is employed and how long the employment has lasted. In no state did the maximum cutoff for AFDC eligibility in 1988 for a family of three even reach 100 percent of the poverty level, and it was as low as 15 percent in Alabama, a monthly income of $118. With "work disregards" (i.e., allowing higher incomes if the recipient gets a job), the maximum cutoff reached as high as 140 percent of poverty in a small number of states (Congressional Research Service, 1988b).

Another factor discouraging enrollment in Medicaid and other public programs is the length and complexity of the application process. Applicants are faced with long and complex forms, often for multiple programs, and are expected to produce extensive documentation of their financial situation. For low-income people, who are less likely than others to have advanced formal education or to speak English, the application process may be daunting. Others may be unaware that they qualify. Recertification can also be burdensome. The period for recertification varies by state—some are monthly, some are every three months, and some are every six months. Persons whose income fluctuates from month to month, therefore, may not be able to depend on consistent coverage.

OTHER PUBLIC PROGRAMS

Fewer than 5 percent of nonelderly Americans are covered by public programs other than Medicaid. These include Medicare and military-related coverage, including the Veterans Administration, CHAMPUS, the Civilian Health and Medical Program of the VA (CHAMPVA), and other programs for the uniformed services.

Medicare. Medicare is a uniform, federally sponsored program for the aged and the disabled. Virtually all persons over age 65 are covered (over 30 million), plus about 3 million persons with permanent disabilities or ESRD. Medicare is financed by payroll taxes, general revenues, and premiums. It is a two-part program. Part A is financed through mandatory payment of payroll taxes and covers inpatient hospital care, some nursing home services, and some home health services. Part B is optional. It is financed via premiums and general tax revenues that account for 25 percent and 75 percent of its costs, respectively. Part B covers physicians and ambulatory services, medical equipment, and other services. Both Part A and Part B require cost-sharing on the part of the beneficiary. Very poor elderly persons may be eligible for "dual coverage," where Medicaid pays premiums for Part B, and the deductibles and copayments for Medicare covered services.

Although not as explosive as Medicaid, Medicare expenditures also grew rapidly during the 1980s, rising from $35 billion in 1979 to about $85 billion in 1989 (Congressional Research Service, 1988b). This growth has been attributed to an increase in the eligible population, increasing use of technology, and overall medical care inflation.

Military-Related Programs. Certain veterans with service-connected disabilities are able to obtain services for free in Veterans' Administration (VA) hospitals. Eligibility is determined by a complicated set of rules based on income and the extent of service-related disability. CHAMPVA provides care for selected dependents and survivors of veterans. Active duty members of the armed services have virtually all of their medical needs attended to at military health care facilities. CHAMPUS covers care for dependents and care received off-base.

Other Public Programs. A variety of programs exist to pay for the medical costs of selected populations, although the initiatives are not normally considered to be insurance programs. Some states cover the needs of the persons not eligible for Medicaid, but who receive General Relief. Others provide care for persons with specific diseases (e.g., tuberculosis). Native Americans living on reservations and prisoners are likewise eligible for special programs.

SUMMARY

In summary, despite the existence of both public and private options for obtaining health insurance, access to health care security remains limited or blocked for many Americans. The majority of insured Americans are covered by private insurance obtained through their employer. However, not all employers provide health benefits, and those that do frequently do not provide them to all workers. The workers who are least able to afford health insurance are often forced either to pay higher percentages of employment-based coverage or to buy non-group insurance. For those lacking employer-subsidized coverage, the high cost of nongroup insurance can be prohibitive. Persons with existing conditions face additional problems because insurers frequently either limit their coverage or exclude them from nongroup coverage altogether. Public programs, which are intended to act as a safety net for those unable to obtain sufficient private insurance, are accessible to only a specific and limited population, and those who are eligible for publicly subsidized health insurance often encounter potentially prohibitive difficulties when attempting to obtain it.

The preceding sections have described the sources and problems of insurance in the United States, but insurance status in this country is dynamic. The challenge is obtaining insurance for some, while it is keeping it for others. Changes in life situations, such as losing a job, getting a job, getting married or divorced, or just getting older, can have important consequences for one's insurance status. The dynamics of insurance coverage in the United States are much more complex than, say, in the Canadian system, one that has been offered by some as an alternative to ours. In Canada, one obtains insurance by becoming a citizen, and one loses insurance by giving up citizenship. Table 2-2 illustrates the contrast between Canada and the United States, where myriad life situations can lead to a change in health care coverage. This is not meant to be an endorsement of the Canadian system; the simplicity of the Canadian approach is not viewed by all as an improvement over the pluralism inherent in ours. The contrast, however, is remarkable and informative. To reform our insurance system one needs to understand how and why the entries in this table play out in real life systems. In the remainder of this chapter, we will present a picture of those who suffer most from the gaping holes in the existing insurance system—uninsured and underinsured Americans.

COUNTING THE UNINSURED: SOURCES OF ESTIMATES

Information on the number and characteristics of uninsured persons is derived from analysis of survey data. The most commonly cited source is the March Supplement of the CPS. The CPS is conducted monthly by the U.S. Bureau of the Census. It is a survey of a representative sample of U.S. households that ascertains information on employment, income, family size, and other sociodemographic characteristics. Approximately 71,000 households are chosen for the survey each month, and approximately 57,000 households containing 148,000 individuals actually complete interviews. The March supplement to the survey includes questions about health insurance coverage. The data are also analyzed annually by the Employee Benefit Research Institute (EBRI),

Table 2-2. How Citizens of the United States and Canada Get and Lose Health Care Coverage

How People Get Coverage		How People Lose Coverage	
United States	Canada	United States	Canada
Get a job that offers insurance	Become a citizen	Lose job	Lose citizenship
Get married (to spouse with insurance)		Change jobs (with a pre-existing condition)	
Have parents with insurance		Get sick, lose job	
Qualify for Medicaid Become pregnant Become disabled Lose job, become poor		Become self-employed	
		Lose income (cannot afford premium)	
Qualify for Medicare Turn sixty-five Become permanently disabled Have end-stage renal failure		Get divorced	
		Grow up and leave home	
Qualify for Veteran's Assistance		Get a job (lose Medicaid)	
Enter prison		Children grow up or leave (lose Medicaid)	
Enter the Army (or be a dependent)		Leave prison	
Buy your own policy		Leave the Army	
Reside in a Native American reservation (as a member of a tribe)		Leave a Native American reservation (leave tribe)	
Purchase individual or group policy		Insurance company denies coverage to group	
		Insurance company folds	
		Insurance carrier cancels contract	

a nonprofit, nonpartisan public policy research organization based in Washington, D.C. Many of the statistics from the CPS presented here are drawn from their reports.

Periodic surveys have also provided information that can allow us to categorize the population that is uninsured. The National Medical Care Expenditure Survey (NMCES) of 1977 provided information on the civilian noninstitutionalized population regarding health insurance as well as health care utilization and expenditures for 1977. The National Medical Expenditure Survey (NMES) of 1987 gathered information on health expenditures by or on behalf of American families and individuals, the financing of these expenditures, and each person's use of services, as well as information on use of nursing homes and facilities for the mentally retarded. These surveys are unique because questions are repeated several times over the course of a year. The results of these surveys have been used by researchers for in-depth analysis of the uninsured. Both surveys were funded and administered by what is now called the Agency for Health Care Policy and Research (AHCPR) (formerly the National Center for Health Services Research). Other sources of information on insurance status include the Survey of Income and Program Participation (SIPP), a longitudinal survey, and the National Medical Care Utilization and Expenditure Survey. Appendix A provides a fuller description of these and other relevant sources of information.

MEASUREMENT ISSUES

Estimating the number of uninsured persons or, conversely, the number of insured persons, is not a straightforward task. The first insurance question for the 1992 CPS is worded, "During 1991, was anyone in this household covered by Medicare (for the disabled and elderly)?" If the respondent answers *yes,* then the interviewer asks who has such coverage and if there is anyone else with such coverage in the household. The interviewer repeats the process until all members of the household with such coverage are counted. This process is then repeated for multiple types of coverage—Medicare, Medicaid, CHAMPUS, other voluntary programs, the military, Veterans Affairs, or private health insurance. All individuals answering *no* to all of these questions are classified as uninsured. While this seems straightforward, the counting of uninsured persons is complicated by people with multiple sources of coverage, by misunderstanding the time period in the question, and by complicated living situations that make it difficult to determine who is a member of the household and who is covered under whose policies.

One problem in identifying or counting the uninsured concerns the time period. The questions in the CPS are designed to produce period-of-time estimates of insurance status for the previous year. This means that a person listed as uninsured during 1991 should have been uninsured for the entire twelve-month period. In addition to identifying this cohort, one might wish to identify persons who were uninsured during any part of the year or at a particular point in time. Demographers call the latter approach a point-in-time estimate.

Some researchers question whether the period estimates of the CPS really measure what they claim to. Swartz (1984) argued that despite the literal formats of its questions, the CPS actually measures lack of insurance at the point-in-time the survey is conducted. This hypothesis, yet unproven, is based on the fact that the CPS estimates were quite similar in magnitude to the point-in-time estimates from other national surveys (see also Brown, 1989). For our purposes, we will assume that the CPS provides a mix between point-in-time and period estimates for the calendar year *before* the annual March survey.

Another problem in estimating the number of uninsured is related to the insurance coverage of dependent children. In the past, the Census Bureau had imputed coverage or lack of coverage to certain dependent children on the basis of answers provided by the main informant. For example, if a parent claimed that his or her policy covered children, the Census Bureau would impute coverage for all unmarried children. Some children under the age of 22, however, were working and had insurance of their own, while some did not have insurance even though their parents did. Beginning in 1988 (insurance status in 1987) questions were added to the cover sheet and other sections of the survey to ask explicitly about children's work-related coverage, Medicaid and other nonemployer-provided coverage by sources outside of the household. The additional children covered by insurance that are identified by these new questions can be counted separately, and are sometimes referred to as "cover sheet children" (Moyer, 1989; Levit, Olin, and Letsch, 1992). Recognizing this discontinuity from pre- and post-1988 is important for analyzing trends in the number of uninsured persons.

The addition of the cover sheet questions in 1988 caused other problems in interpretation. Analysts at the EBRI noted that answers to these questions sometimes conflicted with the main set of insurance questions asked later during the interview. The Census Bureau counts as insured all children for whom there was a positive response to the cover sheet questions, even if they had conflicting answers elsewhere. EBRI, on the other hand, adds other conditions to their determination of insurance status, which has led to a slightly lower estimate of the insured population (and higher estimate of the uninsured) than that used by the U.S. Census. The Census Bureau estimated that 8.4 million children were uninsured in 1991; EBRI uses an estimate of 9.5 million.

HOW MANY AMERICANS ARE UNINSURED?

According to an EBRI analysis of the March 1992 CPS, 36.3 million or 16.6 percent of the nonelderly U.S. population had no health insurance in 1991 (Foley, 1993). The rest of the nonelderly population (181.8 million people or 83.4 percent of the population) were covered by a combination of public and private health insurance (see Table 2-3).

The number of uninsured in the United States has been increasing. Analysts at the Office of National Health Statistics of the Health Care Financing Administration analyzed the CPS data from 1980 to 1991 and found a steady increase in the number of uninsured Americans over this eleven-year period (Figure 2-1). The figure shows the number of uninsured in the United States from 1979 to 1990 according to the estimates from the March CPS of the following year (i.e., March 1980 to estimate the number of uninsured in calendar year 1979). Beginning in 1987 additional sources of insurance were identified based on the cover sheet questions, effectively eliminating these persons from the count of the uninsured. Thus, the bottom line shows the trend of uninsurance based on estimates that exclude cover sheet children from the count of the uninsured. To remove some of the inconsistencies that exist between the data collected before and after 1988, the top line shows what the data would look like if cover sheet children were reclassified as being uninsured. This trend line indicates a steady increase of uninsured through 1986, then a dip in 1987, and a steady increase again through 1990. The temporary decrease in the uninsured coincided with a change in Medicaid eligibility nationwide.

CHARACTERISTICS OF UNINSURED PEOPLE

Despite substantial media interest in the uninsured, there is still a misperception among many Americans as to who these people are (Eckholm, 1993). The popular image of the poor, chronically unemployed uninsured person living without a family is misleading and likely reduces political support for health system reform. Until Middle America understands lack of insurance and underinsurance as an "us" problem rather than a "them" problem, the motivation for change will be diminished.

In this section we describe the characteristics of the uninsured in two ways. We first assess the risk factors associated with lack of insurance by looking at groups of people and estimating the proportion in each who are uninsured; we then compare these proportions. Groups with higher proportions of uninsured, say 18- to 24-year-olds, are said to be at elevated "risk" for being uninsured. However, 18- to 24-year-olds do not account for most of the uninsured, because 18- to 24-year-

Table 2-3. The Total Number of Uninsured Persons: Elderly and Nonelderly Populations, 1991

Population	Number of Persons (millions)	Number Uninsured (millions)	Percentage Uninsured
Nonelderly	218.1	36.3	16.6
Elderly	30.6	0.3	0.9
Total	248.7	36.6	14.7

Source: Adapted from Foley, 1993, Table 1; data from U.S. Bureau of the Census, 1992.

olds do not represent a very large segment of the U.S. population. Therefore, at times we also describe the uninsured in terms of the percentage that different subgroups contribute to the whole. In the following, we will look at breakdowns by employment status, attachment to the work-force, income, age, sex, race, family type, and geography.

EMPLOYMENT AND INDUSTRY CHARACTERISTICS

As described earlier, one of the strongest determinants of health insurance coverage is employment. Members of families headed by full-time workers in 1991 were much less likely to be uninsured (i.e., were less at risk) than members of families headed by part-time or part-year workers (12.6 percent of full-time worker families were uninsured versus 28.3 percent of other working families). Families with nonworking

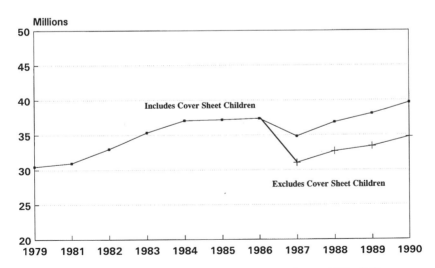

Figure 2-1. The number of Uninsured Persons in the United States, 1979–1990.
Source: Data from Levit, Olin, and Letsch, 1992.
Note: All ages were included. Data were not available for 1980.

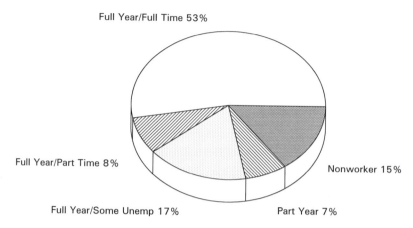

Figure 2-2. The Percentage of Total Uninsured Persons, by Employment Status of the Family Head, 1991.
Source: Foley, 1993, chart 2, p. 8; data from March 1992 CPS.
Note: Part year = thirty-five weeks or less. Nonelderly population.

heads fell somewhere in between (22.5 percent uninsurance rate) because many more of these families were poor and eligible for Medicaid. Despite higher risk of being uninsured among nonworking families, the majority of the uninsured (53 percent) were members of full-time, full-year working families (Figure 2-2). Only 15.3 percent of the unin-

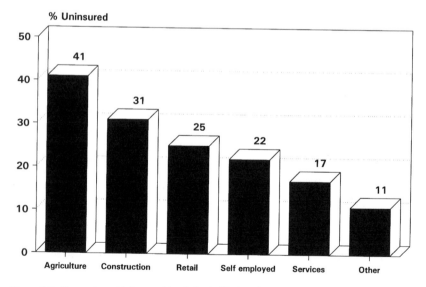

Figure 2-3. Percentage Uninsured by Selected Industries, 1991.
Source: Foley, 1993, chart 3, p. 9; data from March 1992 CPS.
Note: Ages eighteen to sixty-four.

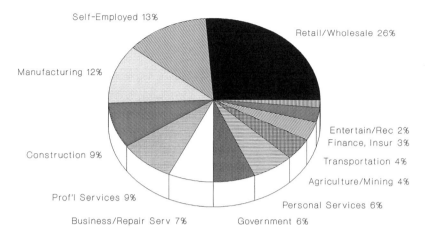

Figure 2-4. The Percentage of Total Uninsured Workers, by Industry of Main Employment, 1991.
Source: Data from Foley, 1993, Table 26; March 1992 CPS.
Note: Ages eighteen to sixty-four.

sured population were members of families with nonworking heads (Foley, 1993).

Workers who lack insurance tend to be employed in selected industries, work in small firms or be self-employed. For example, 41 percent of workers in agriculture, 31 percent in construction, 25 percent in retail trade, and 17 percent in the service industries are uninsured (Figure 2-3). High turnover of employees and/or seasonality of employment are often cited as the reasons for low coverage rates in these industries. However, the majority of the working uninsured are in the retail, trade, services, and manufacturing industries because these industries employ the majority of the work-force (Figure 2-4).

The size of the firm in which a worker is employed is also a determinant of health coverage. In general, the smaller the firm (by number of employees), the more likely it is that an employee in that firm will be uninsured. For comparison, 32 percent of employees in firms with fewer than 10 employees and 22 percent of self-employed workers were uninsured in 1991, while only 9 percent of employees in firms with more than 1,000 employees were uninsured (Table 2-4). The groups at high risk of uninsurance are generally well represented in the ranks of the working uninsured. Nearly half (47.7 percent) of all uninsured workers were either self-employed or working in firms with fewer than 25 employees in 1991.

Dependents of workers are traditionally covered by employer-based health insurance plans or so-called family plans. However, a large percentage of the uninsured are children or adult dependents of workers,

Table 2-4. Uninsured Workers Aged Eighteen to Sixty-Four, by Firm Size and Work Status, 1991

Work Status and Firm Size	Total Workers (millions)	Number Who Lack Health Insurance (millions)	Percentage Uninsured within Each Firm Size Category	Percentage of Total Uninsured Workers
Wage and salary workers by firm size				
Fewer than 10	14.4	4.6	31.7	22.3
10–24	10.4	2.6	25.0	12.7
25–99	15.8	3.3	20.8	16.1
100–499	17.6	2.3	13.3	11.4
500–999	7.0	0.7	9.9	3.4
1,000 or more	47.1	4.4	9.4	21.5
Total wage and salary workers	112.3	17.9	15.9	87.3
Self-employed	12.1	2.6	21.5	12.7
Total workers	124.4	20.5	16.5	100.0

Source: Adapted from Foley, 1993, Table 28; data from March 1992 CPS.
Note: Rounding errors may occur in Totals.

who make up 31.3 percent (11.4 million) of the total uninsured in 1991, while the workers themselves made up 56.4 percent of the total (Table 2-5). The remaining 12.3 percent of the uninsured were nonworkers and their dependents.

The characteristics of nonworking uninsured dependents of workers tend to parallel those of uninsured workers, aggregating in families where the primary breadwinner is employed in a small firm or a specific industry. About half of all dependents of workers without employer health benefits were in firms with less than 25 employees (Needleman et al., 1990) and were concentrated in the retail trade, construction, and professional services industries. Smaller firms are less likely to offer dependent coverage at the same level as large firms.

The percentage of employers who offer dependent coverage has decreased. A report prepared by the Congressional Research Service (1988a) concluded that between 1979 and 1986 decreased coverage for dependents accounted for approximately a 3 percent overall decline in the health coverage rate nationally. The report emphasized that the decline was attributable to demographic shifts caused by the aging of the baby boomers (who became adults and lost their insurance under their parents' plans) and reduced coverage for spouses and children, generally.

Table 2-5. Uninsured Population by Employment Status of Family Head and by Dependent Status, 1991

Family Head	Number without Health Insurance (millions)	Percentage of Total Uninsured
Worker, full-time, full-year	9.7	26.6
Adult dependents	2.1	5.9
Children	5.5	15.0
Other worker	10.8	29.8
Adult dependents	1.0	2.6
Children	2.8	7.8
Nonworker	2.0	5.6
Adult dependents	1.2	3.2
Children	1.2	3.4
Total	36.3	100.0

Source: Adapted from Foley, 1993, Table 7; data from March 1992 CPS.
Note: Nonelderly population. The definition of full-year worker in this table is slightly different from previous usage. In this table, EBRI analysts consider workers to be full-year only if they were never unemployed and looking for work. In previous usage, workers could be full-year even if they had short periods of unemployment.

INCOME AND EDUCATION

Income is related to insurance status for at least three reasons. First, poor persons are generally less able to afford the cost of insurance, whether or not the premium is subsidized. Second, low-wage industries like retail and personal services are less likely to offer group insurance (which tends to be cheaper than individual coverage). Third, low-wage industries also make the lowest employer contributions to health insurance (Foley, 1993). It should not be surprising, then, that the triumvirate of low incomes, low availability, and low subsidies results in low coverage rates.

The link between low income and lack of insurance coverage occurs despite the existence of Medicaid, the program designed to insure the poor. Among workers aged 18–64 in 1991, those earning under $10,000 per year were ten times more likely to lack health insurance than those who earned greater than $50,000 per year (30.4 percent uninsured versus 2.9 percent uninsured). Individuals who lived in families with household incomes less than 1.5 times the federal poverty level were more than five times more likely to be uninsured than those with household incomes greater than 4.0 times the poverty level in 1990 (Figure 2-5). An interesting "step" effect occurs where Medicaid eligibility drops off. Due to the impact of the Medicaid program, those who were "near-poor" (1–1.5 times the poverty level) were slightly more likely to be uninsured than were those who had household incomes below the poverty level (Figure 2-5).

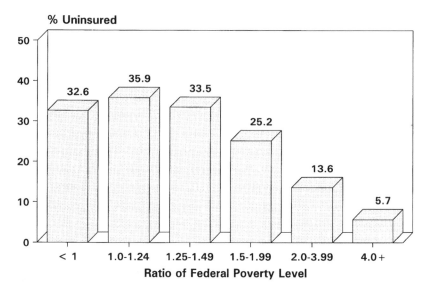

% Uninsured

Figure 2-5. Percentage Uninsured, by Federal Poverty Level, 1991.
Source: Foley, 1993, chart 6; data from March 1992 CPS.
Note: Nonelderly population.

As a result of this income link, the poor and near-poor are dispro-portionately represented among the uninsured. While 14.7 percent of the nonelderly population in the United States were below the poverty level in 1991, they comprised 28.8 percent of the uninsured (Figure 2-6). Overall, low-income families (defined as at or below two times the poverty level) comprised 32.6 percent of the total nonelderly popula-tion but made up 60.8 percent of the nonelderly uninsured. Of course, the flip-side of this figure is that nearly two in five uninsured persons have incomes more than twice the poverty level, and one in ten earn more than four times the poverty level.

Education of the family head is usually correlated with income. It is not surprising, then, that the lower one's education, the higher the risk of being uninsured (Table 2-6). Nevertheless, 66 percent of the unin-sured have at least a high-school education.

AGE

For a variety of reasons, elderly persons, nonelderly adults, and chil-dren have different risks of being uninsured and also make up different proportions of the uninsured. Age may act as a proxy for other demo-graphic and personal characteristics, such as employment status. Also, both Medicare and Medicaid have eligibility criteria tied in part to age.

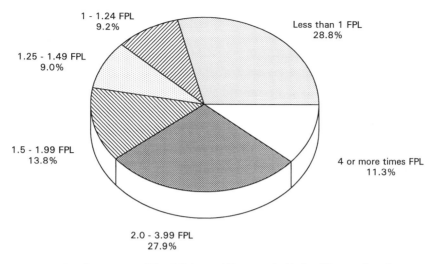

Figure 2-6. The Percentage of Total Uninsured Persons, by Federal Poverty Level (FPL), 1991.
Source: Data from Foley, 1993, Table 14; March 1992 CPS.
Note: Nonelderly population.

ELDERLY PEOPLE

It has been said that you can judge a society's moral fiber by how it treats its most aged members. Since the passage of the Social Security Act of 1965, elderly Americans have had much of their health costs covered by Medicare. CPS estimates for 1991 indicate that approximately 276,000 elderly Americans or only 0.9 percent of the elderly population are uninsured, some of those because a small number of the elderly who worked as domestics or farm laborers never paid Social Security taxes and therefore are not eligible for Medicare. Others are either unaware of their eligibility, are ineligible because of their citizenship status, or chose not to apply for coverage.

WORKING-AGE ADULTS

Working-age adults are the economic providers for their families and dependents and traditionally are assumed to be the key to obtaining health insurance in this country. Subgroups of this population account for disproportionately high numbers of the uninsured. Young adults aged 18–24 are the most likely to be uninsured among both men and women (Table 2-7). As a group, those aged 18–29 comprise 28.6 percent of the adult, nonelderly population, but they make up 41.9 percent of uninsured nonelderly adults. Young people were most often uninsured because they have lost family coverage (which is often age-dependent), have not yet established themselves in the work-force, and

Table 2-6. Uninsured Population by Educational Level of Family Head, 1991

Educational Level of Family Head	Number of Persons (millions)	Number with No Health Insurance (millions)	Percentage Uninsured in Each Category	Percentage of Total Uninsured
No high school	15.1	5.7	38.0	15.8
Some high school	23.9	6.7	27.8	18.3
High school graduate	75.7	13.4	17.7	36.8
Some college	37.8	5.5	14.6	15.2
Associates degree	13.6	1.6	11.6	4.4
Bachelors degree	32.9	2.5	7.5	6.8
Masters degree	13.2	0.7	5.4	2.0
Professional degree	3.7	0.2	4.7	0.5
Doctoral degree	2.2	0.1	4.8	0.3
Total	218.1	36.3	16.6	100.0

Source: Adapted from Foley, 1993, Table 9; data from March 1992 CPS.
Note: Nonelderly population. Rounding errors may occur in totals.

therefore do not receive insurance as a benefit of employment. Also they may not purchase health insurance because they are risk-takers and perceive themselves to be young and healthy, or they simply cannot afford it (Foley, 1993).

CHILDREN

Despite the importance of receiving health care early in life, a surprising number of children are without coverage. Estimates of the number of uninsured children in the United States are included in the CPS each year. The EBRI analysis of the March 1992 CPS estimates the number of uninsured children under 18 in 1991 at 9.5 million, or 14.6 percent of all children (Table 2-8). A controversy over interpretation of questions regarding insurance coverage of children has led to differing estimates of the number of uninsured children based on data from CPS (see previous discussion on measurement issues). The Bureau of the Census estimated the number of uninsured children in 1991 at 8.4 million or 14.0 percent of all children. Children of different age groups are at approximately the same risk of being uninsured, although those aged 13–17 may be at slightly higher risk (16 percent).

Using data from the NMCES and the NMES, Cunningham and Monheit (1990) demonstrated trends in the coverage of children between 1977 and 1987 with respect to various demographic factors. During this time period they found a sharp rise (40 percent) in the percentages of children who were uninsured from 12.7 percent in 1977 to 17.8 percent in 1988. These estimates are point-in-time estimates during the first quarters of 1977 and 1987, respectively. The changes were not dis-

Table 2-7. Uninsured Population by Gender and Age, Working-Age Adults, 1991

Gender (Age in Years)	Number of Persons (Millions)	Number of Uninsured (Millions)	Percentage Uninsured in Age Category	Percentage of Total Uninsured
Men	75.0	14.9	19.9	55.8
18–20	4.8	1.2	25.0	4.5
21–24	7.1	2.5	35.9	9.5
25–29	9.8	2.8	28.7	10.5
30–44	30.2	5.6	18.4	20.7
45–54	13.1	1.6	12.5	6.1
55–64	10.0	1.2	11.5	4.4
Women	78.1	11.8	15.2	44.2
18–20	5.0	1.1	22.5	4.2
21–24	7.2	1.7	23.7	6.4
25–29	9.9	1.8	18.2	6.7
30–44	30.9	4.1	13.1	15.2
45–54	13.9	1.7	12.2	6.3
55–64	11.1	1.4	13.0	5.4
Total	153.0	26.8	17.5	100.0
18–20	9.8	2.3	23.8	8.7
21–24	14.3	4.2	29.8	15.9
25–29	19.7	4.6	23.4	17.3
30–44	61.1	9.6	15.7	35.9
45–54	27.0	3.3	12.3	12.4
55–64	21.1	2.6	12.4	9.8

Source: Adapted from Foley, 1993, Table 23; data from March 1992 CPS.
Note: Rounding errors may occur in totals.

tributed evenly across family types. Children in two-parent families in which both parents worked experienced virtually no change in coverage over the decade. In contrast, the percentage of children who were uninsured in households with employed single-parents, increased from 14.2 percent in 1977 to 22.1 percent in 1987. It may have been in response to these striking trends, noticed by policy-makers in the early 1980s, that subsequent legislation was enacted. In fact, the passage of the Deficit Reduction Act (DEFRA) of 1984 and the Omnibus Budget Reconciliation Act (OBRA) of 1989, each requiring states to extend health coverage through Medicaid to pregnant women and young children, seems to have ameliorated the problem, as reflected in the lower rate of uninsured children reported in 1991.

GENDER

By the age of twenty-five, women have started having babies in large numbers and are more likely than men to obtain insurance. In addition, women are more likely than men to be covered by Medicaid through the AFDC Program because they are more likely to be caring for children.

Table 2-8. Uninsured Children by Age Group, 1991

Age Group (years)	Total Population (millions)	Number without Health Insurance (millions)	Percentage Uninsured within Age Group	Percentage of All Uninsured Children
Infants	3.9	0.6	14.1	5.8
1–5	18.9	2.5	13.5	26.7
6–12	25.7	3.8	14.8	39.7
13–17	16.6	2.7	16.0	27.8
Total	65.1	9.5	14.6	100.0

Source: Adapted from Foley, 1993, Table 37; data from March 1992 CPS.

While men made up 49 percent of the total adult nonelderly population in 1991, they made up 55.8 percent of the uninsured. Men were more likely to be uninsured than women at all ages except 55–64 (Table 2-7). Both men and women were most likely to be uninsured at ages 21–24 and least likely to be uninsured at ages 55–64. The largest discrepancies by gender are for persons aged 18–29.

RACE AND ETHNICITY

By all estimates, minorities are more likely than whites to be uninsured. Compared with other races, whites were at least risk with 13.0 percent uninsured. African Americans had a significantly higher risk (23.7 percent), while Hispanics had the highest risk (33.9 percent) of being uninsured (Table 2-9). These higher rates of uninsurance are reflected in the distributional figures. While whites accounted for 73.9 percent of the nonelderly population in 1991, they made up only 57.8 percent of the total uninsured. The situation is reversed for blacks and Hispanics. Blacks made up 12.8 percent of the nonelderly population but 18.2 percent of the uninsured; Hispanics accounted for 9.5 percent of the nonelderly population, yet 19.4 percent of the uninsured in 1991. Furthermore, between 1977 (from NMCES) and 1987 (from NMES) the increase in the proportion of blacks who were uninsured was twice that of whites (from 17 to 25 percent among blacks versus 12 to 15 percent among whites), while the change among Hispanics, from 20 to 35 percent, was five times the increase among whites (Short, Cornelius, and Goldstone, 1990).

Researchers at the UCLA School of Public Health and the UCLA/RAND Center for Health Policy Studies used data from the March 1980 and March 1990 CPSs to investigate further the high rates of uninsurance among Latinos (Valdez et al., 1993). They found that Mexican-Americans and Central and South Americans had the lowest rates of insurance coverage of all Latinos. Furthermore, during the ten-year period from 1979 to 1989, the number of uninsured Mexicans

Table 2-9. Uninsured Population by Race, 1991

Race/ Ethnic Group	Number of Persons (millions)	Percentage of Total Population	Number Uninsured (millions)	Percentage Uninsured in Each Racial/Ethnic Category	Percentage of Total Uninsured
White	161.1	73.9	21.0	13.0	57.8
Black	27.9	12.8	6.6	23.7	18.2
Hispanic	20.8	9.5	7.0	33.9	19.4
Other	8.4	3.9	1.7	20.1	4.7
Total	218.1	100.0	36.3	16.6	100.0

Source: Adapted from Foley, 1993, Table 15; data from March 1992 CPS.
Note: Nonelderly population. Rounding errors may occur in totals.

increased by 150 percent (42 percent of Mexican-Americans were uninsured in 1989); concurrently, the number of uninsured Central and South Americans living in the United States increased by 328 percent (44 percent of U.S. Central and South Americans were uninsured in 1989). These figures reflect both increases in populations as well as increases in the risk of being uninsured.

FAMILY COMPOSITION

Single individuals and members of single-parent households are more likely to be uninsured than those who are married (Table 2-10). The risk of being uninsured is highest among single childless individuals (27.9 percent of whom were uninsured) and second highest (20.1 percent) among members of single-parent families. Married couples with or without children are least likely to be uninsured (12.9 percent and 13.5 percent, respectively), for a number of reasons. They are more likely to have higher family incomes than either single individuals or single-parent families, since two-worker families are increasingly the norm. Members of a married couple in which both individuals are employed are more likely to have health insurance coverage through employment or indirectly as a dependent of the employed spouse.

Families with children are less likely to be uninsured than comparable households without children. One reason is that families with children are more likely to receive Medicaid through AFDC. Of poor or near-poor families (less than 125 percent of poverty level), 67 percent of persons in single-parent families *with children* received Medicaid in 1991 while only 25 percent of married couples without children received Medicaid (Foley, 1993).

GEOGRAPHY

There is wide variation in health insurance coverage by area of the country. Geographic differences in health coverage are associated with differences in wage rates, firm size, work-force attachment, Medicaid el-

Table 2-10. Uninsured Population by Family Type, 1991

Family Type	Number of Uninsured (millions)	Percentage Uninsured within Each Family Type	Percentage of Total Uninsured
Married with children	12.9	12.9	35.5
Married without children	6.8	13.5	18.8
Single with children	5.9	20.1	16.2
Single without children	10.7	27.9	29.5
Total	36.3	16.6	100.0

Source: Adapted from Foley, 1993, Table 10; data from March 1992 CPS.
Note: Nonelderly population.

igibility, right-to-work laws, and industry type (Congressional Research Service, 1988b). According to the March 1992 CPS, the Pacific and West South Central States had the highest percentages uninsured (19.8 and 24.0, respectively); the New England, Middle Atlantic, East North Central, and West North Central regions had the lowest percentages uninsured (11.9, 12.6, 12.2, and 12.2, respectively); the Mountain, South Atlantic, and East South Central regions had rates of uninsurance in the 17–19 percent range (Levit, Olin, and Letsch, 1992) (Figure 2-7).

The percentage of persons lacking health insurance coverage also varies within regions. The District of Columbia had the highest proportion uninsured in 1991 (30.3 percent), followed by Texas (25.3 percent), New Mexico (24.5 percent), and Florida (23.5 percent) (Foley, 1993). Connecticut and Hawaii had the lowest percentages (8.8 percent and 9.0 percent,[2] respectively) (Foley, 1993). With Hawaii's recent reform of its health insurance laws to cover the "gap group" (a term used by the state to refer to the portion of the population without insurance) the proportion of uninsured persons has dropped and is currently estimated at 3 percent (Miike, 1993).

THE DYNAMICS OF UNINSURANCE COVERAGE

Estimates of the uninsured derived from survey data convey a static image of insurance coverage, implying that individuals rarely change their status. In fact, there is surprisingly high turnover in this population, with some people experiencing short one-time spells without insurance, others experiencing loss of insurance periodically, and still others who are consistently uninsured over time. To design policies that can effectively provide coverage to the uninsured, the number of people experiencing short versus long spells and/or frequent spells without health insurance as well as the population correlates of these phenomena must be known.

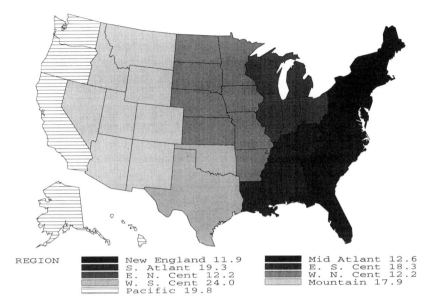

REGION

New England 11.9
S. Atlant 19.3
E. N. Cent 12.2
W. S. Cent 24.0
Pacific 19.8

Mid Atlant 12.6
E. S. Cent 18.3
W. N. Cent 12.2
Mountain 17.9

Figure 2-7. Percentage Uninsured by Geographic Region, 1991.
Source: Data from Foley, 1993, March 1992 CPS.
Note: Nonelderly population.

Survey designs that use repeated interviews of a cohort or panel of households allow us to track insurance coverage longitudinally and to describe its dynamics. The NMES measured health insurance status throughout 1987 with data from four household interviews held during 1987 and early 1988. Those who were listed as uninsured all year reported being uninsured for each of the four interviews (Short, Cornelius, and Goldstone, 1990). Analysts estimated the number of persons uninsured for at least part of 1987 at 47.6 million; 24.3 million for the entire year and 23.3 million for part of the year. The interpretation of these figures is more precise than those derived from the CPS because of the repeated waves at more frequent intervals (refer to previous discussion of measurement issues). Referring to these figures, the CPS estimates of 31–35 million uninsured for that time period apparently signify a mix of period and point-in-time estimates since they fall in between the numbers from NMES that indicate persons uninsured for the entire year and persons uninsured for *at least* part of the year.

Point-in-time estimates of the uninsured can miss people who are uninsured for short spells and bias estimates of size or characterizations of the uninsured toward those who experience long-term spells of uninsurance. Swartz, Marcotte, and McBride examined spells without health insurance by analyzing data from the 1984 SIPP panel, a lon-

Table 2-11. Transitions in Health Insurance Status from Private Coverage to No Coverage.

Number of Transitions	Percentage of All Privately Insured (N = 152 million)	Percentage of All Privately Insured Losing Coverage (N = 30 million)
0	80.4	
1	14.5	73.6
2	4.2	21.2
3+	1.0	5.2

Source: Monheit and Schur, 1988, p. 318; data from 1984 SIPP panel.

gitudinal household survey designed to provide detailed information on the economic circumstances of the noninstitutionalized civilian U.S. population (Swartz and McBride, 1990; Swartz, Marcotte, and McBride, 1993a, 1993b). With use of hazard rates derived from life tables (a way to summarize types of events that last different lengths of time), durations of uninsured spells were determined during a twenty-four-month period (N = 5,233). The researchers found that most spells without insurance ended within one year, while only 15 percent lasted longer than twenty-four months. Furthermore, as individuals continue to be uninsured over time (i.e., as their spell lengthens), the chances that they will obtain insurance and end the spell decrease substantially. In other words, people who are uninsured for long periods of time tend to stay uninsured.

Other investigators of the uninsured, using the SIPP panel data, have noted substantial movement between insured and uninsured status. Monheit and Schur (1988) followed cohorts of privately insured and uninsured persons from the 1984 SIPP panel for a 32-month period. They found that most people (80 percent) who were privately insured at the beginning remained privately insured throughout the 32-month period, but approximately one in five experienced one or more transitions from private coverage to no coverage. Of these, most (74 percent) experienced only one transition; 26 percent (approximately 8 million people) experienced two or more transitions in the thirty-two-month period (Table 2-11). Of those who lost coverage only once, 64 percent regained private coverage and 3 percent obtained public insurance and kept that insurance through to the end of the period. Most of those who lost coverage two or more times, however, were uninsured at the end of the period.

Among the cohort of persons uninsured in the first month of the SIPP panel, the researchers found much more instability in health insurance status. Of course, instability in this case would be viewed as positive, since it means that people gained health insurance. Approximately one-quarter (27 percent) of the uninsured remained uninsured

Table 2-12. Transitions in Health Insurance Status from Uninsured to Insured

Number of Transitions	Percentage of All Uninsured (N = 31 million)	Percentage of Uninsured Obtaining Coverage (N = 22 million)
0	27.3	
1	46.6	64.1
2	20.5	28.3
3+	5.6	7.6

Source: Monheit and Schur, 1988, p. 318; data from 1984 SIPP panel. Reprinted with permission.

for the entire 32-month period. Most (47 percent) experienced one transition to insured status. The rest (26 percent, or 8 million people) experienced two or more transitions to insured status (Table 2-12). Those uninsured for longer periods were more disadvantaged economically, with far less labor market attachment and thus less access to employment-related insurance than those who lacked coverage for shorter periods.

Jensen (1992) argued that policy-makers should pay particular attention to the dynamics of health insurance among the near elderly (ages 55–64) because this group is medically at high risk (and therefore more likely to incur large medical expenses), is particularly vulnerable to loss of insurance, and has short spells of uninsurance that are missed by point-in-time surveys. Among a cohort of 3,163 adults aged 55 to 64 from the 1984 SIPP panel, 21 percent experienced some time without health insurance (the modal spell was four months or less) and only 4 percent were continuously uninsured during the thirty-two-month period. The authors did not make comparisons with other age groups. Among those who lost insurance, the type of coverage lost by the near-elderly was typically individually purchased coverage (about 55 percent of cases), unlike the employer coverage most commonly lost by younger individuals. Specific reasons for insurance loss were difficult to determine precisely. A sudden loss in income (20 percent or more) was the most common reason cited (22 percent of the time), but 45 percent of respondents gave no answer that could be codified. Reform proposals, it was suggested, should aim to reform the individually purchased insurance market to prevent widespread short episodes of insurance loss among the near elderly.

THE UNDERINSURED

In addition to those who lack insurance altogether, there is a large segment of the U.S. population that has health insurance that may be inadequate in the event of serious illness or that discourages use of preventive services. Insurance plans that require large out-of-pocket expenditures[3] relative to personal income or that lack coverage for specific conditions may be inadequate for specific individuals. Among insured individuals there are at least six major causes of high out-of-pocket expenditures in the U.S. health care system (Bodenheimer, 1992): (1) lack of adequate coverage for catastrophic medical expenses due to dollar limits on lifetime medical benefits that are exceeded by many patients with serious and/or long-term illnesses; (2) exclusion from coverage or long waiting periods (mean = 9 months) for coverage of preexisting conditions when new coverage is obtained (most commonly at a new job); (3) failure to cover needed services (e.g., vaccinations, well-baby care, routine physical exams), particularly by private insurance; (4) widespread and increasing use of deductibles and coinsurance payments by employment-based group health plans; (5) cost-sharing occurring in public programs (Medicare, even when supplemented with Medigap—which not all elders purchase—covers only about half of the medical expenses of the elderly, and about one in five spend 15 percent of their income on medical care); and (6) the high cost and virtual nonexistence of private coverage for long-term care for the nonpoor (2 percent of nursing-home expenditures are paid by Medicare, and only 1 percent by private long-term care policies). To qualify for long-term care under Medicaid, the elderly must "spend down" their financial resources to below poverty levels.

According to a report by the Congressional Budget Office, any person with out-of-pocket expenditures for health care that exceed 10 percent of income is underinsured (Monheit et al., 1985). Under this retrospective criterion, families at or near the poverty level may be considered underinsured when out of-pocket expenditures for health care costs exceed $1,000 to $1,500; a family with income in excess of $100,000 would not be considered underinsured until health care costs exceeded $10,000.

The problem with applying criteria retrospectively in defining underinsurance is that persons with inadequate coverage who happen to be lucky enough to stay healthy are not captured in estimates. At the same time, individuals with good coverage but who are unlucky enough to experience a catastrophic illness are classified as underinsured. As an alternative, one could instead count the number of persons having policies with prespecified characteristics that suggest lack of catastrophic coverage, such as no limit on out-of-pocket hospital expenses. These data are hard to collect, however.

To address this definitional problem, Farley (1985) used income and health status data to develop probabilistic models of utilization and high out-of-pocket expenditures based on the NMCES of 1977. Using actuarial estimates, Farley defined underinsurance for preliminary estimates alternately as a 1 or 5 percent *expectation* that out-of-pocket expenditures would exceed 5, 10, or 20 percent of income. In the end, Farley settled on two working definitions of underinsurance: (1) persons who have a 5 percent or greater likelihood of incurring out-of-pocket health expenditures in excess of 10 percent of family income; and (2) persons who have a 1 percent chance of incurring out-of-pocket expenditures in excess of 10 percent of family income.

Estimates of the number of underinsured persons were sensitive to the definition chosen. Farley found that 7.9 percent of nonelderly persons in the United States covered by private health insurance plans had a 5 percent or greater chance of incurring out-of-pocket health expenditures in excess of 10 percent of income. This translates into 12.5 million Americans according to 1991 estimates of the number of privately insured. Approximately 13 percent had a 1 percent chance or greater of incurring out-of-pocket health expenditures in excess of 10 percent of income (20.5 million Americans by the 1991 value for the number of privately insured individuals).

Farley described the underinsured in terms of the size of their group plan, income, age, and other characteristics. Higher risk of underinsurance was associated with smaller group plans. Using the "5 percent chance" definition, 7 percent of individuals in group plans with fewer than 25 members were underinsured, while only 4.5 percent of those in plans with greater than 2,500 members were underinsured. Those purchasing nongroup insurance were seven times more likely to be underinsured than those in group plans (35.8 percent of those covered by nongroup insurance were underinsured).

It is not surprising that Farley also found that the likelihood of being underinsured was very strongly related to income (48 percent of the poor or near-poor versus only 2.3 percent of high-income people). Persons within the 55- to 64-year-old age group were at the highest risk of being underinsured in this analysis (20 percent of this age group was considered underinsured). Reasons cited for the higher risk among the near elderly include their higher chances of failing health and thus of incurring health care costs, and their likelihood of being insured through individual plans that typically offer less comprehensive coverage. Farley found that although the *size* of the underinsured population was sensitive to the definition, the characteristics were less so. In other words, relative to adequately insured individuals, the characteristics of underinsured persons in terms of employment, age, and income remained about the same even when different definitions of underinsurance were applied.

CONCLUSION

In this chapter we have explored sources of insurance and their limitations, summarized data on the size and the characteristics of the uninsured population, described the dynamic nature of insurance status, and examined the phenomenon of underinsurance. The uninsured can be quantified by either point-in-time or period estimates based on surveys such as the CPS or NMES. The numbers vary somewhat depending on the approach and the interpretation of answers to certain questions. We know that the risk of being uninsured is highest for single young adults who are poor or unemployed, although many uninsured persons are older and employed with moderate incomes. We also know that the problem of the uninsured goes far beyond the group of individuals who are continually without coverage. Millions of individuals experience short and/or multiple spells each year without health insurance. Last, it is clear that, although the large majority of Americans have health insurance coverage, many of them lack enough coverage to protect themselves from financial hardship in the event of serious illness.

Recent changes in coverage levels may impact on the motivation for health system reform. The number of uninsured has been growing steadily. In addition, employers have increased the amount of front-end cost sharing in the form of higher insurance premiums and increased deductibles. If this trend continues, the extent of underinsurance may continue to rise. Each of the three circumstances—permanent uninsurance, transient uninsurance, and underinsurance—has different implications for policy making. Understanding the size and characteristics of these populations is an important first step toward health system reform.

3

HEALTH STATUS

Mothers have probably always told their children, "If you have good health, you have everything." Maternal wisdom aside, health status is important to examine in the context of access to care for two reasons. As a medical outcome, poor overall health may indicate the existence of a problem due to lack of insurance. This effect may be indirect or direct. To the extent that insurance acts as a financial mechanism that enables persons to consume health care services, the effect on health outcomes is indirect, since it is really health services that lead to changes in health status. However, there may also be a *direct* effect of insurance on health. For example, if having health insurance provides a sense of well-being growing out of security, if it allows easy access to simple, everyday health questions, or if insured persons are provided with more timely and higher-quality care, then the mere fact of having insurance may enhance one's overall health status (see Hahn and Flood, 1993b, for a fuller discussion).

The direction of causality of the insurance–health relationship is controversial. As described in Chapter 1, it is theoretically possible that persons self-select into various levels of insurance plan if they know or believe themselves to be at higher risk. This is certainly the case with women planning a pregnancy, and also applies to the safety net aspects of Medicaid and its coverage of disabled and medically needy persons. Under this model, insurance status is "caused" by health status, not the other way around. Even if insurance status "causes" health, causal relationships are difficult to prove. Many factors beyond health care influence health status (environment, stress, and health knowledge and behaviors are some of the most obvious), and, therefore, it is difficult to isolate the influence of health insurance. Was the uninsured child (in a hypothetical study) hospitalized for asthma because that child could not see a doctor, or because the air quality in the child's tenement was poor?

A second reason for examining overall health status is that it is a strong predictor of the use of health services. For example, those who say they are in fair or poor health or who restrict their activity have nearly double the number of hospitalizations, physician visits, and prescription drugs of healthier persons (Wilensky and Berk, 1982). Thus, in assessing whether utilization is equitable, one needs to account for initial health status, which can determine the need for services.[1]

The most common measures of overall health status in the literature include perceived health status (measured as poor, fair, good, or excellent), days of limited activity, and number of chronic conditions. The relationship between payment status and overall health status in terms of each of these measures is described in the following.

PERCEIVED HEALTH STATUS

Uninsured persons report themselves to be in fair or poor health more often than do privately insured persons, and less often than do Medicaid recipients (Table 3-1). Since Medicaid was designed for the poor and sick, these figures are not surprising. Indeed, many beneficiaries may have become eligible under programs for the medically needy.

One potential confounder of the relationship between payment status and health status is age, since younger people tend to be healthier and are more likely to be uninsured. Two studies have tried to control for age. In a study of differences in health status by insurance coverage based on the 1980 NMCUES, uninsured respondents were healthier, but also younger, than the insured group. Upon closer inspection, the authors noted that the uninsured people reported worse health in every age stratum and, with statistical adjustment for age, were found to be in worse health, overall (Needleman et al., 1990).

A second study minimized confounding by age by restricting the data to low-income children. Rosenbach (1985) found that fair/poor health or limitations on activity were reported more frequently by the uninsured (9.7 percent) than the insured (6.7 percent) (Table 3-1). Children with Medicaid all year or part of the year (not shown in the table) were more likely to report fair/poor health or activity limitations than were the other groups (11.1 percent and 14.2 percent, respectively). Adverse selection may explain the finding that children insured by Medicaid for just part of the year reported worse health than those covered all year. Poor children who may not otherwise be eligible for Medicaid because their incomes are too high can obtain coverage under a program for medically needy people (in most states) if they incur high medical costs.

Income is also known to be related to health status (Freeman et al., 1987). Since Medicaid recipients are disproportionately poor, they could be sicker just because they are poorer. Analyses of the 1984 and the 1986 National Health Interview Survey (NHIS) examined both income and health status with respect to insurance coverage. The results

Table 3-1. The Percentage of the Population Reporting Fair or Poor Health, by Insurance Coverage, in Various Studies, Various Years

Study	Uninsured	Medicaid	Insured/ Other Insured
1977 NMCES			
Davis and Rowland, 1983	15		11
Wilensky and Berk, 1982[a]	19	34	18
1980 NMCUES			
Needleman et al., 1990[b]	4.1		2.5
Rosenbach, 1985[c]	9.7	11.1	6.7
Leicher et al., 1985	11.8	20.6	7.3
1982 RWJF Access Survey			
Andersen et al., 1987	25[d]		14
1984 NHIS			
Rowland and Lyons, 1989	11.3	19.4	6.6
1986 RWJF Access Survey			
Robert Wood Johnson Foundation, 1987[e]	12.2		11.7
1986 NHIS			
Congressional Research Service, 1988a	10		7
1989 Massachusetts survey			
Blendon et al., 1992	10		6

Note: Insured/Other Insured includes Medicaid if a separate figure is not provided.

[a] Poor/near poor, all ages.
[b] Age-adjusted; figures refer to poor health only.
[c] The study is restricted to low-income children. Outcome measures assessed were fair/poor health or activity limitation.
[d] Below 150 percent of poverty.
[e] All ages.

conflict. In 1984, both poverty level and insurance status were important correlates of health status (Table 3-2) (Rowland and Lyons, 1989). Among both uninsured and privately insured groups, those who were below poverty had substantially lower health status than the group as a whole. Likewise, within income groups, differences by payer appear to persist. Within each income and geographical grouping, there is a clear pattern. About 20 percent of Medicaid recipients report their health to be poor, but the proportion of privately insured persons reporting the same results is about one-third to one-half. The figures for uninsured persons consistently fall somewhere in the middle.

In a study based on data from just two years later, the relationship between insurance coverage and health status was not apparent. Analyses of the 1986 NHIS, this time stratified by family income rather than poverty status, showed little difference in reported health by insurance status after stratification (Table 3-3) (Congressional Research Service, 1988a). In this analysis Medicaid patients were analyzed together with privately insured persons, which certainly accounts for some of the discrepancy between the two studies, at least for those families with very low incomes.

Table 3-2. The Percentage of the Population under Age Sixty-Five Reporting Fair or Poor Health, by Residence, Poverty Status, and Insurance Coverage, 1984

Residence/ Poverty Status	Uninsured	Medicaid	Private/Other
Total	11.3	19.4	6.6
MSA			
Total	10.5	19.0	6.2
Below poverty	15.3	18.8	9.2
Non-MSA			
Total	12.8	20.5	7.5
Below poverty	15.9	21.0	12.8

Source: Adapted from Rowland and Lyons, 1989, Table 6, p. 992; data from National Health Interview Survey, 1984. Reprinted by permission of the Hospital Research and Educational Trust.

MSA = Metropolitan statistical area.

All of the previous studies tend to be limited in their failure to control for possibly spurious factors. Lacking extensive data on confounders makes it difficult to tease out evidence of a link between insurance coverage and health status. A study using the NMES data takes a step in the right direction. Hahn and Flood (1993a) examined the self-reported health status[2] of persons aged 18–64 and differentiated among those privately insured, publicly insured, and uninsured part or all of the year. In multiple regressions, they controlled for age, gender, race, education, family income, health-related lifestyle (obesity, activity level, smoking), disability status (SSI or Medicare), and utilization rates. They performed stratified analyses by age (18–44 and 45–64) and income (low, middle, high), and found consistent and positive effects on health status associated with private insurance. Persons with public insurance had the lowest levels of health, even lower than those of uninsured persons. Although the study's use of disability status as a control for prior health status is weak, and self-reported health can be somewhat subjective, the significant effects they found add considerable weight to arguments suggesting a direct link between insurance and health.

OTHER MEASURES OF HEALTH STATUS

LIMITATIONS IN ACTIVITY

Medicaid patients more frequently report limitations in activities than do privately insured or uninsured people. This pattern is no doubt in part an artifact of the disability category of eligibility for Medicaid. Among the poor and near-poor in 1977, Medicaid beneficiaries had on average eleven bed days, compared with seven for the other insured

Table 3-3. The Percentage of the Population under Age Sixty-Five Reporting Fair or Poor Health, by Family Income and Insurance Coverage, 1986

Family Income	Uninsured	Insured	Difference[a]
<$15,000	13	15	−2
$15,000–24,999	9	8	1
$25,000–49,999	5	4	1
>$50,000	2	2	0
All persons	10	7	3

Source: Data from 1986 National Health Interview Survey, Congressional Research Service, 1988a, p. 170.

[a] Difference in percentage points, uninsured minus insured.

and five for the uninsured. Likewise, 21 percent of Medicaid recipients reported limited activity, compared with 19 percent for privately insured and 12 percent for uninsured people (Wilensky and Berk, 1982).

Using the 1980 NMCUES, Howell (1988) found consistent differences among insurance status groups in the mean number of days of restricted activity, stratified by poverty status. Medicaid recipients reported the most days, followed by privately insured and then uninsured people. Differences by insurance status were consistent across poverty strata. Furthermore, based on the 1982 Robert Wood Johnson Foundation (RWJF) survey, total nonhospital disability days (another indicator of activity limitations) were greatest for the uninsured below 150 percent of poverty level (15 days), followed by the insured (12 days) and the uninsured above 150 percent of poverty (9 days) (Andersen et al., 1987).

As in the analysis of overall health status, the age distribution of the different insurance groups may affect overall figures. A subsequent analysis using the 1980 NMCUES compared uninsured with all insured persons in terms of limitation in activity, with adjustment for age. Crude rates were higher for the insured, but after adjustment a higher proportion of uninsured than of the insured reported some limitation in activity (6.4 percent versus 5.7 percent) (Needleman et al., 1990). Finally, in a survey of nonelderly Massachusetts residents performed in 1989, Blendon et al. (1992) found that 16 percent of uninsured people had a disability that limited their activity, while only 8 percent of insured people indicated that this was true. We are unaware of any analyses of these health status measures that controlled for both age and income.

CHRONIC OR SERIOUS DISEASE, AND SYMPTOMS

The RWJF 1986 access survey reported that 12.4 percent of uninsured persons have chronic or serious disease, compared with 20.9 percent of insured persons (Robert Wood Johnson Foundation, 1987).[3] Other evidence, however, suggests that the uninsured are no different from the privately insured in terms of their prevalence of specific chronic conditions, including back problems, heart disease, asthma, and others (Rundall et al., 1991). It may seem unlikely that persons with chronic or serious illnesses would fail to purchase insurance, yet that appears to be the case, at least in some instances. One explanation is that preexisting conditions can prevent individuals from obtaining insurance policies outright or can make available policies extraordinarily expensive.

Finally, other studies have examined the number of symptoms reported by respondents and evaluated their seriousness. Persons on public insurance were the sickest, followed by uninsured persons and then privately insured persons (Andersen et al., 1987).

CONCLUSIONS

The evidence on the relation of health status to insurance status is mixed. Without adjusting for confounders, investigators have found that Medicaid patients are more likely to report fair or poor health status than uninsured patients and privately insured patients. In studies that controlled for income, the results on perceived health status conflict, although there is evidence suggesting true difference in health status by payer. In studies of limitation in activity and the presence of chronic or serious disease, Medicaid patients are again sicker, although the findings comparing uninsured and privately insured patients are inconsistent.

The poorer health status of Medicaid recipients is due at least in part to the adverse selection that occurs as a result of categorical eligibility for the disabled or programs for the medically needy. We are not aware of any studies that show how the health status of Medicaid beneficiaries varies in relation to the eligibility criteria set up by different states. Age and income adjustments are clearly appropriate for comparisons of health status by insurance coverage, yet have not always been made in previous studies. Overall, existing knowledge suggests that analyses of utilization by payer are likely to be confounded by health status, and the relationships between the two variables may be subtle.[4]

4

INTERMEDIATE PROCESS INDICATORS

When asked to talk about problems with access to care, most people tell you about problems getting to see the doctor, whether it be for a runny nose and cough or for a painful hip that limits mobility. These problems may influence the frequency of visits or the nature of one's relationship with a provider. In the next two chapters we review evidence on disparities in what we call the "process of care." The *process of care* is a phrase that describes the character and quantity of health care services received by patients.[1] In this chapter we are concerned with particular aspects of health care delivery that are commonly believed to represent barriers to the receipt of optimal care. We look at four types of "intermediate" access indicators that might prevent people from seeing their doctor in a timely way: patients' usual source of care, the location of their care, the convenience of services, and the use of municipal hospitals. In Chapter 5 we will examine the utilization of care provided by physicians and hospitals—the two principal components of mainstream medical care—by comparing the quantity and quality of patient–provider interactions while highlighting research that considers the medical need for these services in its analysis.

HAVING A USUAL OR REGULAR SOURCE OF CARE

There are two principal concerns over the source of medical care: whether persons have a "usual" or "regular" place to get care, and the site or location of their care. Persons without a regular source of medical care may lack an entry point to the health care system when an acute problem strikes. Therefore, they may be less likely to receive necessary treatment in a timely manner.[2] Research has shown that persons without a regular source are less likely to report that important health problems have been cured (Cornelius, 1991) and have lower levels of satisfaction with care (Andersen et al., 1987). Patients may be less willing to seek out preventive services of proven efficacy when they lack a regular source of care. For example, women without a regular source of care are significantly less likely to have had a Pap smear in the past year (for women 20 years old and older), to have had a breast examination by a physician (women 40 years old and older), or a mammogram (women 50 years old and older) (Hayward et al., 1991).

The second issue about sources of care concerns the location where persons receive their care (i.e., whether it occurs in a physician's office, an emergency room, or a clinic). When the usual source of care is a hospital outpatient department or emergency room, organizational impediments can result in a lack of continuity with a particular provider, or services that are episodic and not comprehensive. Children receiving routine care at a clinic, for example, are ten times as likely to go elsewhere for sick care as are children who receive routine care at a private physician's office (St. Peter, Newacheck, and Halfon, 1992). At the forefront of policy concerns over the location of care are the use and possible abuse of emergency departments by poor people, particularly those with public insurance. There is little debate over the value of emergency rooms; they provide twenty-four-hour coverage and technologically advanced care. Emergency rooms, however, are probably not an optimal source of primary care. They provide little continuity of care because patients rarely see the same physician each time they visit. They may be unnecessarily expensive if overhead costs are high or if health care providers order superfluous tests because they are not familiar with the patient's medical history. Clinics in hospital outpatient departments potentially offer advantages over emergency rooms in terms of the cost and continuity of care, but their use still implies care that may be less continuous and comprehensive than that in a community-based alternative (Freeman et al., 1990).

Uninsured persons are more likely than either privately or publicly insured persons to lack a usual source of care, as highlighted by figures from numerous surveys (Table 4-1). Between the years 1980–1982 and 1986–1987, the proportion of persons not having a usual source of care appears to have increased for all payer groups, but especially for the uninsured. The figures reported by Rosenbach (1985) and by Bloom (1990) refer only to children, which may explain the lower percentages of uninsured people without a usual source of care in those studies.

The influence of income, health status, and other factors in combination with insurance has been examined with respect to the presence of a usual source of care, and the differences by payer appear to hold. At least four studies include a multivariate analysis of the probability of having a usual source, with two of them using RWJF data. In an analysis of the 1982 RWJF sample that controlled for age, sex, income, health status, race/ethnicity, and urban/rural residence, the uninsured were 1.6 times as likely as the insured not to have a regular source of care (Hayward et al., 1988a). Similar results were found in a subset of the

Table 4-1. Persons without a Usual Source of Care, by Insurance Coverage, in Various Studies, Various Years

Study	Uninsured	Public Insurance	Private Insurance
1980 NMCUES			
Howell, 1988	25	15	13
Rosenbach, 1985[a]	18	16	13
1982 RWJF Survey			
Needleman et al., 1990[b]	22	11	10
1986 RWJF Survey			
Robert Wood Johnson Foundation, 1987[c]	31		16
1987–1988 Orange County Survey			
Hubbell et al., 1989	39	13[d]	
1987 NMES			
Cornelius, Beauregard, and Cohen, 1991	35	13	18
1988 NHIS			
Bloom, 1990[e]	21		8
St. Peter, Newacheck, and Halfon, 1992	22[f]		9[g]

Source: Weissman and Epstein, 1993, p. 248. © 1993 by Annual Reviews, Inc. Reprinted with permission.

Note: Davis and Rowland (1983) reported that NMCES confirms these findings, but specific figures are not provided.

[a] Low-income children (below 150 percent of poverty).
[b] Lewin/ICF tabulations from the 1982 Robert Wood Johnson Foundation Access Survey.
[c] Includes persons aged sixty-five and older.
[d] All insured low-income adults (below 200 percent of poverty).
[e] Children seventeen years of age or younger.
[f] Poor children without Medicaid.
[g] Poor children with Medicaid.

1986 sample (Hayward et al., 1991). Hubbell et al. (1989a) found that insured low-income persons were three times as likely to have a regular source of care as low-income uninsured persons, with control for income, ethnicity, and employment status. Finally, in a study of low-income children in the 1980 NMCUES, uninsured low-income children were more likely than Medicaid recipients or privately insured children to lack a regular source of care (18 percent, 15 percent, and 13 percent, respectively) (Rosenbach, 1985).

Just as people have different ideas of how to use medical care in general, they may have different preferences about seeing a doctor regularly. Understanding the reason for not having a regular source of care may therefore be important in determining whether there is a problem in access. Analyzing RWJF data, Hayward and colleagues (1991) noticed that of individuals *without* a regular source of care, 61 percent did not want one! These patients may not perceive an access problem in their situation. Of course, there are reasons for lacking a regular source of care that suggest real barriers to access, such as financial problems or difficulty getting appointments. Only 13 percent of respondents fell into this category, however (Hayward et al., 1991). To investigate more deeply, the authors next specified several regressions for the probability of *not* having a regular source for any reason (overall) and for specific reasons (e.g., financial), with control for age, sex, health status, income, race, urban/rural residence, and education. Uninsured respondents were significantly more likely than insured respondents to report no regular source overall and were also more likely to lack a regular source because of financial problems ($p < .05$).

Whether having a regular physician is a matter of patient preference, as suggested earlier, or of financial necessity, the impact of having no insurance coverage on having a regular medical contact may be felt especially by those who are poor. In a study of the loss of Medicaid status among medically indigent adults in California, Lurie et al. (1984, 1986) noted a considerable drop in the proportion of persons who reported having a regular physician—from a baseline figure of 96 percent down to 40 percent after six months, and then back up to only 50 percent after one year—while the control group who kept their Medicaid status remained the same as their baseline at 94 percent. It is very unlikely that these patients had a sudden change in their preference for a regular source of care. One can therefore conclude from these results that the chances of keeping a regular physician are drastically reduced when a poor person loses insurance.

THE LOCATION OF CARE

Where one receives health services is often linked to whether the care is regular or "continuous." Most of the surveys listed in Table 4-1 also examined the location of patients' usual source of care and found differences by insurance class.[3] We present the most recent findings from the 1987 NMES in Table 4-2. Of those with a usual source, uninsured and publicly insured patients were less likely than privately insured patients to have a physician's office as their usual source of care and more likely to rely on hospital-based or other sources. These patterns are probably related to the finding (not shown in the table) that both uninsured and publicly insured patients were also less likely to see a specific physician at their usual source. Thus, taken together with the findings from the previous section, those with public insurance had about the same likelihood of having a usual source as the private insured, but they closely resembled the uninsured in their access to a physician's office as a usual source.

These figures on the location of the usual source of care may underestimate the reliance of groups on hospital-based ambulatory care,

Table 4-2. Location of the Usual Source of Care, by Insurance Coverage, 1987

Location	Uninsured	Public Insurance	Private Insurance
Hospital outpatient or emergency room	11	14	5
Physician's office	74	71	88
Other nonhospital sources[a]	15	16	7

Source: Data from Cornelius, Beauregard, and Cohen, 1991.

[a] Includes health centers, company and school clinics, walk-in centers, patient's home.

since they derive only from individuals who claim to have a consistent source of care. For people who were with or without a usual source of care, the RWJF 1986 access survey included questions about the location of recent visits. The researchers found that 24.3 percent of the uninsured reported the emergency room or the outpatient department was the site of their most recent ambulatory visit (regardless of whether it was a usual source), compared with 13.2 percent of the insured ($p < .05$) (Freeman et al., 1990). In a study of children, the proportion of care that Medicaid recipients and other insured youths received in the emergency department was twice as high if they reported not having a regular source of care (Orr et al., 1991).

Perhaps because of their reliance on the emergency department as a regular source of care, uninsured and Medicaid patients are also far more likely than others to be admitted to the hospital via this route. In a recent study of patients hospitalized in a group of five Massachusetts hospitals, uninsured and Medicaid patients were approximately three times as likely as insured patients to have entered the hospital via the emergency room (Stern, Weissman, and Epstein, 1991).

The hypotheses presuming to explain the apparent overutilization of emergency room visits by Medicaid and uninsured patients are myriad. Poor and uninsured patients may have more urgent health care problems or may be unable to receive care elsewhere during normal working hours. It may be that for those receiving free care or care paid for by Medicaid, there is no incentive to use cheaper sources. Given the extremely long waiting times in some emergency departments (Baker et al., 1991; Bindman et al., 1991), it seems just as likely that other, more pressing factors may come into play. Poor neighborhoods often lack easily accessible community-based alternatives, and physicians tend to locate their practices in affluent neighborhoods. The lack of alternatives may be reinforced by positive or attractive elements of certain facilities. The staff at public hospitals are often known to be sensitive to the special needs of patients with low incomes and tolerant of varied lifestyles (see, for example, Altman et al., 1989). In addition, institutional providers in general may be more receptive to uninsured patients because they have more options to cost-shift or to receive explicit funding for uncompensated care that might not be available in other settings.

One of the side effects of our fragmented, two-tiered medical care system is that the poorest and the sickest are often left to wander through the system without guidance or oversight or incentives to use services appropriately. While apocryphal anecdotes of abuses are rare, at least some authors have charged that the absence of preutilization review and lack of financial disincentives (i.e., cost-sharing) for welfare patients result in wasted resources and inefficient care-seeking behavior (Dickhudt, Gjerdingen, and Asp, 1987). For example, in a study involving 1,200 insured persons (all ages) in Minnesota, the authors codified visits to an emergency room as "essential," "marginally appropriate," and "inappropriate." The last category was defined to comprise emergency visits for mild acute problems and chronic conditions. Sixty-one percent of emergency room visits for Medicaid patients were inappropriate, compared with 19 percent for HMO patients and 33 percent for privately insured individuals. The figures for essential visits were 13 percent, 22 percent, and 20 percent, respectively; these results persisted after stratification by the time of the visit (daytime versus after-hours) (Dickhudt, Gjerdingen, and Asp, 1987). The authors did not control for age in this analysis, yet older persons may suffer from a greater preponderance of serious conditions warranting emergency care. If Medicaid recipients in the AFDC program were younger than the insured groups, this might account for some of the difference in patterns of use. Nevertheless, the pattern of data suggests that Medicaid patients receive substantial amounts of care in emergency rooms for problems that are not truly medical emergencies.

The preceding data supply information on the *proportion* of care provided at different locations. Analyses based on *rates* of use offer a slightly different slant. The uninsured make fewer ambulatory visits overall than insured groups (see the more complete discussion in the section on physician use, following). Even though they are relatively more likely to use the outpatient department as a source of care, they have lower absolute rates of outpatient department visits—about 0.5 per year overall, compared with about 0.6 visits per year for the insured (Needleman et al., 1990). This finding holds for all age groups under age 65, with the exception of pregnant women. Uninsured pregnant women have much higher rates of outpatient department use than the insured (1.8 versus 1.3 per capita). This fact may reflect the lack of private obstetric care in urban areas where outpatient departments are prevalent. Other studies, as well, suggested that low Medicaid reimbursement rates may cause care to be shifted to institutional sources (Long, Settle, and Stuart, 1986; Cohen, 1989).

Table 4-3. Travel Time and Waiting Time for Persons with a Usual Source of Care, by Insurance Coverage, 1977–1987

	Uninsured	Public Insurance	Private Insurance
Davis and Rowland, 1983 (1977 NMCES)			
Traveling ≥ 30 minutes	25		18[a]
Leicher et al., 1985 (1980 NMCUES)			
Traveling ≥ 60 minutes	5.5	4.5	2.5
Waiting ≥ 60 minutes	24.0	29.4	18.0
Cornelius, Beauregard, and Cohen, 1991 (1987 NMES)			
Traveling ≥ 60 minutes[b]	3.9	4.9	1.7
Waiting ≥ 60 minutes[b]	15.5	19.8	8.5

Source: Weissman and Epstein, 1993, p. 250. © 1993 by Annual Reviews, Inc. Reprinted with permission.

[a] Includes all insured.
_ [b] All differences $p < .05$.

CONVENIENCE

The convenience of care (measured by travel and waiting times) may be associated with rates of service, especially for minor problems or visits for preventive care. The NMCES, NMCUES, and NMES have all queried patients on travel and waiting times. Uninsured persons in 1977 were more likely than others to travel thirty minutes or more to receive care (25 percent versus 18 percent, $p < .05$); somewhat surprisingly, this occurred within the confines of standard metropolitan statistical areas as well as outside of them (Davis and Rowland, 1983) (Table 4-3). The authors did not report on the mode of transportation, but it seems reasonable to surmise that part of the explanation of longer travel times is that they also must rely more often on public transportation. When they arrive at their site of care, uninsured individuals generally have to wait longer, particularly if they are minorities or live in the South (Davis and Rowland, 1983). Note, however, that in studies that examine publicly insured patients separately, the differences between uninsured and Medicaid patients are minor compared with differences between these two groups and the privately insured. For example, in a more recent study of persons with a usual source of care (reported in the 1987 NMES), those with public insurance or no insurance were each more than twice as likely as the privately insured to travel sixty minutes or more to their usual site or to have to wait sixty minutes or more once they arrived ($p < .05$) (Table 4-3) (Cornelius, Beauregard, and Cohen, 1991).

Extremely long waiting times may have an important impact on patients' health. At a public hospital in California, Baker, Stevens, and Brook (1991) studied patients who left an emergency department without being seen and compared them with those who waited.[4] The average waiting times were 6.2 hours for those who waited to be seen and 6.4 hours for those who left. The acuity of the patient's condition was determined by nurse triage ratings and by retrospective review of medical charts by the authors based on prospective clinical criteria. Nearly half of those who left were judged to need immediate medical attention and 11 percent were subsequently hospitalized within one week.

THE USE OF MUNICIPAL HOSPITALS

Public hospitals have long been characterized as the provider of last resort for the poor and uninsured. During the 1940s and 1950s, poor patients flocked to these facilities, which in turn grew in number and size. Since the advent of Medicaid, however, large numbers of patients have taken advantage of their newfound insured status and "voted with their feet," choosing to use other hospitals because of convenience, a perception of better quality, or some other reason (Altman et al., 1989). In fact, the bulk of uncompensated care is actually provided by voluntary and private hospitals, simply because there are so many of them. Nevertheless, municipally owned hospitals are still an important source of care for the poor, the uninsured, and the underinsured. Several authors have noted the disproportionate burden of uncompensated care borne by public hospitals (Coffey, 1983; Kelly, 1985; Sloan, Valvona, and Mullner, 1986; Sulvetta and Swartz, 1986).[5]

When municipal hospitals are absent or are closed down, access to care by those who rely on them may suffer due to the inability or unwillingness of other area facilities to serve the needy population. A national study of metropolitan areas adjusted the number of hospital admissions (to reflect outpatient use) and then compared numbers of uncompensated "adjusted admissions" among cities with and without public hospitals. The authors found between 31 and 34 uncompensated adjusted admissions per 100 uninsured poor persons in cities with public hospitals, versus 24 per 100 in cities without public hospitals (Thorpe and Brecher, 1987). When the public hospital in Shasta County, California, shut down, Bindman, Keane, and Lurie (1990) surveyed patients who had been discharged from the hospital. One year later they found that the percentage of persons who had no regular provider, were denied medical care, had to wait seven or more days for an appointment, or missed medications before refill had all increased. A similar group in another county reported decreases in all of those categories ($p < .05$ for all comparisons).

5

THE QUANTITY AND QUALITY OF CARE

This chapter continues with the discussion of process. The quantity and quality of specific services constitute "ultimate process indicators"—measures of medical care that represent actual encounters (or the absence of any) between patients and providers. The stage for this review is set with a look at overall per capita expenditures and how they differ among persons with varying levels and types of insurance coverage. Next, findings from research on use of physicians and hospitals are presented for the key comparison groups. This is followed by a short section on prescription drug use. Combined, these sections describing service use offer insights into how uninsured persons fare compared with insured groups in their use of mainstream medicine. The chapter concludes with a review of topics that reflect problems in achieving timely access (e.g., foregone care, delayed care and patient dumping), and with an examination of the use of preventive services.

With respect to the topics covered in this chapter, it is important to weigh carefully the quality of the research performed. One of the challenges to studying access is the ability to compare "apples with apples." Finding differences in visits or hospital days among different populations is not very meaningful unless one has some confidence that the populations being compared are similar in terms of health status or other variables associated with the need and demand for care. Otherwise, it may just be that some groups use less care because they are less sick. Thus, the more thoughtful investigations control explicitly for prior health status. There is also a branch of access studies that control *implicitly* for health status. To do this, researchers try to zero in on important and necessary care, so they ask people about delays or denial of health services that were "needed." This approach suffers from a reliance on subjective opinions by nonphysicians, but at least one can compare utilization between groups with similar wants. Studying the use of preventive care is another way to think about access for an implied need. The assumption is that certain preventive services are clinically appropriate for all patients falling in predetermined age or gender categories. Knowing individuals' health status, then, is not so important. For example, nearly all adult women should receive regular breast exams, even if they are healthy. When people fail to receive recommended preventive services, questions of access arise.

PER CAPITA AND OUT-OF-POCKET EXPENDITURES FOR HEALTH CARE

One common way to measure health care utilization is to examine total health care expenditures. Differences in aggregate spending figures are suggestive but not conclusive evidence of access problems. Low health costs in one group relative to another may occur for a variety of reasons unrelated to access. For example, patients with low total expenditures may use services less frequently than others to treat identical problems. Others may receive less intensive or less sophisticated services when they use them, or they may buy services at lower prices. Differences in overall cost between insured and uninsured persons in particular may result from differences in underlying sociodemographic characteristics or health status. Nevertheless, there is the lingering suspicion that higher cost indicates better overall care. Out-of-pocket expenditures are a subset of total expenditures and tend to measure the financial burden of health care. They are most meaningful when analyzed relative to disposable income. However, neither total expenditures nor out-of-pocket expenditures are normally considered to be valuable indicators of access for the reasons discussed earlier.

During the past fifteen years, three major national surveys of health care use sponsored by the National Center for Health Statistics and other organizations have provided information on these topics (see Appendix A for descriptions of NMCES, NMCUES, and NMES). In this section we will review published data from the two most recent surveys—NMCUES and NMES.

Uninsured persons are responsible for far fewer health care dollars per capita than insured individuals in this country. An estimate prepared by Lewin/ICF using 1980 NMCUES data indicates that aggregate spending levels by uninsured persons were 40 percent below those of insured persons (Table 5-1) (Needleman et al., 1990). Furthermore, uninsured persons had lower per capita health care expenditures in every category of service. The distribution of expenditures among the categories of use also paints a different picture of patterns of care. Uninsured patients rely disproportionately on hospital care (36 percent of expenditures versus 27 percent for the insured). This pattern has at least four possible explanations relevant to concerns over access. First, higher reliance on inpatient treatment may be indicative of better sources of funding for uncompensated care, leading patients and their

Table 5-1. Estimated per Capita Personal Health Care Expenditures (Percentage of Total) for Noninstitutionalized Nonelderly Persons, by Insurance Coverage, 1988

Category of Use	Insured		Uninsured	
Hospital inpatient	$ 396	(27.2%)	$313	(36.0%)
Hospital emergency room and outpatient	143	(9.8)	90	(10.3)
Physicians office visits	459	(31.6)	239	(27.6)
Dentists	212	(14.5)	91	(10.7)
Other professional	81	(5.6)	31	(3.4)
Prescription drugs and medical sundries	92	(6.3)	67	(7.8)
Eyeglasses and appliances	40	(2.7)	22	(2.5)
Other health care	34	(2.3)	13	(1.7)
Total	$1,457	(100.0)	$866	(100.0)

Source: Needleman et al., 1990, p. 45; data from Lewin/ICF estimates using the health Benefits Simulation Model using the 1980 National Medical Care Utilization and Expenditure Survey.
Note: The 1980 data have been updated to reflect trends in utilization and population characteristics.

doctors to gravitate toward institutional facilities rather than small ambulatory settings. Second, insured persons might overuse ambulatory care to a greater extent than uninsured persons. A third argument, and one that is gaining prominence in the access literature, is that people who face financial barriers might defer seeking primary care or other ambulatory treatment until the condition worsens and warrants hospitalization. To the extent that these hospitalizations can be avoided, public dollars might be better spent in improving cost-effective uses of ambulatory care[1] (see further detail in Chapter 6). Finally, a fourth explanation behind the contrary patterns of hospital use is that young uninsured people may rely with greater dependence on hospital care as their first contact with the health care system since their health needs are more likely to be due to accidents and pregnancy.

One of the original goals of the Medicaid legislation was to reduce the out-of-pocket financial burden of receiving medical care. Medicaid recipients do indeed have drastically lower out-of-pocket burdens than other payer groups. Data from the 1987 NMES provide detailed information on the key insurance classes. Lefkowitz and Monheit (1991) began their investigation of out-of-pocket expenditures by identifying persons with at least some contact with the system. It was determined that 87.3 percent of privately insured respondents younger than age 65 reported at least some use of medical services in 1987, compared with 82.9 percent of similarly aged respondents with public insurance only,[2] and 63.7 percent of those who were uninsured all year. Of those with any use, the total expenditure was highest for those with public insurance and lowest for the uninsured (Table 5-2). Mean out-of-pocket expenditures are actually highest for privately insured users. As might be

Table 5-2. The Mean Total and Out-of-Pocket Expenditures per Person Using Services, by Insurance Coverage, 1987

	Uninsured All Year		Public Insurance[a]		Private Insurance	
	All	Poor[b]	All	Poor	All	Poor
Total expenditures[c] ($)	915	1,008	2,619	2,946	1,316	1,627
Mean out-of-pocket expenditures ($)	346	318	226	167	380	367
Proportion spent out of pocket[d] (%)	77	74	17	13	53	52

Source: Lefkowitz and Monheit, 1991, Table 1.

[a] Medicare, Medicaid, CHAMPUS/CHAMPVA, or other public insurance.
[b] Family income below 100 percent of the federal poverty level.
[c] Expenditures do not include health insurance premiums.
[d] Computed for each person and then averaged.

expected, the order is dramatically altered when looking just at the *proportion* of total expenditures represented by out-of-pocket expenditures since the population without insurance tends to have lower incomes than average. The highest figures (77 percent) are for the uninsured, and the lowest figures (17 percent) are for the publicly insured. This ordering stays the same even when the authors focused on people with incomes below poverty. A note of caution in interpreting these figures is warranted. Out-of-pocket expenditures for health insurance premiums are not included, and this omission could substantially affect the figures for people who pay for their own private insurance.

PHYSICIAN VISITS

Disparities in the use of physician services have long been used as indicators of possible inequities in access. This section begins by describing some of the advances in access to physicians attributable to Medicaid in its early years. The focus then turns toward the uninsured. The chapter is structured so that studies limited to crude (unadjusted) physician use rates are presented first, followed by studies that controlled for sundry confounders, one at a time. The section ends with a review of multivariate analyses that compare service use for the three key comparison groups (Medicaid, uninsured, and privately insured) while simultaneously controlling for a number of potentially important confounders.

It is useful to view the use of physicians from two complementary perspectives. The percentage of persons who do not see a physician at all during a year is a gross indicator of initial access to the system—a physician cannot prescribe medicines or make a referral to specialists if there is no initial contact. There is also an underlying assumption that the first decision to seek care usually belongs to the patients, while the level of use once care is initiated is in the provider's realm of decision making. Measuring total use or the mean number of visits per user

Table 5-3. The Percentage Reporting No Visits to Physicians during One Year, Various Studies

	Uninsured	Medicaid	Private/Other
1977 NMCES			
Wilensky and Berk, 1985[a]	50	30	36
1980 NMCUES			
Kasper, 1986[b]	43.7	21.2	24.4
Rosenbach, 1985[c]	36.3	24.8	31.0
1982 RWJF			
Andersen et al., 1987	30	15	18
1984 NHIS			
Rowland and Lyons, 1989	40.8	17.2	25.9
1986 RWJF			
Freeman et al., 1990[d]	44		35.7
1987–1988 Orange County Survey			
Hubbell et al., 1989a[e]	32		11

Source: Weissman and Epstein, 1993, p. 252. © 1993 by Annual Reviews, Inc. Reprinted with permission.

[a] Poor/near poor (below 150 percent of poverty), all ages, figure given is 1 minus the probability of a visit.
[b] Calculated from age-specific rates.
[c] Low-income children.
[d] Adults only.
[e] Low-income, below 200 percent of poverty levels.

is a second way to measure basic access to physicians. These data describe the intensity of use for those who are able to cross the threshold of initial access to the system.

THE USE OF PHYSICIANS BY MEDICAID RECIPIENTS

The arrival of Medicaid in 1966 had an enormous effect on the ability of the very poor to see physicians. Until that time, the poor routinely had utilized physicians less often than more advantaged Americans, despite having more health problems. By 1974, the trend had reversed itself and persons with low incomes had 13 percent more physician visits than did persons with higher incomes. These figures were not adjusted for health status. Although low-income children still saw physicians less often than children in families of higher income, between 1964 and 1974 the differential was substantially reduced (Davis, 1976; Donabedian, 1976).

More recent evidence affirms the role of Medicaid in assuring that recipients are able to gain access to physicians. Medicaid recipients are less likely than either the uninsured or the privately insured to go without seeing a physician for one year. Table 5-3 includes results from studies that provide unadjusted data on this measure and explicitly compare Medicaid recipients with other payer groups. This pattern is especially evident among poor persons. In a study of 652 low-income persons in California, those without Medicaid were more than twice as

Table 5-4. The Mean Number of Visits to Physicians, by Insurance Coverage

	Uninsured	Medicaid	Private/Other
1977 NMCES			
Wilensky and Berk, 1985[a]	2.4	4.5	3.5
1980 NMCUES			
Leicher et al., 1985	2.0	5.0	3.8
Taube and Rupp, 1986[b]		5.9	5.0[c]
1984 NHIS			
Rowland and Lyons, 1989	2.6	5.7	3.3

[a] Poor/near poor (below 150 percent of poverty), all ages.
[b] Poor/near poor with at least one use.
[c] All poor/near poor not enrolled in Medicaid.

likely not to have seen a physician in the past year than those with in-surance (assumed to be enrolled in Medicaid) (Hubbell et al., 1989a). Medicaid recipients also visit physicians more often on average than patients with private insurance or those who are uninsured. The find-ings presented in Table 5-4 (and Table 5-5) are from studies that com-pare unadjusted mean number of physician visits for Medicaid with similar data for other insurance groups. Physician visit rates per capita for those on Medicaid are nearly twice as high as for the uninsured and are consistently higher than for the other insured populations.

It is often difficult to translate research statistics into the perspective of actual policies. Yet, Blendon et al. (1986) were able to use national data and a special survey in Arizona to confirm the importance of Medicaid in providing access to physicians for the poor. Using results from the RWJF 1982 access survey and a similar survey conducted in Arizona, which did not have a Medicaid program at the time of the study, the authors found that low-income persons in Arizona and in

Table 5-5. The Mean Number of Visits to Physicians for Low-income Persons in Arizona and the United States, by Age and Medicaid Coverage, 1982

	Location		Medicaid Coverage of States	
Age	Arizona	United States	Top Third	Bottom Third
0–16	3.2	5.3[a]	6.7[a]	4.8[a]
17–64	6.1	7.0[a]	7.7	6.5
65+	6.5	6.0	na	na

Source: Adapted from Blendon et al., 1986, p. 1162. Reprinted by permission of the *New England Journal of Medicine.*
Note: States were ranked by the proportion of the low-income population covered by Medicaid.
[a] Differed significantly from Arizona, $p < .05$.
na = not applicable.

Table 5-6. Visits to Physicians by the Uninsured as a Percentage of Insured Use, in Various Studies, Various Years

Survey	Percentage
1977 NMCES	
Davis and Rowland, 1983	65
Wilensky and Berk, 1982[a]	68
1980 NMCUES	
Leicher et al., 1985	53
Long and Settle, 1985 (low-income adults and children)	68
1984 Survey of Income and Program Participation	
Long and Rodgers, 1989	63
1984 NHIS	
Rowland and Lyons, 1989	46–79[b]
1986 NHIS	
Congressional Research Service, 1988	64
Congressional Research Service, <$15,000 income	53
Long and Rodgers, 1989	75
1986 Robert Wood Johnson Survey	
Freeman et al., 1987	72
1989 NHIS	
Hafner-Eaton, 1993	0.5–0.62[c]

Source: Weissman and Epstein, 1993, p. 253; based on Garrison, 1990, Table 1. © 1993 by Annual Reviews, Inc. Reprinted with permission.

[a] Wilensky and Berk included all ages.
[b] Lower figure with respect to Medicaid; high figure with respect to privately insured.
[c] These figures are odds ratios; the lower is for well patient and chronically ill patients; the higher is for acutely ill patients.

states with limited Medicaid programs made substantially fewer physician visits than low-income persons in other states (Table 5-5). The authors argued convincingly that the results could not have been due to differences in practice styles between Arizona and the rest of the country because differences in use of physicians by the elderly, virtually all of whom are insured by Medicare, were negligible.[3]

THE USE OF PHYSICIANS BY THE UNINSURED

As displayed in Table 5-3, uninsured persons are more likely than other insurance groups to go without seeing a physician for at least one year. Results showing that insurance coverage is also a strong predictor of the average number of physician visits, an indicator of the intensity of use, have been replicated many times (Table 5-6).

Some of the uninsured are able to obtain Medicaid coverage for part of the year, and one might expect to find an incremental effect for this group, given the higher usage rates for Medicaid beneficiaries presented previously. Rates of ambulatory visits for the poor and near poor increased from 2.4 per year for the always uninsured to 3.1 for

Table 5-7. The Average Number of Reported Contacts with Physicians per Person, by Insurance Coverage and Age, 1986

Age (years)	Uninsured	Insured	Ratio
0–17	2.9	4.4	.66
18–24	2.7	4.7	.57
25–45	3.4	5.0	.68
46–64	5.0	6.7	.74
All nonelderly	3.3	5.2	.64

Source: Congressional Research Service, analysis of 1986 National Health Interview Survey public use tape, 1990, p. 171.
Note: Contacts include telephone calls to physicians and home visits.

those with Medicaid part of the year (uninsured otherwise) and to 4.5 for those always on Medicaid all year (Wilensky and Berk, 1982).[4]

OTHER FACTORS AFFECTING PHYSICIAN VISITS

Numerous factors other than insurance status, including age, sex, race, income, residence, and health status, are all known to be associated with service use and thus are suspected of confounding the association between payment source and utilization. A person's age, sex, and health status provide the basic context of need, or predisposing characteristics, while the factors of race, income, or residence may indicate the presence of behavioral differences or other access barriers (Aday, 1984; Dutton, 1986). Each of these possible confounders is considered in the following by reviewing the results of studies that controlled for one or at most two factors at a time.

Age and Sex. When 1980 NMCUES data were stratified by age and sex, uninsured persons were consistently found to have lower utilization of physicians. Uninsured children, adults, and pregnant women all saw physicians about two-thirds as often as insured persons (Needleman et al., 1990). More recently, in the 1986 NHIS, the uninsured also reported seeing physicians less often in all age groups, with the greatest discrepancy by payer for those aged 18–24 years (Table 5-7) (Congressional Research Service, 1988a). Persons aged 18–24 years comprise a disproportionate share of the uninsured population compared with the overall population. Nevertheless, the lower utilization rates of the uninsured do not seem to be due to their age distribution.

Race and Geography. Data from the 1977 NMCES survey suggest that differences in visit rates by insurance status persist when examined in strata defined by race and geographic region (Table 5-8) (Davis and Rowland, 1983). The effect of race is apparent, since whites saw doctors more often than blacks in each insurance stratum. Furthermore,

Table 5-8. The Mean Number of Visits to Physicians for the Population under Age 65, by Insurance Coverage, Residence, Race, and Health Status, 1977

Residence	All		In Fair/Poor Health	
	Uninsured	Insured	Uninsured	Insured
Total	2.4	3.7[a]	4.1	6.9[a]
South	2.1	3.5[a]	3.8	6.1[a]
White	2.3	3.7[a]	4.4	6.4[a]
Nonwhite	1.5	2.8[a]	2.2	5.0
Non-South	2.6	3.8[a]	4.5	7.4[a]
White	2.7	3.8[a]	4.6	7.6[a]
Nonwhite	1.9	3.5[a]	3.5	6.5

Source: Adapted from Davis and Rowland, 1983, Table 5, p. 161; data from National Medical Care Expenditure Survey, 1977.
Note: This table excludes those uninsured for part of the year.
[a] Significant difference between insured and uninsured, $p < .05$.

insured Southern whites saw a physician nearly 2.5 times as often as uninsured blacks, but only about 30 percent more than insured blacks, thereby suggesting a role played by insurance coverage as well. The effects of insurance, race, and residence were similar when analysis was restricted to those respondents in fair or poor health (Table 5-8).

Income. Analyses of the 1984 NHIS survey data stratified by income demonstrate that differential usage by payer persists and suggest that insurance status is a stronger predictor of physician use than income. In terms of the proportion of individuals without any visits in one year and the mean number of visits, the differences across poverty levels are far smaller than the differences across insurance groups (see Tables 5-9 and 5-10) (Rowland and Lyons, 1989). Data from the 1986 NHIS also show that insurance status was a more important predictor than income, although the size of the effect shrank as family income grew. In that survey, the discrepancy in physician use between the insured and the uninsured was highest for families with incomes below $15,000 (6.6 visits per person annually for insured individuals versus 3.5 for uninsured) (Congressional Research Service, 1988a).

Health Status. Perhaps the most compelling analysis of access to care is for those who are sick. Stratified analyses address this concern by examining use of physicians by persons in poor or fair health. Large variations by insurance status are apparent. Among those in poor or fair health, insured patients saw physicians almost 70 percent more often then uninsured persons in 1977 (Davis and Rowland, 1983) and nearly twice as often than the uninsured in 1980 (Leicher et al., 1985). Similarly, among the poor/near-poor[5] with poor or fair health status, those

Table 5-9. The Percentage of the Poor and Near-Poor Population under Age 65 Reporting No Visits to Physicians, by Insurance Coverage and Poverty Status, 1984

Poverty Status	Uninsured	Medicaid	Private/Other
Total (all United States)	40.8	17.2	25.9
Poor (below poverty)	41.3	17.5	29.5
Near poor (100–149 percent of poverty)	41.2	16.4	29.1

Source: Adapted from Rowland and Lyons, 1989, Table 7, p. 994; data from National Health Interview Survey, 1984. Reprinted by permission of the Hospital Research and Educational Trust.

on Medicaid saw a physician 7.1 times per year, compared with 5.7 for other insured and 3.9 for uninsured (Wilensky and Berk, 1982). This pattern of differences was also noted for poor/near poor persons who had limited activity or reported more than eight bed days during the course of one year (Wilensky and Berk, 1982).

Years later, the usage gap among the sickest Americans persisted. Insured persons reporting fair or poor health in 1986 were more than twice as likely to visit a doctor as uninsured sick persons ($p < .05$), while the ratio of visits by insured and uninsured patients with chronic or serious illnesses was 1.5 ($p < .05$) (Table 5-11) (Freeman et al., 1990).

Another approach to controlling health status is to construct a use–disability ratio. The ratio is usually defined as the number of physician visits per 100 days of restricted activity. Howell (1988) used data from the 1980 NMCUES to examine the use–disability ratio for persons with at least one restricted activity and found lower ratios among uninsured persons (12.0) than by persons with private or Medicaid coverage (19.4 and 18.1, respectively). Andersen et al. (1987) found similar discrepancies among insurance types in the 1982 RWJF access survey.

MULTIVARIATE ANALYSES CONTROLLING FOR MANY VARIABLES AT ONCE

Given the important effects of variables such as age, sex, race, and income on the use of health services, it makes sense to control for their

Table 5-10. The Mean Number of Visits to Physicians for the Poor and Near-Poor Population under Age 65, by Insurance Coverage and Poverty Status, 1984

Poverty Status	Uninsured	Medicaid	Private/Other
Total (all United States)	2.6	5.7	3.3
Poor (below poverty)	2.6	5.5	3.2
Near poor (100–149 percent of poverty)	2.7	6.1	3.3

Source: Adapted from Rowland and Lyons, 1989, Table 8, p. 995; data from National Health Interview Survey, 1984. Reprinted by permission of the Hospital Research and Educational Trust.

Table 5-11. The Mean Number of Ambulatory Visits for Working-Age Adults, by Insurance Coverage and Health Status, 1986

	Insured	Uninsured	Ratio of Insured to Uninsured
Fair or poor health	11.9	5.6	2.1[a]
Other measures			
Chronic/serious illness	10.1	6.6	1.5[a]
Hypertension	7.6	5.7	1.3

Source: Adapted from Freeman et al., 1990, Tables 4 and 5, pp. 819–20. Reprinted by permission of the Hospital Research and Educational Trust.

[a] $p < .05$.

independent effects all at the same time if we are to make any strong conclusions about the impact of insurance on use. Several studies have investigated access to physicians while controlling for multiple factors or stratifying by multiple important characteristics. The results generally point in the same direction as described earlier. After adjustment for health status, significant disparities in the proportion of low-income children not seeing a physician in 1980 were present by insurance status (uninsured, 36 percent; privately insured, 31 percent; Medicaid full year, 27 percent; Medicaid part year, 17.1 percent) (Rosenbach, 1985). Likewise, children on Medicaid part of the year who saw a physician at least once had significantly more visits during the year than other groups. As explained elsewhere, in interpreting these figures it is important to note that coverage of the medically needy is probably the explanation for the exceptionally high utilization by those on Medicaid part of the year.

In a subsequent analysis of the same data, Rosenbach (1986) found that, among low-income children, Medicaid beneficiaries were significantly more likely ($p < .05$) to have made at least one visit to a physician in an office setting than either the uninsured or the privately insured. The analysis controlled for age, race, education, income, health status, and physician supply variables. Rosenbach concluded that Medicaid eligibility for poor uninsured or underinsured children would improve access to physician services.

Another way of describing the access limitations faced by the uninsured is to estimate the level of utilization they would have had were they to be insured. Lewin/ICF used the 1980 NMCUES to simulate the expected level of utilization and the utilization shortfall for the uninsured, assuming that the uninsured would use services at the same rate as the insured after adjustment for age, sex, income, and health status (Needleman et al., 1990). Estimates from 1980 were projected to 1988 on the basis of utilization trends and population characteristics. Comparing expected to actual utilization, the authors estimated a 36.9 percent shortfall for physician visits for the uninsured.

In a study based on more than 92,000 persons from the 1982 NHIS, Newacheck and Halfon (1988) assessed the effect of Medicaid on health care utilization by constructing a multivariate model with control for age, sex, race, and family size (predisposing characteristics); perceived health status and restricted activity (variables indicating need); and region and urban/nonurban location. The authors compared the utilization experience of poor persons having Medicaid with poor and nonpoor persons not having Medicaid, regardless of whether the latter group had another source of insurance. The results are presented in Table 5-12. After adjustment for the other variables in the model, poor persons with Medicaid had about the same or slightly higher number of adjusted physician contacts as persons above poverty in each age group.[6] Poor persons without Medicaid had significantly lower mean annual visits in every age category under 65 years and overall. The effect of Medicaid may be understated in these models because the non-Medicaid group included both the insured and the uninsured.

In a particularly rigorous study of NHIS survey data, Hafner-Eaton (1993) analyzed physician utilization for over 100,000 subjects. Using logistic regression to predict the likelihood of any utilization, the author controlled for geographic location, family size, education, and family income in addition to determining whether individuals reported themselves to be well, acutely ill, or chronically ill. The well and chronically ill uninsured population were about one-half as likely to see a physician, while the acutely ill were about two-thirds as likely.

Although the studies cited earlier suggest that differences in physician visits by insurance coverage persist even with control for many other characteristics, we know of two studies that did not find significant associations or found associations that were inconsistent. Yelin, Kramer, and Epstein (1983) examined patients with specific symptoms and discrete diagnoses (e.g., back pain, emphysema, diabetes) in the 1976 NHIS. The number of patients with each condition ranged from 238 (rheumatoid arthritis) to 2,284 (tendinitis). The authors found no consistent differences in the use of physicians by payment source.

In a study of the Community Hospital Program originally funded by RWJF in eleven sites nationally, Cornelius (1991) estimated the likelihood of any ambulatory utilization and the number of visits for over 1,000 patients, controlling for demographic variables, health status, residence, and the usual source of care. The findings pointed toward lower use for uninsured patients, but the coefficients were not statistically significant. The studies by Yelin et al. and Cornelius both had small numbers of subjects for stratified or multivariate analyses. Because of this limitation, and the lack of other contradictory studies, we conclude that the weight of the evidence leans toward supporting less use of physicians by the uninsured.

Table 5-12. Adjusted[a] Mean Annual Contacts with a Physician[b], by Age, Poverty, and Medicaid Status, 1982

	All Ages[c]	Under 17	17–44	45–64
Above poverty	5.3	4.4	4.8	6.5
Below poverty				
With Medicaid	5.7	4.2	6.3[d]	4.0
Without Medicaid	3.9[e]	3.3[e]	3.9[e]	1.6[e]

Source: Adapted from Newacheck, 1988, Table 4, p. 411. Reprinted by permission of the Hospital and Educational Trust.

[a] Adjusted for age, sex, race, family size, perceived health status, restricted activity, region, and urban/nonurban location.
[b] Includes telephone contacts and contacts with nurses and other persons working under direct supervision of physician; ambulatory care, only.
[c] Includes persons over age sixty-five.
[d] $p < .01$.
[e] $p < .05$—compared with group "above poverty."

SUMMARY

There appear to be substantial differences in use of physician services by payer. These differences are evident both in the likelihood of seeing a physician and in the intensity of use among those who receive at least some services. Compared with privately insured individuals, persons covered by Medicaid see doctors as often or more, and persons who are uninsured see doctors less often. The available literature is fairly extensive, and a number of studies suggest that these differences by payer are not merely artifacts of sociodemographic characteristics or health status.

HOSPITAL CARE

The use of hospital care is important for at least two reasons. First, hospital care is usually provided for diseases or conditions that are considered to be much more serious than those treated on an outpatient basis; therefore, they may have greater implications for health status. Second, because hospital care is so expensive, differential utilization has a large financial impact. Thus, the incentives on the part of hospitals to implicitly ration care to those who cannot pay is stronger than it is for ambulatory care.

The research on access to hospitals draws on two types of data. Self-reported data from community-based surveys provide the best source for population-based rates of use. For utilization of services within the hospital (i.e., during the stay), most researchers rely on the hospital discharge abstract, which is often collected and computerized in large data bases on a statewide basis. Unfortunately, lack of insurance is not recorded explicitly in the abstract. A person whose expected payer is listed as "Self-Pay" or "Free Care" is presumed to be uninsured. The expected payer is not a perfect representation of eventual payer status, since poor patients who seem to be uninsured at the time of admission (or even at discharge) may find that they eventually are eligible for Medicaid. Also, persons who believe they are insured may find that their insurance lapsed or does not cover a particular hospitalization. Thus, the eventual payment source does not always match the expected payer status. The expected payer, however, is the best *presumption* of a patient's insurance status. In fact, self-pay patients are the ones most likely to have unpaid bills (Weissman et al., 1992).[7] Perhaps more important, the expected payer status better fits the research hypothesis that treatment decisions are made on the basis of insurance, since patterns of care are presumably based on perceptions about coverage at the time treatment decisions are made, not about what happens to be the source of payment later on.

The first part of this section examines evidence on rates of admission and total hospital days by payer as a rough approximation of use. Where possible, studies that control for demographic variables and health status are noted. Later, material is reviewed that examines more closely the care received in hospital, including the intensity and the quality of treatment. These include studies on the length and cost of hospital stays, the number of procedures, measures of treatment aggressiveness, and the occurrence of adverse events caused by negligence.

ADMISSION RATES AND HOSPITAL DAYS

Numerous surveys examining differences in overall hospital use by payer consistently demonstrate less use by uninsured patients and more use by Medicaid patients, compared with the privately insured. Depending on the study, hospital use in Table 5-13 was measured by percentage of the population hospitalized at least once, per capita admissions, or total days. In every study, hospital use by the uninsured is substantially lower than that by the privately insured. Medicaid patients are hospitalized more often than either of the other two groups, and so the percentage figures comparing the uninsured with Medicaid patients are even lower where statistics for each group were available.

It is possible that discrepancies in access to hospital care for the uninsured may have narrowed in recent years. Freeman et al. (1987) reported a 39 percent hospitalization gap in 1982, compared with a 19 percent gap in 1986. This finding is consistent with other research that shows increases in the number and proportion of self-pay patients in U.S. hospitals between 1980 and 1985 (Sloan, Morrisey, and Valvona, 1988). In recent years managed care programs may also have lead to reduced hospital utilization for privately insured persons.

As with the analyses of physician use, a number of other factors influence hospitalizations. Age, of course, is an important predictor. Admission rates for the uninsured were consistently lower in each age

Table 5-13. The Use of Hospital Services by the Uninsured as a Percentage of the Use by the Privately Insured and Medicaid Recipients, in Various Studies, Various Years

Survey	Percentage of Privately Insured	Percentage of Medicaid Recipients
1977 NMCES		
Davis and Rowland, 1983	52	
Wilensky and Berk, 1982[a]	50	39
1980 NMCUES		
Kasper, 1986	50	30
Long and Settle, 1985 (low-income adults and children)	33	
1982 Robert Wood Johnson Survey		
Aday, Fleming, and Andersen, 1984	86	42
Aday and Andersen, 1984	66	35
Freeman et al., 1987	61	
1984 Survey of Income and Program Participation (SIPP)		
Long and Rodgers, 1989	31	
1984 NHIS		
Rowland and Lyons, 1989	72	36
1986 NHIS		
Congressional Research Service, 1988	76	
Congressional Research Service, < $15,000 income	60	
Long and Rodgers, 1989	63	
1986 Robert Wood Johnson Survey		
Freeman et al., 1987	81	72

Source: Adapted from Garrison, 1990, Table 1, p. 169.
Note: The use of hospital services is measured by hospital days, mean admissions, or percentage hospitalized. Therefore, figures may vary within the same data source. Privately insured may include publicly insured (Medicaid) if a separate figure is not provided.
[a] Wilensky and Berk included all ages.

category in the 1980 NMCUES (Kasper, 1986). In analyses of 1986 NHIS data, however, total hospital days for children aged 0–17 years were nearly 50 percent higher for uninsured patients (Table 5-14) (Congressional Research Service, 1988a). There is no obvious explanation for the discrepancy between the two studies, although it should be kept in mind that the calculation of total days is influenced both by admission rates and by average lengths of stay.

The extent or continuity of Medicaid coverage may also be associated with hospital use. Wilensky and Berk (1982) found an incremental impact on hospital use for the poor and near poor depending on how much of the year they were covered by Medicaid. The number of hospital stays increased from 0.09 stays per year for the always uninsured, to 0.18 for those with Medicaid part of the year (uninsured otherwise), to 0.23 for those on Medicaid all year.[8] This trend is consistent with the figures supplied earlier on ambulatory care by Wilensky and Berk, but it contrasts slightly with the results of the multivariate analysis by Rosen-

Table 5-14. The Average Number of Reported Hospital Days per Person, by Insurance Coverage and Age, 1986

Age	Uninsured	Insured	Ratio of Uninsured to Insured
0–17	0.38	0.26	1.46
18–24	0.34	0.44	0.77
25–45	0.39	0.56	0.70
46–64	0.64	0.97	0.66
All nonelderly	0.42	0.55	0.76

Source: Congressional Research Service analysis of the 1986 National Health Interview Survey public use tape, 1990, p. 171.

bach (1985) that showed the highest ambulatory utilization for low-income children was for those covered by Medicaid for just part of the year.

Other studies have examined hospital use with control for income. In one study using 1984 NHIS data, the differences in the number of hospital stays within insurance class, comparing all persons to the poor and near poor, were minor compared with the differences across insurance classes (Table 5-15) (Rowland and Lyons, 1989; also see Wilensky and Berk, 1982). However, in another study using NHIS data two years later, the figures on average number of hospital days indicate strong effects of both income *and* insurance (Table 5-16) (Congressional Research Service, 1988a). Despite using a similar data source, family income was defined differently in these two studies, one using total income and the other using poverty status which adjusts income for family size. Although the influence of income changes, the association of insurance status with hospital use is strong in both cases.

The disparities in hospital use by insurance class persist across racial lines, and apparently outweigh them. In the South, insured nonwhites (presumably poorer than whites) use about 20 percent more hospital days on average than insured whites, while the differences in utilization between insured and uninsured persons within races are almost threefold (Table 5-17) (Davis and Rowland, 1983). The differences were less drastic in the non-South regions.

Table 5-15. The Number of Hospital Discharges per 100 Persons, by Insurance Coverage and Poverty Status, 1984

Poverty Status	Uninsured	Medicaid	Private/Other
Total	7.4	20.6	10.2
Poor (below poverty)	8.0	19.4	11.4
Near poor (100–149 percent of poverty)	8.1	24.8	13.4

Source: Adapted from Rowland and Lyons, 1989, Table 9, p. 997; data from National Health Interview Survey, 1984. Reprinted by permission of the Hospital and Educational Trust.

Table 5-16. The Average Number of Reported Hospital Days per Person, by Insurance Coverage and Family Income, 1986

Family Income	Uninsured	Insured	Ratio of Uninsured to Insured
< $15,000	0.52	0.84	0.62
$15,000–24,999	0.33	0.59	0.56
$25,000–49,999	0.34	0.44	0.77
> $50,000	0.14	0.55	0.25
All individuals	0.42	0.55	0.76

Source: Congressional Research Service, 1988a, p. 171; data from National Health Interview Survey, 1986.

A few studies used multivariate techniques to compare hospital use among persons with different insurance coverage. Yelin, Kramer, and Epstein (1983) found significantly fewer hospitalizations among the uninsured population in the 1976 NHIS for five of nine chronic conditions. Chen and Lyttle (1987) studied hospital utilization in the RWJF surveys, and after adjusting for demographic and supply characteristics as well as perceived health status, they found that the uninsured had significantly fewer hospitalizations and total hospital days than either Medicaid or privately insured persons. In a study of the Community Hospital Program originally funded by RWJF in eleven sites nationally, Cornelius (1991) examined hospital utilization for 1,150 persons who had an episode of illness that forced them to curtail their usual activities for three or more days in a row. The uninsured were significantly less likely ($p < .05$) to have any inpatient use from 1978 to 1981 than the privately insured. Using comprehensive survey data, Cornelius was able to control simultaneously for age, sex, race, income, health status, usual source of care, and use of ambulatory services.

Table 5-17. Hospital Patient Days per 100 Persons for the Population under Age 65, by Insurance Coverage, Residence, and Race, 1977

Residence	Uninsured	Insured
Total	47	90[a]
South	35	104[a]
White	33	100[a]
Nonwhite	40	119[a]
Non-South	56	84
White	51	81[a]
Nonwhite	89	114

Source: Adapted from Davis and Rowland, 1983, Table 6, p. 163; data from National Medical Care Expenditure Survey, 1977.
Note: This table excludes those uninsured for part of the year.
[a] $p < .05$ for insured versus uninsured.

Table 5-18. Estimated Utilization Shortfall for Uninsured Persons

	Current Policy	Expected Utilization If Insured	Shortfall (%)
Hospital inpatient admissions per 1,000 persons	91	133	46.3
Hospital outpatient visits per 1,000 persons	490	675	37.7

Source: Adapted from Needleman et al., 1990, p. 59; data from Lewin/ICF estimates with the Health Benefits Simulation Model using the 1980 NMCUES aged to depict 1988.

Although overall rates for hospitalization may be lower for unin-sured patients, rates may be higher for selected illnesses. Weissman, Gatsonis, and Epstein (1992) examined hospitalization rates for thir-teen conditions such as cellulitis, asthma, or bleeding ulcers for which patients were more likely to require admission if ambulatory care was less than optimal. Uninsured persons had higher rates of hospitaliza-tion for these conditions than the privately insured population, with control for race and income. Billings and Teicholz (1990) also found a higher proportion of "preventable" admissions by the uninsured and those insured by Medicaid compared with the privately insured. These results are discussed in greater detail in the chapter on outcomes.

Finally, using the same simulation methods described previously, Needleman et al. (1990) estimated shortfalls for the uninsured of 46 percent in inpatient admissions and 38 percent in hospital outpatient visits, with adjustment for age, sex, income, and health status (Table 5-18). These simulations provide very strong evidence of differences in hospital use that cannot be explained by need or predisposing factors.

INTENSITY: RESOURCE USE IN THE HOSPITAL

In spite of evidence that access to the health care system may be com-promised for some groups, until recently many felt that once initial entry was achieved, all patients received uniform care appropriate to their medical condition. This belief was reinforced by the 1977 NMCES data, which showed that, *for people who used the hospital at least once,* the average number of stays was nearly equivalent across insur-ance groups (Wilensky and Berk, 1982).[9] Even when differences in care were found to be associated with coinsurance levels in the RAND Health Insurance Experiment, the bulk of the effects were presumed to occur on the ambulatory level (Lohr et al., 1986). However, there is growing evidence to the contrary, that is, treatment in the hospital varies with payment status. A summary of all known studies relating to service intensity in hospitals is provided in Table 5-19.

Table 5-19. The Use of Hospital Services by the Uninsured (Self-Pay/Free Care) and Medicaid Recipients, Expressed as a Percentage of the Use by the Privately Insured, in Various Studies, Various Years, Various Conditions

Survey	Uninsured	Medicaid Recipients
Length of Hospital Stay		
Braveman et al., 1991[a]	0.84	0.94
Hadley, Steinberg, and Feder, 1991[b]		
Chronic tonsillitis	0.88	—
Noninfectious gastroenteritis, NOS	0.82	—
Acute bronchitis	0.85	—
Unilateral inguinal hernia	0.62	—
Uterine leiomyoma, NOS	0.77	—
Acute myocardial infarction, interior wall, NEC	0.89	—
Epstein, Stern, and Weissman, 1990[c]	—	1.12
Melnick and Mann, 1989[d]	0.91	1.05
Weissman and Epstein, 1989[e]	0.93	1.01
Yergan et al., 1988[f]	0.86	0.86
Duncan and Kilpatrick, 1987[g]	0.82	—
Hospital Trustees, 1987[h]	>1	—
Dowd, Johnson, and Madson, 1986[i]		
373 uncomplicated normal delivery	0.83	0.94
371 uncomplicated caesarean section	0.92	1.03
355 uncomplicated hysterectomy	n.s.	1.07
162 uncomplicated hernia	n.s.	1.20
183 uncomplicated stomach disorder	0.90	1.21
243 medical back	n.s.	1.19
430 psychoses	0.73	n.s.
Kelly, 1985[j]	0.92	—
Martin, Frick, and Shwartz, 1984[k]	—	1.15
Becker and Sloan, 1983[l]	0.75	—
Hornbrook and Goldfarb, 1983[m]	>1	—
Overall Cost of Care		
Braveman et al., 1991[a]		
Total charges	0.72	0.87
Charges per day	0.89	0.95
Melnick and Mann, 1989[d]	0.93	1.03
Martin, Frick, and Shwartz, 1984[k]	—	1.07
Procedures (during inpatient stay)		
Haas, Udvarhelyi, and Epstein, 1993		
C-section rates[n]	0.86	0.80
Hadley, Steinberg, and Feder, 1991[b]		
Total hip replacement	0.55	—
Coronary artery bypass graft surgery	0.71	—
Total knee replacement	0.26	—
Stapedectomy	0.50	—
Surgical correction of strabismus	0.44	—
Stafford, 1990[o]		
Vaginal birth after C-Section (VBAC)	2.2	1.2
Stafford, 1990[o]		
C-Section rates	0.66	0.79

Table 5-19. (cont.)

Survey	Uninsured	Medicaid Recipients
Wenneker, Weissman, and Epstein, 1990[p]		
Angiography	0.95	3.6
Bypass grafting	0.94	n.s.
Angioplasty	n.s.	n.s.
Weissman and Epstein, 1989[e]		
All hospital procedure	0.93	0.94
Greenberg et al., 1988[q]		
Undergoing surgery for non–small cell lung cancer	0.66	—
Receiving radiation, chemotherapy, or both	0.64	—
Rate of Poor Process Quality		
Burstin, Lipsitz, and Brennan, 1991[r]		
Adverse event rate	n.s.	n.s.
Percentage adverse events due to negligence	2.35	n.s.
Hand et al., 1991[s]		
Late stage of diagnosis	[t]	[t]
Omitted hormone receptor test	[t]	[t]
Omitted adjustment therapy	n.s.	n.s.
Omitted radiotherapy after p. mastectomy	n.s.	n.s.
Omitted lymph node dissection	n.s.	n.s.

Source: Adapted and expanded from Weissman and Epstein, 1993, p. 260. ©1993 by Annual Reviews, Inc. Reprinted with permission.

Note: Only statistically significant figures are provided.

N.S. indicates that hypotheses were tested but results were not significant.

[a] California newborns with evidence of serious problems.
[b] Ratios calculated from reported relative regression-adjusted average lengths of stay, national sample, 1987.
[c] Length of stay for adult patients (excluding obstetrical and psychiatric patients) in five Massachusetts hospitals, 1987. The figure 1.12 represents the average affect in three of the five hospitals with significant results.
[d] Patients in New Jersey hospitals, 1982.
[e] Patients in Boston area hospitals, 1983.
[f] Patients with the diagnosis of pneumonia in seventeen hospitals in the Professional Activity Study, May 1970 to December 1973.
[g] Patients in 130 Florida hospitals. Privately insured includes patients with some third-party payment, including a public source (Medicaid).
[h] Cited in Needleman et al., 1990.
[i] Patient discharges in seven diagnosis-related groups (DRGs) from community hospitals in Minneapolis and St. Paul, 1982.
[j] Patients in short-term general nonfederal hospitals, 1970–1977. Ratio of the length of stay in hospitals with great amounts versus average amounts of uncompensated care.
[k] All Medicare, Medicaid, and Blue Cross Plan patients discharged from twenty-eight hospitals in New York State, 1978.
[l] National sample, 1974.
[m] Sixty-three New England hospitals, 1969–1970. The statistic (>1) indicates an elasticity showing longer lengths of stay in hospitals with higher proportions of self-pay patients.
[n] Massachusetts hospitals, 1987; rates were standardized for mother's age, race, parity, marital status, and education.
[o] All California nonmilitary hospital births and discharges, 1986.
[p] All patients in Massachusetts hospitals with circulatory disorders or chest pain, 1985. Ratios are based on reported odds ratios.
[q] All patients given this diagnosis in New Hampshire and Vermont, 1973–1976. Ratios are reported odds ratios.
[r] New York hospital patients, 1984. Ratios are reported odds ratios.
[s] Ninety-nine Illinois hospitals, 1988.
[t] A percentage figure could not be calculated. However, a higher proportion of "poorly insured patients" (Medicaid and uninsured) was significantly associated with lower rates of procedures representative of higher quality.

The weight of the evidence on length of stay for hospital patients indicates that self-pay or free-care patients stay fewer days in the hospital (Becker and Sloan, 1983; Kelly, 1985; Dowd, Johnson, and Madson, 1986; Sloan, Valvona, and Mullner, 1986; Duncan and Kilpatrick, 1987; Yergan et al., 1988; Melnick and Mann, 1989; Weissman and Epstein, 1989; Hadley, Steinberg, and Feder, 1991). To our knowledge, only two investigations have discovered longer lengths of stay among self-pay patients—a study of New England hospitals in 1970 by Hornbrook and Goldfarb (1983) and a more recent study of New York patients (Hospital Trustees, 1987, cited in Needleman et al., 1990).

Some of the earlier studies showing shorter lengths of stay for uninsured patients were based on hospitalizations that occurred before the advent of the Prospective Payment System, and so may not reflect the more competitive environment of today's hospitals. Other research did not control for the clinical condition of the patients or examined only a few conditions. More recent studies, however, have addressed these shortcomings.

The study by Weissman and Epstein (1989) included patients in the Boston metropolitan area in 1983. After controlling for DRG case mix, severity of illness and type of hospital, uninsured patients were discharged sooner for similar illnesses than were Blue Cross or Medicaid patients. These findings were supported by results of a study using similar methods in New Jersey (Melnick and Mann, 1989). More evidence was provided in a national study of nearly 600,000 patients hospitalized in 1987. Uninsured patients had 12–38 percent shorter stays than privately insured patients for highly discretionary conditions ($p < .01$).[10] There were smaller, nonsignificant differences in length of stay for low-discretion diagnoses (Hadley, Steinberg, and Feder, 1991).

A few studies have examined resource use of Medicaid patients and found, with control for case mix, that they stay longer and cost more than either Blue Cross or uninsured patients (Martin, Frick, and Shwartz, 1984; Melnick and Mann, 1989; Weissman and Epstein, 1989; Epstein, Stern, and Weissman, 1990).

One possible explanation for the disparities in length of stay between uninsured and insured patients is that the uninsured receive equivalent services, but in a shorter period of time. In the Boston study, however, uninsured patients underwent fewer procedures than Blue Cross patients, but about the same number as Medicaid recipients (Weissman and Epstein, 1989). The New Jersey study found that self-pay patients stayed about 10 percent fewer days on average and also had 10 percent lower costs than Medicaid or Blue Cross patients, with control for DRG, age, sex, area wages, and hospital type. Apparently, shorter lengths of stay were not counterbalanced by more intensive use of services (Melnick and Mann, 1989).

Some researchers have suggested that differences in resource use by payer may be explained by other factors such as location of service or race. The idea is that uninsured persons are disproportionately represented in minority groups and may be more likely to be admitted to certain hospitals. Thus, differences in treatment patterns may be due to racial factors or to practice styles of certain institutions, rather than to financial incentives. In the study by Yergan et al. (1988), significant differences in health status-adjusted procedure rates among Blue Cross, Medicaid, and self-pay patients with pneumonia disappeared after controlling for patients' race and the hospital site. The authors proposed therefore that differences in treatment patterns may be the result of where uninsured patients seek care (location) or their race, or both factors.

Other attempts to control for hospital type and/or race have nevertheless led to strong residual insurance effects. For example, Braveman et al. (1991) examined data for 29,751 sick newborns discharged in 1987 from California hospitals. After controlling for race and diagnosis, they found that uninsured newborns had 16 percent shorter lengths of stay, 28 percent lower total charges, and 10 percent lower charges per day. The findings were consistent across all hospital ownership types. The study by Weissman and Epstein (1989) that showed shorter lengths of stay for uninsured patients in the Boston area controlled for hospital type and case mix, but not race.

Not all deficits in care provided to the uninsured can be presumed to indicate deficiencies in the process of care. One should ideally examine the appropriateness of every admission and each procedure and compare patterns across payment types. This has not been done. Obstetrical care is one area where high procedure rates, especially for cesarean sections, have been challenged as unnecessary, and therefore may provide prima facie evidence of overuse. Stafford (1990) examined the records of nearly one-half million deliveries in California in 1986, of which nearly one-quarter were delivered by cesarean section. The privately insured were about 50 percent more likely than the self-pay patients and nearly twice as likely as indigent patients[11] to undergo this procedure (Table 5-20). The data for Medicaid, HMO, and other payers in the table, adjusted for age, race, and pregnancy-related problems, also demonstrate a link between insurance status and procedure rate. At least for this procedure, the results in Table 5-20 suggest that lower rates may be more appropriate, since the rates for Kaiser HMO are closer to self-pay and indigent rates than private rates. In a follow-up investigation, Stafford (1991) noted similar trends for vaginal births after cesarean (VBACs); in this case significantly *lower* rates of VBAC were present (again implying higher C-section rates) for women covered by private insurance than for those self-paying or covered by indigent services.

Table 5-20. Rates of Cesarean Section, by Payer, California, 1986

Payer	Rates (%)
Privately insured	29.1
Non-Kaiser HMO	26.8
Medi-Cal	22.9
Kaiser HMO	19.7
Self-pay	19.3
Indigent[a]	15.6

Source: Adapted with permission from Stafford, 1990, p. 314. © 1990 by the American Public Health Association.
Note: The author ran parallel analyses, adjusting for age, race, and pregnancy-related problems, and reported that the adjusted rates closely agreed with those recited here. Hospital deliveries only.
[a] Mostly public hospitals.

At least two studies examined high-technology, high-cost procedures and found that the uninsured were significantly less likely to undergo these treatments. Wenneker, Weissman, and Epstein (1990) controlled for clinical condition and demographic factors including age, sex, and race among patients admitted to Massachusetts hospitals in 1985 with circulatory disorders or chest pain. They found that privately insured patients were 28–80 percent more likely to undergo angiography, angioplasty, or bypass grafting than either uninsured or Medicaid patients. Hadley, Steinberg, and Feder (1991) found that rates of five high-cost or high-discretion procedures were 29–75 percent lower for uninsured patients than for those privately insured.

Hadley, Steinberg, and Feder (1991) hypothesized that significantly high rates of "not abnormal" (i.e., normal) biopsy results indicate aggressive treatment. They found that, for five of seven selected procedures, the insured were about twice as likely as the uninsured to have "not abnormal" results (p values ranged from $p < .01$ to $p < .10$).

Finally, there is evidence that the uninsured may receive less aggressive life-saving therapies from hospitals. A study team reviewed 1,808 hospital charts of cancer patients in New Hampshire and Vermont and found that insured patients were more likely than uninsured to be treated by surgery (odds ratio 1.52, $p < .05$) (Greenberg et al., 1988). Of those not treated by surgery, the insured patients were more likely than the uninsured to receive some other form of treatment, such as radiation therapy or chemotherapy (odds ratio: 1.57). The authors found no significant differences in survival after diagnosis, however.

POOR QUALITY OF CARE IN HOSPITALS

Capturing solid evidence of poor quality is often difficult due to the detailed data-gathering effort required. Two studies of hospital quality included insurance status as explanatory variables. In a subsidiary analysis of The Harvard Malpractice Study (Hiatt et al., 1989), Burstin, Lipsitz, and Brennan (1992) explored the distribution of adverse events (injuries suffered as a result of medical management) and *negligent* adverse events among more than 30,000 patients hospitalized in New York State in 1984. The mean rate for adverse events was 4.2 percent; about 27 percent of the adverse events were determined to be negligent. The likelihood that an adverse event was due to negligence was significantly associated with payer. Among self-pay patients, 40.3 percent of adverse events were negligent, compared with 29.1 percent for Medicaid and 20.3 percent for private patients (p = .017). Self-pay patients were also more likely than others to suffer disability leading to death as a result of their injuries. The second study used the facility rather than the patient as the unit of analysis. Insurance status was associated with two of five indicators of deficient quality (Hand et al., 1991). Hospitals with higher proportions of "poorly insured patients" (i.e., Medicaid or uninsured) had higher rates of late stage diagnosis or omitted hormone receptor tests. Differences in three other measures were not significant. The correlations were adjusted for a variety of hospital characteristics.

SUMMARY

Patients who are uninsured clearly have lower rates of hospital care than other groups. There is also evidence that suggests that even after hospitalization their use of hospital services as measured by length of stay and number of procedures is lower. At least two studies have suggested that the quality of hospital care provided to the uninsured is lower, although the data are preliminary.

According to the RWJF surveys, the gap in rates of hospital care narrowed between 1982 and 1986 at the same time that the number of uninsured persons grew. One possible explanation is that, given more restrictive Medicaid eligibility and growing costs of insurance, some of the newly uninsured did not "choose" to be uninsured, and may therefore have been sicker than prior cohorts (requiring more hospital use). The growth of managed care may also have led to reduced hospital utilization by the privately insured. Although the results of earlier studies are generally consistent, it seems important to update existing information since the trends in use by the privately insured may also alter the traditional pattern.

THE USE OF PRESCRIPTION DRUGS

The prescription of medication is the linchpin of medical management that offers the major alternative to surgery in modern medicine. Yet very little information is available about differences in prescription drug use by payment source, particularly for the uninsured. We know that the poor who are covered by Medicaid use more prescription medications, presumably in large part because the program pays for prescription medications as a covered benefit. The number of prescription drugs for the poor and near poor was found to be 2.0 per year for the always uninsured, 3.0 for those with Medicaid part of the year (uninsured otherwise), and 6.0 for those always on Medicaid all year (Wilensky and Berk, 1982).[12] Because Medicaid patients are sicker, on average, control for health status is useful. The figures for the same populations who perceived their health to be fair or poor were 5.6, 6.8, and 12.1, respectively. In spite of these higher figures for Medicaid, restrictive drug approval procedures have had the effect of severely restricting access to new drugs, especially for drugs in psychopharmacological and anti-infective categories (Grabowski, 1988).

Some states have tried to control the use of expensive (and possibly nonessential) drugs by Medicaid recipients. These states have employed a variety of strategies such as imposing utilization review, set formularies, limits on number of prescriptions, or copayments (Jencks and Benedict, 1990). These strategies, especially the latter three, may cause access problems. A study of over 10,000 Medicaid recipients (all ages) in New Hampshire found that the imposition of a limit of three prescriptions per month caused a meaningful drop of 30 percent in the number of prescriptions filled (Soumerai et al., 1987). No change was observed in a comparison state. The reduction in use was greatest for "ineffective" drugs (58 percent). However, surprisingly large reductions in utilization were observed for medications normally considered to be essential, including insulin (28 percent), thiazides (28 percent), and furosemide (30 percent). A change to a $1 copayment returned drug use to just below precap levels. A later article by Soumerai et al. (1991) exploring the effect of the drug payment limits on nursing home use is described in the chapter on outcomes.

INDICATORS OF TIMELINESS
PROBLEMS GETTING CARE

A fundamental idea of fairness underlying America's safety net is that people who truly need help are able to get it. That is why it is disturbing to learn of instances where patients feel they must forego or delay receiving needed care as a consequence of their insurance status, and it is why these types of reports make for a powerful indictment of the system. There are medical and economic consequences, too. Untimely care may result in unnecessary morbidity since patients entering the health care system after a delay may appear with greater severity of illness and more health care needs and thus cost more to care for. Thus, instances where persons who need care cannot receive it provide direct evidence of important problems with access.

This section contains reports on the association of insurance status with the prevalence of foregone or delayed care by insurance status. The health consequences of delayed care, such as advanced cancer or greater severity of illness upon admission to hospital, will be presented in Chapter 6.

An abundance of researchers have examined various facets of foregone care, and the evidence clearly points to access problems among those without private insurance (see Table 5-21). Perhaps one of the most telling statistics from the RWJF surveys, for example, is the number of persons who needed care but did not receive it. In 1982, 15 percent of the uninsured reported not receiving needed care, compared with 5 percent of insured, a ratio of 3:1; 4 percent of those having no insurance or public insurance had been refused care for financial reasons, compared with 1 percent of the privately insured (Aday and Andersen, 1984; see also Hubbell et al., 1989a, for evidence of denied care among uninsured patients in Orange County, California).

Reports of delays or denials of needed care represent important access problems no matter what the subject's age, income status, or residence. Yet, if certain characteristics are associated with both insurance status and the likelihood of encountering access problems independent of one another, then multivariate analyses can shed more light on the difficulties of achieving care and help to isolate the influence of financial barriers. In an analysis of the 1986 RWJF Access Survey (Robert Wood Johnson Foundation, 1987), access problems were discovered even after controlling for age, gender, income, health status, race/ethnicity, and urban/rural residence. Investigators used logistic regression to estimate relative risks (RR) for uninsured versus insured in the reporting of: (1) financial barriers to having a regular source of care (RR = 2.9); (2) a need for supportive medical care but not getting it (RR = 1.9); and (3) an illness causing a major financial problem (RR = 2.3) ($p < .05$ for all RRs) (Hayward et al., 1988a). Supportive care was defined as prescription drugs, physical therapy, nursing care, medical equipment, or nursing home care. The authors also found that uninsured persons with any one of eleven chronic medical conditions were more likely *not* to have seen a physician in the last year; however, the findings were not statistically significant (RR = 1.3, $p > .05$).

Investigations seeking to uncover or document differences in access often fail to distinguish underservice in one group from overservice in another. It seems critical, then, to focus some of this review on those studies that examined important and necessary care, with the assumption that at least some treatment is appropriate.[13] This matter was addressed by the 1986 RWJF Access Survey, which asked whether respondents had any one of five serious symptoms in the prior month for which they did not seek medical care. The symptoms included bleed-

Table 5-21. Problems with Getting Care, in Various Studies, Various Years

Study, Author, Year	Type of Problem	Percentage of Subjects with Indicated Problem		
		Uninsured	Public	Insured
1977 Michigan Gortmaker, 1981	Unmet dental needs reported by parents (for children ages 3–17)		18	8
1980 NMCUES Needleman et al., 1990	Health care condition during the year for which care was desired but not received	8.9		5.0
	Among those who did not obtain care, those who did not for economic reasons	66		33
1982 RWJF Survey Aday and Andersen, 1984 (all ages)	Needed help but did not get it	15	8	5
	Were refused care for financial reasons	4	4	1
	Found it more difficult to get care now than in previous years	11	4	0
1986 RWJF Survey Freeman et al., 1987	Needed care but did not get it for economic reasons	13		6[a]
	Of persons with serious symptoms, did not get care	67		41[a]
Hayward et al., 1991	Relative risk of needing supportive medical care but not getting it	1.9[b]		
	Relative risk of not seeing a physician in the past year for respondents with one or more chronic conditions	1.3[b]		
1988 DCHA Uninsured Patient Survey, Washington, D.C. Billings and Teicholz, 1990	Unable to get care thought needed	21.4		
	Unable to fill prescription	17.7		
	Unable to get diagnostic test recommended by M.D.	9.4		
	Unable to get advice of specialist	15.6		
1989 Massachusetts Survey Blendon et al., 1992	Unable to get care for financial reasons	10		1

Table 5-21. (*Cont.*)

		Percentage of Subjects with Indicated Problem		
Study, Author, Year	Type of Problem	Uninsured	Public	Insured
	Failed to receive care for a serious or chronic condition	48		19
	Failed to receive care for a serious symptom	51		28

Source: Weissman and Epstein, 1993, pp. 255–256. © 1993 by Annual Reviews, Inc. Reprinted with permission.
Note: Public includes Medicaid; Insured refers to private insurance, but includes Medicaid if a separate figure is not provided.
[a] All United States, insured and uninsured.
[b] Adjusted relative risk compared with the insured, controlling for age, sex, income, health status, race.

ing, shortness of breath after light exercise, loss of consciousness, chest pain when exercising, and severe weight loss unrelated to dieting. Among the cohort of persons surveyed, 41 percent with one or more of these symptoms did not see or tell a physician about that problem (Table 5-21). The rate for the uninsured (67 percent) was substantially higher, but the figure for low-income individuals (42 percent) was virtually identical (Freeman et al., 1987).

The studies just reviewed focus on care that was not obtained. Because uninsured and underinsured patients face financial and other barriers to care, they may delay seeking or receiving treatment when symptoms first appear even though access is eventually achieved. In its least insidious form, delays may simply prolong minor suffering, the sort that all of us have encountered waiting for an appointment or when we were too busy to see a doctor. If treatment for more severe symptoms is delayed, however, one's health can be seriously threatened.

Delays in seeking care may be particularly important for cancer patients since diagnosis and treatment during early stages may prolong survival. Two studies from the 1970s raised fundamental concerns with respect to payment source. Berg, Ross, and Latourette (1977) and Friedman, Parker, and Lipworth (1973) both identified delays in seeking treatment for cancer among patients whose payment source was not private insurance. Friedman, Parker, and Lipworth (1973) found that women who were uninsured or insured by Medicaid were more likely than women with private insurance to delay. Because the rates for the first two groups did not differ, the authors concluded that better insurance status would not have a profound effect on delayed cancer care among the poor. Other socioeconomic factors might be more powerful predictors.

Two studies specifically investigated the prevalence of delayed care among uninsured hospitalized patients. Billings and Teicholz (1990) interviewed 955 uninsured hospital patients in Washington, D.C., in 1988 and found that almost 20 percent reported delays in treatment of the medical problem that ultimately resulted in admission. Unfortunately, comparisons with insured patients were not reported. Weissman et al. (1991) interviewed more than 17,000 hospitalized patients in the Boston area to determine socioeconomic characteristics and their association with delayed care. The patients were asked whether they delayed seeking or receiving care for the condition that eventually led to their hospitalization, and if yes, the reason. Patients who were poor, black, uninsured, or did not have a regular doctor were 40–80 percent more likely to report delay than others ($p < .01$). Most of the delays were because the patient miscalculated the severity of their condition, and so may not be indicative of an access problem in any obvious way. To get a clearer picture, the analysis was repeated for those who said that the principal reason for their delay was the cost of care. The odds of reporting delay because of cost for persons who were both poor and uninsured were twelve times greater than for other patients ($p < .01$). One of the limitations of this approach is that self-reports by patients can be subjective and biased. If patients who are uninsured and poor delay no more than others but simply have a propensity to say so, then the results could be misleading. This investigation did take one other step in addressing this concern. In a multiple regression controlling for the principal reason behind the admission (the Diagnosis-Related Group, or DRG) and other clinical measures, patients who reported delays ended up staying 9 percent longer in the hospital, or about one-half day on average, than those who did not have delays. This result goes at least part of the way in validating the patient reports (i.e., in supporting the idea that the delays were real and had medical consequences). Those who delayed were apparently sicker than others *with the same clinical condition,* and this resulted in longer hospital stays. Still, one would not know for sure whether people who delay also tend to use hospitals differently for behavioral reasons that are not related to the severity of their illness. Of course, it is difficult to distinguish between cases where people delayed *seeking* care from those cases where they were unable to receive timely care. The weight and consistency of the evidence is extraordinary, however.

PATIENT DUMPING

Hospitals that find themselves squeezed by increasing competitive pressures are known to institute policies that limit admission of poorly insured patients to their hospitals (Congressional Research Service, 1988a; Weissman, Crane, and Sager, 1987; Sofaer, 1990). In a national survey of physicians conducted in 1984, 5.7 percent reported that their hospitals discouraged admissions of Medicaid patients; the figure was 21 percent for uninsured patients (Schlesinger et al., 1987).

One of the more extreme practices that has been documented to limit admissions is to transfer emergency room patients who are economically or socially undesirable to other hospitals, usually municipally owned facilities. In some cases patients are transferred for purely economic reasons even when they are medically unstable. This practice has become known as patient dumping. The danger of dumping is that patients consequently receive delayed care or experience unnecessary medical risk (Himmelstein et al., 1984; Kellerman and Hackman, 1988).

Anecdotal evidence abounds of private hospitals that distribute lists of the closest public hospitals for the uninsured who arrive on their doorstep (Dallek, 1985). Before 1986, it was estimated that approximately 250,000 patients in need of emergency care were dumped annually (Ansell and Schiff, 1987). The findings of four empirical studies that investigated the insurance status and medical condition of economic transfers are summarized in Table 5-22. Patients without insurance or insured by Medicaid are clearly at greater risk of economic transfer than other insurance classes. The proportion of economic transfers lacking insurance ranged from 46 to 89 percent, the figures for Medicaid are 21–46 percent, and the proportion who were medically unstable or in need of emergency hospitalization ranged from 7 to 44 percent.

Dumping patients who are medically unstable or in active labor has been outlawed since 1986 under the Emergency Medical Treatment and Active Labor Act. Enacted as part of the 1986 Consolidated Omnibus Budget Reconciliation Act (COBRA), Medicare-participating hospitals with emergency departments must screen and stabilize emergency patients unless a physician certifies that the benefits of transfer outweigh the risks. The receiving hospital must also agree to the transfer in advance. However, the concept of medically stable may be hard to define (Ansell and Schiff, 1987). In addition, consumer groups note that HCFA has not issued final regulations implementing the law, and in the four years subsequent to passage only 19 hospitals were penalized (140 were cited) (Faulkner and Gray, 1991). Kellerman and Hackman (1988) reported that the implementation of COBRA in the midst of their study period apparently had no effect on the rate of economic transfer of unstable patients to their hospital. In a follow-up study published two years later, they confirmed that any change in observed numbers of economic transfers were due principally to a change in the receiving hospital's policies (in response to its own overcrowding problem), and that COBRA has had little impact on other hospitals' dumping activities (Kellerman and Hackman, 1990).

Table 5-22. Insurance Coverage and Medical Stability of Economic Transfers

	Percentage of Patients		
	Uninsured	Medicaid	Medically Unstable
Himmelstein et al., 1984 (N = 458)	63	21	7
Schiff et al., 1986 (N = 467)	46	46	24
Andrulis and Gage, 1986 (N = 1,066)	50		44[a]
Kellerman and Hackman, 1988 (N = 190)	89		27

[a] Required emergency hospitalization.

PREVENTIVE CARE

While poor persons, in particular those covered by Medicaid, may have similar levels of physician use when they are sick, they are less inclined to use preventive services when they are healthy (Newacheck, 1988). Preventive care is more likely than other types of care to be initiated by the patient and perhaps to be more discretionary. Certain types of preventive care have obvious and cost-effective benefits. In this section we review evidence demonstrating differences in the use of preventive care by payment source. Because preventive services for children, adults, and pregnant women are often financed in different ways, each topic is covered separately.

THE USE OF PREVENTIVE CARE BY CHILDREN

Although most children are insured, they are often not covered for preventive services. The notable exceptions are children who are beneficiaries of Medicaid, since they are eligible for the Early and Periodic Screening, Diagnosis, and Treatment program (EPSDT). The services provided under the aegis of EPSDT include physical examinations, vision and dental checkups, and follow-up care, although the thoroughness of required screening and follow-up services varies considerably by state.

The evidence on the ability of Medicaid to encourage the use of preventive visits is mixed. In one study Medicaid children were more likely than others to obtain physical examinations at the recommended intervals, as well as vision and dental checkups and other preventive services (Newacheck, 1988). This study did not separate out poor, privately insured children from the poor uninsured. On the other hand, Ball (1985) found no significant differences between low-income uninsured and Medicaid children in their use of general checkups, immunizations, or eye examinations. The 1982 RWJF survey provides some statistics on the use of specific preventive medical procedures by children under the age of 17 years (Aday and Andersen, 1984). Uninsured children were less likely than those with private insurance to receive a tuberculosis skin test, a polio vaccination, or a measles vaccination, but the differences were not very large (Table 5-23).

A multivariate analysis of the 1987 NMES provides insight concerning the impact of Medicaid insurance coverage on the use of preventive services. For children who would otherwise be uninsured, being insured by Medicaid for an entire year was found to increase the probability of well-child visits by 17 percent and to increase compliance with the guidelines of the American Academy of Pediatrics for well-child visits by 12 percent (Short and Lefkowitz, 1991). The Medicaid reimbursement level was not associated with the magnitude of these effects. The authors noted that behavioral factors other than insurance, especially educational attainment, explain a large proportion of the gap in service use between children of different income levels.

THE USE OF PREVENTIVE CARE BY ADULTS

Discrepancies in the use of preventive care by payer occur among adults as well as children. Substantial differences by payer in the percentage of persons having a blood pressure reading occurred in 1982 (Table 5-24) (Aday and Andersen, 1984). These figures were not adjusted for age or prevalence of the disease condition in the community. Poor blacks, for example, may have a much higher prevalence of high blood pressure and other coronary heart disease risk factors than other populations (Maynard et al., 1986).

Other analysts have studied these effects while controlling for health status. Woolhandler and Himmelstein (1988) used multiple logistic regression to control for overall health status and demographic variables and found that uninsured women were 64 percent more likely than insured women to lack adequate blood pressure screening (Table 5-24). Ball (1985) reported on data from the 1980 NMCUES and found that women on Medicaid were 47 percent more likely to have a general checkup and 600 percent more likely to have an eye exam than low-income uninsured women. The RWJF survey focused

Table 5-23. Preventive Medical Procedures Received by Children Less than Seventeen Years of Age, by Insurance Coverage, 1982

	Percentage of Children with Indicated Procedure		
	Uninsured	Public Only	Private Only
TB skin test	77	76	81
Polio vaccine	94	95	97
Measles vaccine	91	95	94

Source: Adapted with permission from Aday and Andersen, 1984, Table 7, p. 1336. © 1984 by the American Public Health Association.

Table 5-24. Patients without Blood Pressure Checks, by Insurance Coverage, 1982 and 1986

	Percentage of Subjects		
	Uninsured	Public Only	Private Only
Patients without blood pressure reading, 1982 (Aday and Andersen, 1984)	36	18	22
Women without a blood pressure checkup, 1982 (Woolhandler and Himmelstein, 1988)	18		11[a]
Patients with hypertension without blood pressure reading, 1986 (Freeman et al., 1987)	22		20[b]

[a] Includes all insured, adjusted for demographic and health status variables.
[b] This figure represents all United States, not just the privately insured.

just on persons with hypertensive disease and found smaller differences by payer (Freeman et al., 1987).

The National Cancer Institute recommends the delivery of preventive care, and has set as a goal for the year 2000 that four-fifths of all women should receive adequate Pap smears and breast exams. In the 1982 RWJF access survey, 60 percent of all women had received a Pap smear and 65 percent had received a breast exam. These figures actually declined to 54.1 percent and 54.5 percent, respectfully, by 1986 (Hayward et al., 1988b). Several investigations have therefore focused on preventive health care services targeted at women.

- Women with private insurance in the 1982 RWJF survey were about 40 percent more likely to have a Pap smear or have a breast examination by a physician than the uninsured or publicly insured (Aday and Andersen, 1984).
- Approximately 10,000 adult women were interviewed in the 1982 NHIS. Uninsured women were 28–38 percent less likely than insured women to receive a Pap smear, a breast examination, or a glaucoma test (Table 5-25) (Woolhandler and Himmelstein, 1988). Only about one-half of uninsured women had undergone a breast examination. The authors noted that uninsured women are more likely to be poor and therefore to be at elevated risk for contracting the diseases that these tests discover.
- By 1986, insured women in the RWJF survey were still more than twice as likely to report a Pap smear, a breast exam, or a mammography, within the recommended periods (Hayward et al., 1988b).

PRENATAL CARE

Prenatal care is a highly cost-effective service for low income women. Prenatal care is known to reduce the risk of low-birth-weight babies

Table 5-25. The Percentage of Women Who Do Not Obtain Basic Diagnostic Tests, 1982

Test	Overall	Uninsured	Insured
Pap smear	27	39	25
Breast examination	38	50	36
Glaucoma test	30	43	28

Source: Adapted from Woolhandler and Himmelstein, 1988, p. 2873.

and to help avoid the high costs associated with neonatal intensive care units (U.S. General Accounting Office, 1987) (see also Schramm, 1985, for a discussion of the favorable cost–benefit ratios of the Women and Infant Children [WIC]program with respect to Medicaid). Dollars spent on prenatal care repay dividends in terms of fewer high risk births, lower use of neonatal intensive care, and lower infant mortality. Medicaid is a major source of payment for deliveries in this country, financing from 16 to 24 percent of all births in selected states in 1983 and 1984 (Howell and Brown, 1989). Nevertheless, one-third of pregnant women do not get adequate prenatal care, in large part because of financial barriers that take the form of lack of insurance for maternity care for almost one-quarter of pregnant women and very low reimbursement rates for Medicaid providers, which may discourage participation in that program (Torres and Kenney, 1989).[14] A direct link between Medicaid fees for obstetric care and adequacy of prenatal care has not been demonstrated, however.

The adequacy of prenatal care is clearly related to the possession of private insurance, as demonstrated by numerous investigations (Table 5-26). In 1986, 20 percent of uninsured pregnant women failed to get prenatal care during their first trimester, compared with 15 percent for the United States as a whole (Freeman et al., 1987). In a study by the Children's Defense Fund, uninsured pregnant women delayed receiving prenatal care at a rate three times as high as insured pregnant women (cited in Needleman et al., 1990; not listed in the table). In another investigation, researchers from the U.S. General Accounting Office (GAO) interviewed 1,157 women who were Medicaid recipients or uninsured in 32 communities (U.S. General Accounting Office, 1987). About 63 percent of women interviewed obtained prenatal care that GAO deemed insufficient because they did not begin care within the first three months of their pregnancy or made eight or fewer visits for care. Late or insufficient prenatal care was a problem among this group of Medicaid recipients and uninsured women across all ages, all races, and all sizes of communities. The researchers also compared the care received by the disadvantaged sample with that received by 4,047 privately insured women. Among women with uncomplicated pregnancies, 16

Table 5-26. The Use of Prenatal Care, by Insurance Coverage, in Various Studies

	Uninsured	Public/ Medicaid	Insured/ National Average
St. Clair et al., 1990			
Percentage of underutilizers among low-income women (N = 185)[a]	43	64	42
Freeman et al., 1987			
Percentage who failed to get care during first trimester	20		15[b]
Adler and Emmerich, 1990			
Mean estimated gestational age at first prenatal visit (N = 98)[a]	18 weeks	13 weeks	8 weeks
Norris and Williams, 1984			
Percentage with prenatal care in first trimester (white/hispanic/black)		65/56/67	82/60/70
Buescher et al., 1987			
Percentage with inadequate prenatal care	44[c]	38	14[d]
Piper, Ray, and Griffin, 1990			
Effects of Medicaid expansion on prenatal care	No significant effects noted		
Howell et al., 1991			
Percentage who began care in first trimester	70[e]	69[f]	92[g]
Schwethelm et al., 1989			
Percentage in first trimester	84	76	91
Percentage in third trimester	1.8	3.1	0.8
Freund et al., 1989			
Percentage of deliveries with prenatal care in first trimester (4 Medicaid Competition Demonstration sites)		32–36	76[h]
U.S. General Accounting Office, 1987			
Percentage with inadequate prenatal care for noncomplicated pregnancy	24	16	2
Haas et al., 1993			
Percentage with satisfactory prenatal care[i]	88	87	96

Source: Weissman and Epstein, 1993, p. 259. © 1993 by Annual Reviews, Inc. Reprinted with permission.

[a] p < .05 for differences across groups.
[b] The figure is for all United States as a whole.
[c] Received care in public health department.
[d] All other live births in county.
[e] Non-Medicaid residents of low-income areas.
[f] Enrolled for four or more months of pregnancy.
[g] Non-Medicaid residents of high-income areas.
[h] National average.
[i] Massachusetts, 1987.

percent of Medicaid, 24 percent of uninsured, and 2 percent of private insured women received inadequate prenatal care, in this case defined as beginning in the third trimester or comprising four or fewer visits. Lack of money to pay for care along with lack of transportation and lack of awareness about the pregnancy were cited as the principal barriers to care among those Medicaid and uninsured women interviewed.

Table 5-27. The Percentage Distribution of Medicaid and Non-Medicaid Prenatal Care, by Principal Site, 1986–1987

Site of Care	Poor non-Medicaid	Medicaid	All Deliveries
Physician's office	22	39	76
Hospital clinic	21	28	14
Health department	47	23	10
Other	10	9	
Total[a]	100	100	100

Source: Data from Jencks and Benedict, 1990, Table 2, p. 49; Singh et al., 1989; U.S. General Accounting Office, 1987.

[a] May not total to 100 due to rounding errors.

As part of an effort to evaluate the Healthy Start Program for near poor uninsured pregnant women in Massachusetts, Haas et al. (1993) measured access to satisfactory prenatal care. Satisfactory care was defined according to criteria developed by the Institute of Medicine and was classified according to the number and timing of prenatal visits, adjusted for the length of gestation. Nearly 60,000 births were classified according to insurance status. Relatively large deficits occurred for both uninsured and Medicaid women compared with privately insured women (88, 87, and 96 percent obtained satisfactory care, respectively). Statistical tests of the differences, however, were not reported because the researchers were more interested in changes over time as a result of the program.

It is possible that some of the problems women face in obtaining prenatal care are related to the source or location of care. As we know from other research, this is also related to insurance status. The data in Table 5-27, for example, are a compilation of two studies showing that Medicaid recipients have better access to private physicians for prenatal care than the non-Medicaid poor, but both fall far short of the experience for the average mother-to-be. Likewise, in a small study (N = 149) in Minneapolis of women obtaining prenatal care, 52 percent of privately insured women, 23 percent of Medicaid insured, and only 2 percent of uninsured women got their care from private physicians (Oberg et al., 1991). Women who visited clinics subsequently experienced longer waiting times ($p < .01$) and were more likely than privately insured women to see different physicians on different visits ($p < .01$).

6

OUTCOMES OF CARE

In contrast to the numerous studies documenting unequal *use* of health care services by poor and uninsured people, many fewer have explored whether barriers to care have been sufficiently large to affect health *outcomes*. Because improving health status is an essential goal of medical care, health outcomes are obvious indicators of access. One might draw an analogy between measuring access and rating the success of your favorite baseball team. The team may have the best pitchers, fielders, and hitters, make the fewest errors, and might even have the highest payroll, but unless they win ballgames, you are bound to be disappointed. The same holds true for health care, only it is more diffi cult to measure the "wins."

One reason why health care "wins" are hard to measure is that myriad influences external to the medical care system (environmental or social factors, for example) have noticeable impacts on health status. It is often difficult to link differential outcomes to specific medical interventions or components of the health care system. For example, consider the hypothetical situation where two similar groups of patients are hospitalized, but one group suffers higher rates of complications several weeks after discharge from the hospital. Was there an access problem? Did the hospital treat one group differently (i.e., better) than the other? Without careful investigation, it is difficult to know whether the causes of the poor outcomes were initiated during the hospital stay or after discharge in the ambulatory setting, were affected by differences in home environments or individual health behaviors, or were instead influenced by unmeasured differences between the groups in severity of illness. In spite of these methodological limitations, health outcomes are valuable objects for study because they provide a bottom-line, ultimate indicator of access to health care.

This chapter begins with a review of those outcomes having some association with hospital care, including mortality during or after hospitalization, severity of illness upon admission to hospital, and avoidable hospitalizations. This is followed by an inspection of research that addresses two important health concerns at different ends of the life spectrum—perinatal care and cancer treatment. Findings from research on perceived health status are presented next, followed by nursing home entry and discharge. The chapter ends with a discussion of patient satisfaction.

HOSPITAL DEATHS

Most Americans die in the hospital. Differences in the rates of death that occur during or shortly after hospital stays, however, especially for nonelderly persons, may indicate problems with access or quality of care. At least three studies have determined that uninsured patients have higher in-hospital mortality rates than patients with other payment sources (Table 6-1):

1. A study by Yergan et al. (1988) used data from seventeen hospitals randomly selected from a national abstracting service in 1972 to examine outcomes for patients admitted with pneumonia. Self-pay patients were six times more likely to die in hospital than Blue Cross patients, with control for age, sex, admission test results, and comorbidity.
2. In a national study of hospital patients in 1987, the probability of an in-hospital death for uninsured patients was 1.08 to 1.32 times higher than for privately insured patients in fifteen of sixteen age–sex–race cohorts ($p = < .05$ for ten of the relative probabilities). The research included controls for hospital characteristics and the risk of in-hospital mortality at the time of admission (Hadley, Steinberg, and Feder, 1991).
3. A study of patients admitted with acute myocardial infarction to Massachusetts hospitals was performed in 1987. The odds of dying within thirty days after discharge were one-and-one-half times as great for uninsured patients than for privately insured patients. The relative odds were adjusted for age, race, sex, income of resident, Zip code, clinical factors including anatomic location of the infarct and number of comorbidities, teaching status of the hospital and whether it had sophisticated cardiac care facilities (Young and Cohen, 1991).

Once again one must consider alternative explanations. At least some of the findings related to inpatient mortality from the first two studies could instead be explained by a scenario where insured patients are more likely to be discharged to nursing homes or hospices (because insurance will pay for it), where death may occur shortly after release from the hospital. It might look like these privately insured patients had lower in-hospital mortality rates. However, Young and Co-

Table 6-1. Studies of Hospital-Related Mortality, by Source of Payment

Study	Patients and Study Year	Number of Cases	Ratio of Uninsured to Insured
Yergan et al., 1988	Pneumonia admissions, 1972	4,369	1.56[a]
Hadley, Steinberg, and Feder, 1991	All diagnoses, 1987	592,598	1.08–3.20[b]
Young and Cohen, 1991	Emergency admissions for AMI[c], 1987	4,972	1.54, 1.57[d]

[a] Self-pay versus Blue Cross.
[b] Regression-adjusted relative probabilities, in the 15 of 16 age–sex–race cohorts that were >1; $p < .05$ in 10 of 16. The figure for white females age 35–49 years was 0.92 ($p > .10$).
[c] Acute myocardial infarction.
[d] Inpatient and total thirty-day mortality, respectively.

hen (1991) were able to track patients' mortality even after leaving the hospital, so they decided to test this hypothesis. They repeated their analyses on just in-hospital deaths. The differences in the mortality rates by insurance status did not change substantially, suggesting that discharge to terminal care facilities was not causing a bias in their principal findings of discrepant mortality.

It is interesting that none of these researchers was able to posit a reason for these very large differences in rates. Of course, the implication is that the quality of care for uninsured patients is somehow deficient, perhaps due to the rationing of expensive therapies. Other information discussed shortly suggests that quality of care may be lower for uninsured patients and that higher thresholds for admitting uninsured patients may result in greater severity of illness on admission and potentially higher rates of mortality. Nevertheless, none of the three studies discussed earlier established a direct line between differences in process of care and differences in mortality.

SEVERITY OF ILLNESS ON ADMISSION TO THE HOSPITAL

The severity of a patient's condition upon admission to the hospital may be associated with access to care in a way that is analogous to the stage of cancer upon initial presentation in a doctor's office. Suppose a woman encounters delays in her ambulatory care. When she is eventually admitted to the hospital, her condition may be more severe than if she had received prompt medical attention earlier. Alternatively, higher severity on admission to hospital may suggest different thresholds for admission. The woman's physician might not have been eager to admit her until her condition progressed to a more serious stage. Either situation might represent delayed or less intensive care for the patient, thus indicating a problem with access.

One methodological challenge clearly is to accurately measure disease severity. One previous study used disease staging to compare the severity of illness of hospitalized patients with different insurance. *Disease staging* is a severity classification system in which higher stages reflect more extensive disease and presumably greater severity of illness (Gonnella, Hornbrook, and Louis, 1984). Stage 1 has no complications or problems with minimal severity, Stages 2 and 3 represent involvement of more sites and significantly increased risk of complications, and Stage 4 signifies death. For example, patients with diabetes mellitus and an infection in one or more systems are placed in Stage 2; and patients with acidosis or coma are placed in Stage 3. Gonnella, Hornbrook, and Louis (1984) used this method of severity classification and found that uninsured patients admitted to hospital tended to be more severely ill. Sixty-one percent of uninsured hospital patients with diabetes mellitus were at Stage 2 or higher, compared with only 48 percent of Medicaid and Blue Cross patients. Similar results occurred for a number of different conditions, suggesting that the greater severity of illness of uninsured patients may be due to delays in prior care.

In another study of uninsured patients nationwide, Hadley, Steinberg, and Feder (1991) examined sickness on admission by looking at two variables: (1) the proportion of weekend admissions on the assumption that these admissions were more urgent than weekday admissions and therefore the patients might be more severely ill; and (2) the risk-adjusted index of mortality, a predicted figure based on demographic and clinical information found in the discharge abstracts. In analyses performed in sixteen age–sex–race strata, the uninsured had higher rates of weekend admissions in fourteen strata and higher mortality risk indexes in thirteen strata.

AVOIDABLE HOSPITALIZATIONS

In the RAND Health Insurance Experiment, selected participants assigned to a plan with free hospital care and relatively high deductibles for outpatient care had lower use of ambulatory care, were hospitalized *less* frequently than average, and had lower overall costs than those in the free plan (see Chapter 7 for more detail). The most common explanation for these results was that fewer ambulatory visits gave the doctor fewer opportunities to hospitalize the patient. Since then, an alternative and more subtle link between ambulatory care and hospitalization has been explored in the access literature. The basic reasoning is that persons who face financial or other barriers to ambulatory care or who receive poor quality ambulatory care may be hospitalized more often, not less often, than others, at least for selected conditions that may deteriorate if not treated promptly and/or effectively on an ambulatory basis. As with other process–outcome links, a "smoking gun" demonstrating an association has not been found. It is difficult to identify specific instances where individuals received poor quality ambulatory care or should have seen a doctor, but did not. These are concerns of process. Avoidable hospitalizations focus on the outcome, instead. Persons who are *presumed* to have less access to high-quality ambulatory care are more likely in the aggregate to experience an otherwise preventable exacerbation of their illness that necessitates hospitalization (see also Rutstein et al., 1976; Craddick, 1979; O'Kane, 1989; Billings et al., 1993).

A previous investigation of an HMO population supports the general hypothesis that certain types of hospitalizations may be at least partially avoidable or preventable. In a study using chart review at anHMO in the Midwest, Solberg et al. (1990) identified fifteen diagnoses indicating potential links with inadequate prehospital care. Of hospital cases with those diagnoses, 45 percent failed explicit quality criteria for ambulatory care and 10 percent were judged implicitly by physicians to have received poor-quality ambulatory care. The research thus suggests the validity of a potential link with quality.

Support for this idea is also provided by a study that compared the proportions of hospital admissions represented by "preventable" conditions for more than 1,000 insured and uninsured patients in Washington, D.C., hospitals (Billings and Teicholz, 1990). Cases were deemed to be preventable or avoidable on the basis of chart reviews performed by Lewin/ICF (see also Needleman et al., 1990). The authors found that nearly 40 percent of admissions for the uninsured were "preventable/avoidable" compared with 21.2 percent for Medicaid recipients and 12.2 percent for other insured patients. In addition to these chart reviews, the authors interviewed the uninsured patients and found that 38 percent reported access problems prior to admission that were related to their current condition. The problems included difficulty filling prescriptions, getting diagnostic tests, or obtaining consultation with specialists.

Earlier in this book we provided results of studies that examined the frequency of admission to hospitals in an aggregate fashion. The data suggest that uninsured patients are admitted to the hospital less often, overall. When broken down by disease, however, the pattern is less clear cut. For example, Wissow et al. (1988) focused on avoidable hospitalizations for children with asthma. Based on data from Maryland during 1979–1982, Medicaid-enrolled children were 3.2 times as likely to be hospitalized for asthma as were children with other sources of payment. The authors suggested that the lack of preventive services for asthma in the poor may be at the root of the variation in admission rates.

As part of an investigation into the use of hospital care by the uninsured, Weissman, Gatsonis, and Epstein (1992) convened a physician panel that identified 13 avoidable hospital conditions (AHCs), including diabetic coma, ruptured appendix, cellulitis, gangrene, and others. They used data from all hospital discharges in Massachusetts and Maryland in 1987 and figures from the CPS to calculate population-based relative rates for each particular AHC and for all thirteen AHCs combined and, as a contrast, for all other hospital conditions (non-AHCs). Uninsured and Medicaid patients were more likely than privately insured patients to be hospitalized for AHCs. Furthermore, the differences by payer for AHCs were larger than differences in rates for other hospital conditions (non-AHCs). In other words, the differences could not be attributed to a general pattern of high hospital usage. Table 6-2 reproduces results for Massachusetts (the figures for Maryland were similar). These findings persisted in multivariate analyses with control for race and income in six age–sex cohorts in each state.

The practice of using avoidable hospitalizations to monitor quality of ambulatory care is appealing and is growing in popularity. Plans to incorporate the tool for Medicaid patients in Texas, Iowa, and Massachusetts are already in place, but the method needs to be better understood. In thinking about AHCs, two conceptual distinctions seem important. The first is the distinction between sentinel events and rates. Some hospital admissions, such as those for immunizable conditions, are almost always avoidable. Even a single (sentinel) case may be cause for concern. For most AHCs, however, being avoidable is a matter of degree. Because management of patients with chronic conditions such as congestive heart failure is complex, monitoring AHCs may be most useful when their rates deviate substantially from some prescribed norm or when they vary over time in a way that can be traced to a change in public policy.

A second conceptual distinction is between admissions that are avoidable and those that are discretionary. These are very different concepts, which can be easily confused. For example, both appendicitis and ruptured appendix are nondiscretionary admissions. For both, surgery in hospital is accepted as the most appropriate treatment. Yet, only ruptured appendix is potentially avoidable. In a better world, surgeons would only need to remove inflamed appendices, not ruptured ones.

As with any health outcome, the occurrence of avoidable hospitalizations can potentially be traced to multiple causes, including but not limited to poor ambulatory care. As a result, alternative hypotheses might explain higher rates of AHCs among vulnerable populations. For example, higher rates of hospitalization may be due to elevated incidence or prevalence of disease for some conditions. However, the findings from Weissman et al. were fairly consistent across multiple conditions.

The frequency of avoidable hospitalizations may also be affected by patients' health behaviors or by providers' perceptions of barriers to

Table 6-2. Age- and Sex-Standardized Relative Admission Rates of Avoidable and Other Hospital Conditions, Massachusetts, 1987

Condition	Uninsured Relative to Privately Insured			Medicaid Relative to Privately Insured		
	Relative Rates	Adjusted Relative Rates[a]	Confidence Interval[b]	Relative Rates	Adjusted Relative Rates[a]	Confidence Interval[b]
Appendix, ruptured	1.17	1.14	0.93–1.34	1.27[c]	0.58[c]	0.51–0.65
Asthma	1.45[c]	1.42[c]	1.20–1.63	4.03[c]	1.84[c]	1.63–2.05
Cellulitis	2.68[c]	2.62[c]	2.07–3.17	4.41[c]	2.02[c]	1.76–2.27
Congestive heart failure	1.20	1.17	0.90–1.43	5.28[c]	2.41[c]	2.08–2.75
Diabetes (DKA, coma)	2.83[c]	2.77[c]	2.21–3.32	5.06[c]	2.32[c]	2.00–2.63
Gangrene	2.33[c]	2.27[c]	1.57–2.98	3.35[c]	1.53[c]	1.18–1.89
Hypokalemia	1.66[c]	1.62[c]	1.21–2.04	3.31[c]	1.51[c]	1.17–1.86
Immunizable conditions	2.08[c]	2.03[c]	1.09–2.96	3.69[c]	1.69	0.92–2.46
Malignant hypertension	2.44[c]	2.38[c]	1.83–2.93	3.40[c]	1.56[c]	1.29–1.82
Pneumonia	1.64[c]	1.60[c]	1.32–1.89	4.32[c]	1.98[c]	1.73–2.22
Pyelonephritis	1.59[c]	1.55[c]	1.29–1.81	3.07[c]	1.40[c]	1.20–1.61
Ulcer, bleeding	1.62[c]	1.58[c]	1.20–1.97	2.21[c]	1.01	0.86–1.16
All AHCs	1.75[c]	1.71[c]	1.41–2.01	4.02[c]	1.84[c]	1.62–2.05
All non-AHCs	1.02	1.00	—	2.19[c]	1.00	—
High Discretion Non-AHC Conditions	1.14	—	—	2.88[c]	—	—
Low Discretion Non-AHC Conditions	0.77[c]	—	—	1.54	—	—

Source: Adapted from Weissman, Gatsonis, and Epstein, 1992, pp. 2391-2392.

AHC = avoidable hospital condition.
[a] The numbers in this column are the ratios of the relative rates for each AHC divided by the relative rate for all non-AHCs.
[b] Confidence intervals apply only to adjusted relative rates.
[c] $p < .05$ that confidence interval includes 1.

ambulatory care. Disadvantaged patients, for example, may be less likely to comply with physicians' orders or may delay seeking care and thereby present at more advanced stages of illness when they first see a doctor, making hospitalization more likely. If physicians know in advance about problems obtaining high-quality outpatient care, they may have lower thresholds for admitting disadvantaged patients for precisely these sorts of conditions (if they think that outpatient follow-up might be unreliable). If this were true, physicians may be acting as best they can within the constraints of our health system.

Weissman et al. addressed this latter scenario by measuring patient severity. If physicians have lower thresholds for admitting uninsured patients with AHCs, then those patients would presumably be less sick, on average, and would have lower severity levels. Overall, it was found that uninsured patients hospitalized for AHCs were slightly less severely ill and Medicaid patients in AHCs were slightly more severely ill, compared with similar privately insured patients. This suggests a somewhat lower threshold for admitting uninsured patients, but a higher threshold for admitting Medicaid patients. However, the differences in severity for AHCs among insurance groups were not convincing; the overall differences were small and the size and even direction of the differences varied substantially by individual condition. Given these supplemental findings, disparity in the admission threshold was not likely to be an important explanation for the patterns uncovered.

PERINATAL OUTCOMES

A long-standing tenet of public health advocates is that the health of a society is mirrored by the health of its babies. For many years, the infant mortality rate was used to compare the overall health status of different countries. In the United States, women who are uninsured or covered by Medicaid have worse birth outcomes than other women. Many of the studies described in Chapter 5 that examined the process of prenatal care also tried to link their findings to outcomes. In the study by the U.S. General Accounting Office (1987) mentioned earlier, pregnant women who were uninsured or insured by Medicaid were interviewed about the results of their births and their answers were compared to national data from other sources. While 6.8 percent of babies born nationwide were classified as having low birth weight (less than 2,500 grams), 12.4 percent of the babies born to the disadvantaged women GAO interviewed were of low birth weight (U.S. General Accounting Office, 1987).

In another study focusing on the uninsured, Braveman et al. (1989) examined adverse outcomes associated with newborns in an eight-county region of California between 1982 and 1986. Adverse outcomes were defined as prolonged hospital stays, transfers to another facility, or death. Uninsured newborns had 30 percent higher odds of an adverse outcome than privately insured. In addition, the authors reported that the number and percentage of uninsured newborns increased during that period and that this increase was accompanied by a worsening (i.e., increase) in the relative odds of adverse events.

For all its shortcomings, Medicaid may serve a valuable role in preventing poor birth outcomes. In a study of California deliveries, Howell et al. (1991) divided Medicaid beneficiaries into recent enrollees (for three months or less of their pregnancies) and other enrollees, and

Table 6-3. Birth Outcomes: Rates per 1,000 Live Births for Medicaid and Non-Medicaid Groups, California, 1983

Birth Outcome	Medicaid		Non-Medicaid	
	Enrolled 0–3 months of pregnancy	Enrolled 4+ months of pregnancy	Residents of Low-Income Areas	Residents of High-Income Areas
Total deliveries	1,880	5,612	4,054	1,464
<2,500 grams birthweight	78	63	54	42
<260 days gestational age	151	120	103	70
Infant mortality	13.8	8.6	12.6	6.8

Source: Adapted from Howell et al., 1991, Tables 8 and 9, p. 9.

then compared their outcomes with those of non-Medicaid women in a sample of low- and high-income areas (Table 6-3). In this case poor birth outcome was defined as either birth weight less than 2,500 grams, gestational age less than 260 days, or infant death. All three of the low-income study groups, including recent and longer-term Medicaid enrollees and non-Medicaid women, had poorer birth outcomes than the high-income group. However, in a multivariate analysis of low birth weight, only the recent Medicaid enrollees had significantly higher rates of poor outcomes. In other words, women who were covered by Medicaid for the bulk of their pregnancies did well, while those enrolling at the end of their pregnancies did not. These results suggest that both income and payment source are important factors in perinatal outcomes.[1] Norris and Williams (1984) addressed a related topic and found that the birthweights and perinatal outcomes of women covered by Medicaid in California were similar to those not covered and that the outcomes had improved substantially for both groups between 1968 and 1978.

These cross-sectional studies beg the question of whether insuring otherwise uninsured women would actually improve the health of their babies. After all, the mere provision of insurance does not guarantee that women will use the services offered. Three studies have examined whether provision of insurance coverage to poor women who were previously uninsured might improve birth or maternal outcomes. During the 1980s, the Tennessee Medicaid program was expanded to include married women. The income eligibility cut-off remained at approximately 80 percent of the poverty level and the eligibility determination process remained the same. Piper, Ray, and Griffin (1990) found no change in first trimester initiation of prenatal care or birth outcomes, although women affected directly by the regulatory change could not be analyzed separately from the entire statewide sample.

Haas et al. (1993) and Haas, Udvarhelyi, and Epstein (1993) evaluated a program called Healthy Start introduced in Massachusetts in 1986. The aim of Healthy Start was to provide insurance coverage for prenatal care for uninsured women whose incomes were below 185 percent of the Federal poverty level. "Satisfactory" prenatal care was defined using an Institute of Medicine index based on the trimester in which care was initiated and whether there were a sufficient number of visits for the length of gestation. Adverse birth outcomes included birth weight less than 2,500 grams and prematurity. Adverse maternal outcomes included severe pregnancy-related hypertension, placental abruption, and maternal length of stay greater than newborn length of stay. Changes over time were compared (1984–1987, i.e., before and after Healthy Start was initiated) in the process and outcomes of prenatal care for privately insured patients versus women who were uninsured (in 1987 some of the uninsured women received coverage through Healthy Start). For all patients taken together, "satisfactory" care was associated with better birth and maternal outcomes. However, Healthy Start did not increase the proportion of uninsured woman who received satisfactory care, nor did it improve newborn or maternal outcomes relative to privately insured women and their babies.

STAGE AT DIAGNOSIS AND SURVIVAL FOR CANCER

The stage of cancer at presentation is potentially an index of the effectiveness of ambulatory care and hence of access; the assumption is that patients with better ambulatory care are more likely to be diagnosed at an earlier stage of disease. Two of the studies in the literature are based on data from the 1960s or earlier. In a study of early diagnosis of breast cancer in Massachusetts women under the age of 65, researchers found that uninsured and Medicaid patients were significantly more likely to present with advanced tumors (Friedman, Parker, and Lipworth, 1973). Berg, Ross, and Latourette (1977) studied survival in patients with 39 types of cancer who obtained primary care at the University of Iowa from 1940 to 1969. Delays in seeking treatment by patients classified in the indigent payment class (compared with private pay patients) led to a later stage of cancer upon presentation. In addition, the indigent care patients had poorer survival for 20 of 22 types of cancer. These results showing diminished survival among indigent patients persisted even after correction for initial delay and for stage of disease.

Two more recent efforts have examined the association of payment status with cancer survival. In the previous chapter we described how researchers found differences in the aggressiveness of anticancer treatment for 1,400 patients with lung cancer living in New Hampshire and Vermont (Greenberg et al., 1988). The authors also examined length of survival during a four-year period following diagnosis. No significant differences were discovered after control for demographic variables, disease stage, and functional status.

Ayanian and colleagues (1993) examined stage of diagnosis and survival for more than 4,000 patients with breast cancer diagnosed in New Jersey in 1987. Uninsured patients and those with Medicaid coverage had a higher stage at diagnosis than the privately insured. Uninsured and Medicaid patients also had a shorter median survival after control for age, stage, race, and income based on patients' census tract or Zip code.

PERCEIVED HEALTH STATUS AND OTHER MEASURE OF HEALTH STATUS

In Chapter 2 differences in health status by payer were described because medical need is an important predictor of utilization and certain outcomes. Several studies are reviewed in this section that used overall health status indicators as *outcomes* of specific policy interventions. The studies were limited to sites that serve predominantly Medicaid and uninsured patient populations, so it is impossible to make direct comparisons between insured and uninsured patients. Nevertheless, they provide valuable insights into potential areas of access problems for sick people with inadequate insurance.

Patients who are uninsured or insured by Medicaid tend to rely disproportionately on municipal hospitals for their care. When such a hospital closes down, the health status of such patients may be at risk. As described earlier, users of a public hospital that closed down in Shasta County, California, experienced a variety of access problems, including lack of a regular provider and denied care, relative to a similar cohort in a neighboring county (Bindman, Keane, and Lurie, 1990).[2] The authors also examined changes in health status. Patients in Shasta County had significant declines on the Medical Outcomes Study Short Form (MOS-SF) in terms of social and role function, health perception, and pain, relative to patients in the control county. A link also appeared between access problems and health care outcomes. Patients in both counties who reported access difficulties during the study year were more likely to experience worsening health status in terms of pain and deficits in mental health, physical function, and health perception.

Even when municipal hospitals stay open, long waiting lines in the emergency departments and outpatient clinic can frustrate patients and compromise access. Some just give up and leave, even for serious problems. In one hospital in San Francisco,[3] the median waiting time for all patients was nearly three hours (Bindman et al., 1991). Potential patients who left without being seen were more likely to report that their pain or the seriousness of their problem had worsened 7–14 days later than those who stayed. Baker, Stevens, and Brook (1991) also investigated the outcomes of persons who left an emergency department without being seen[4] and found that 11 percent were subsequently hospitalized within one week. Neither study showed a significant difference in the demographic or payer characteristics between those patients who left without being seen and those who stayed. Finally, black and Hispanic patients at two New York City hospitals with hypertension were examined to determine the connection between health insurance and the control of their disease. The study controlled for age, race, gender, education, alcohol and smoking-related problems, noncompliance, and lack of a primary care physician. Uninsured patients were 1.9 times more likely to have severe, uncontrolled hypertension (95 percent CI; 0.8–4.6). Because uninsured and Medicaid patients are more likely than others to rely on hospital emergency departments for their ambulatory care, and are especially likely to visit public hospitals, the implications for avoidable morbidity are noteworthy.

NURSING HOMES

Nursing homes provide the context for two possible outcomes of care: (1) entrance into nursing homes might represent an adverse outcome of medical care in the community; and (2) exit from a nursing home, depending on the destination, reflects the care received in the nursing home. Why might these transitions be noteworthy? Exceptionally high rates of nursing home admissions for patients living in the community (at home) may indicate unacceptable access or quality of ambulatory care or inadequate home support. This situation is especially meaningful for chronically ill patients who may prefer to live at home rather than in a nursing facility. Moreover, in certain cases home care may be a more cost-effective patient management strategy than nursing home admission. These sorts of conclusions have to be balanced by other considerations. For example, higher demand for nursing home admission is probably associated with higher disposable incomes, patient attitudes and preferences, and, of course, insurance.

It may also be important to compare destinations upon *discharge* from nursing homes (i.e., exits). Many patients die in nursing homes and others transfer to an acute care hospital shortly after admission to a nursing home; however, some are discharged back into the community, which suggests a better outcome. Evidence of variation by payment status for any of these outcomes is scant.

Soumerai et al. (1991) scrutinized nursing home admissions for Medicaid patients who were 60 years old or older and who received three or more prescription medications per month. The study was part of a broader investigation into the impact of a cap imposed on prescription drug payment in New Hampshire. During the study period, drug use dropped by 35 percent among the 411 subjects in New Hampshire, but it did not change among the 1,375 controls in New Jersey. The proportion of Medicaid patients entering nursing homes rose from 2.3 percent before the study period to 10.6 percent in New Hampshire, while rising from 2.1 percent to only 6.6 percent in New Jersey. The authors concluded that the money saved through reduction in drug use was almost entirely offset by the excess admissions to nursing homes.

A study that investigated the association of payment source with nursing home discharge status found, overall, that 28.3 percent of patients were discharged to community settings; the remainder either died in the nursing home or were transferred to another institutional setting (Weissert and Scanlon, 1985). Using logistic regression, with control for marital status, age, diagnosis, physical dependency, mental disorders, and aggregate measures of revenue sources for the facility, the authors found that Medicaid patients were 40 percent less likely than the average patient to be discharged to the community. The use of discharge status from nursing homes as a marker of quality suffers from the same limitations as outcome measures for hospitals—outcomes may be inadequately adjusted for health status and other risk characteristics. Moreover, while Medicaid patients may have fewer social supports in the community, which makes their discharge there less likely, they also have better coverage for nursing home services, which could explain the patterns of discharge described here.

SATISFACTION

Despite a growing distaste for the current *system* of health care (Blendon and Donelan, 1990), most Americans are satisfied with the care they receive from their own doctors. Nevertheless, there are data that provide evidence of differences in the level of satisfaction, by payer. Using survey data from 1981–82, Chen and Lyttle (1987) explored differences in the proportion of persons who were generally favorable about their care and found that 31 percent of uninsured persons were "not completely satisfied with their care" versus 23 percent of patients with either public or private insurance (Table 6-4). The difference between uninsured and privately insured patients was significant in a multivariate analysis controlling for demographic characteristics and medical need.

At the other end of the spectrum are those patients who have very negative impressions of their care. For those with at least one ambulatory visit in the last year, uninsured respondents were "not at all satis-

Table 6-4. Satisfaction with Care, by Insurance Coverage

	Uninsured	Public	Private
Chen and Lyttle, 1987 (1982 RWJF Survey)			
Not completely satisfied[a]	31%	23%	23%
Robert Wood Johnson Foundation, 1987			
(1986 RWJF Survey)			
Not at all satisfied[b]	10.2		3.6
Not at all satisfied[c]	4.8		2.0

Note: Private includes all other insured if no separate figure is provided.

[a] After adjustment for demographic and need variables, differences were significant, $p < .05$.
[b] For persons hospitalized at least once in the past year, $p < .05$.
[c] For persons with at least one ambulatory visit in the past year.

fied" with their most recent visit more than twice as often as insured respondents (4.8 percent versus 2 percent, $p > .05$); similarly, of those hospitalized at least once, about 10.2 percent of the uninsured were "not at all satisfied" compared with about 3.6 percent of the insured ($p < .05$) (Table 6–4) (Robert Wood Johnson Foundation, 1987). In general, then, uninsured patients seem to be less satisfied with their care than other groups, although at least one study indicated that persons with public insurance register about the same level of satisfaction as do uninsured persons.

7

SPECIAL CASES: COST-SHARING, CHANGES IN OR LOSS OF INSURANCE, AND MEDICAID MANAGED CARE

The bulk of this book has been devoted to exploring relations between access to care and health insurance for the major payer groups for individuals under sixty-five in the United States today—the uninsured, the privately insured, and those insured by Medicaid. In this chapter we review three special cases introduced in Chapter 1: cost-sharing, loss of insurance, and Medicaid managed care. As in the rest of the book, effects on process and outcome are noted. Cost-sharing focuses on persons who have insurance but face different coverage levels. The questions asked by the research community address whether cost-sharing adversely affects utilization, if so what type of services, and whether cost-sharing affects patients' health outcomes. The review of cost-sharing represents by far the bulk of this chapter. The next section, on loss of insurance, offers an opportunity to study what happens to access when someone loses coverage involuntarily. Although it is limited to just a few studies, they are methodologically quite interesting and powerful because in some instances the effect of insurance can be isolated from the confounders that plague cross-sectional studies. The final section of this chapter reviews the rapidly growing literature on Medicaid managed care. The organizational approach of managed care is spreading like wildfire, as state after state implements managed care programs, hoping to cut costs without cutting eligibility or reimbursement, at least on the surface. Our review may shed some light on the consequences of this movement with respect to access.

COST-SHARING

The effect of cost-sharing on the frequency and type of health care utilization has been recognized for many years; however, this was not always the case. At one time many argued that health care was different from other sorts of economic goods. Physicians would advise the use of medical services based on medical need, not on the ability to pay; consumers, concerned about their health, made sacrifices in other areas of their consumption in order to obtain needed services, even at a high price. This view of behavior made some wary of cost-sharing. Forcing middle class consumers to pay more would not change health-seeking behavior, but would merely place an added financial burden on those needing care.

On the other side of the aisle sit those who believed that health care was similar to other economic goods and that neither doctors nor patients are immune from financial incentives. To them cost sharing might be helpful if it led patients to reduce use of services that provided them with little or no health benefits and thus was not worth the price to individuals or to society. Because these alternative theories have enormous implications for how health care should best be financed, a substantial research literature has evolved.

PROCESS INDICATORS

An early review of the cost-sharing literature from the 1960s and early 1970s noted strong evidence that cost-sharing affects the volume of medical care utilization and that the size of the coinsurance rate is related to the strength of the effect (Ginsburg and Manheim, 1973). In other words, the more that people had to pay for their care, the fewer services they would use. Economists calibrate consumers' responses to changes in prices with a statistic called *price elasticity*. Based on their review, Ginsburg and Manheim concluded that the price elasticity of demand varied by demographic group, that is, the sensitivity of consumers to changes in coinsurance rates was a function of their age, their gender, and other characteristics.[1]

Tables 7-1 and 7-2 summarize research from the 1980s and 1990s by exploring the link between cost-sharing and utilization, with special attention to the effect of cost-sharing on the poor. Table 7-1 is dedicated solely to research emanating from the RAND Health Insurance Experiment (HIE), while Table 7-2 covers findings from other studies. With almost no exceptions, these investigations concluded that cost-sharing reduces health care utilization and expenditures.

The RAND HIE (see Appendix A) has been the most widely cited source of health services research in the 1980s on the question of how cost-sharing affects service use and expenditures. Much of the research on the impact of cost-sharing on utilization is limited because the generosity of coverage is often confounded by self-selection. In other words, persons who expect to incur higher health care expenditures are more likely than others to choose coverage with low coinsurance

Table 7-1. The Association of Cost-Sharing and Health Care Utilization in the RAND Health Insurance Experiment

Study	Utilization Type	Effect Found
Newhouse et al., 1981; Manning et al., 1988; Newhouse, 1991	Numerous	Substantial associations showing less use in cost-sharing group (see Table 7-3)
Keeler and Rolph, 1983	Inpatient and outpatient episodes	Use was 66–80% higher for persons in free plan
Marquis, 1984	Choice of primary care provider	Not related
O'Grady et al., 1985	Emergency care	Use was 16–42% higher for persons with no cost-sharing
Leibowitz et al., 1985a, 1985b	Outpatient and inpatient care for children	Cost-sharing reduced use of outpatient care (including preventive) but had no effect on inpatient care for children
Lohr et al., 1986	Highly effective and rarely effective care	Associations strongest for poor (see Table 7-4)
Shapiro, Ware, and Sherbourne, 1986	Visits for serious and minor symptoms	Cost-sharing group had about 33% fewer visits for minor symptoms and 20% fewer visits for serious symptoms
Siu et al., 1986	Inappropriate hospitalization	There were no significant differences between cost-sharing and free plans in the percentage of admissions or of days classified as inappropriate
Foxman et al., 1987	Antibiotics	Free plan had 80% higher use for both beneficial and questionable use
Wells et al., 1987	Use of general medical provider for mental health care	Not related
Lurie et al., 1987	Preventive care	Children <7 and adults 45–65 received more immunizations under free plan; women received more Pap smears under free plan
Lurie et al., 1989	Eye exams, lens purchases	Persons in free plan were 18% more likely to have eye exams if problem perceived; persons in free plan were 14% more likely to purchase lenses
Anderson, Brook, and Williams, 1991	Office-based care for children	Children in cost-sharing had lower probability of visit and fewer visits; medical and pathology service inputs were also less, but no significant differences for surgical or radiology

Table 7-2. The Association of Cost-Sharing and Health Care Utilization, in Various Studies

Study	Utilization Type	Effect Found
Beck, 1973 (copayments in Canada)	Physician services	Declined 18% in poor families and 6–7% in nonpoor
Roemer et al., 1975 (Medicaid copayment experiment)	Ambulatory visits, hospital care	Ambulatory visits declined, but after several months, hospital rates rose to higher levels than the control group
Scheffler, 1984 (introduction of 40% coinsurance[a])	Ambulatory and inpatient	Ambulatory and inpatient use both declined 30% after introduction of 40% coinsurance
Roddy et al., 1986 (introduction of copayments[a])	Acute (self-limiting), preventive, and other visits	Acute, self-limiting visits declined 41% over 1 year, 44% over 2 years; preventive visits declined 25% over 1 year, 28% over 2 years; other visits declined 29% over 1 year, but *rose* 10% over 2 years
Farley, 1986 (NMCES)	Hypertension visits	Persons with comprehensive insurance (i.e., first dollar coverage) had 11% more visits
Greene and Gunselman, 1986 (Blue Cross employer groups choosing coinsurance plans)	Admission rates, hospital days/1,000, amount paid by employer	Admission rates declined 11.3% versus 3.4% for the control groups; days per 1,000 declined 14.4% versus 3.4% for the control groups; expenditures per employer declined 5.6% versus a 17% *rise* in the control group
Cherkin, Grothaus, and Wagner, 1989 ($5 co-payment in an HMO)	Visits	Declined 11%
Richwald et al., 1991 (introduction of $20 fee in STD clinic in LA County, 1986–88; fee was then dropped)	Visits, syphilis cases	Visits dropped 17% after the imposition of the fee and then increased 14% after the fee was dropped; reported cases of syphilis rose 9% during the period of the fee, then decreased 14% in the twelve-month period after the fee was dropped.

[a] Cost-sharing provisions applied to the United Mine Workers Health Plan.

rates. A strong point of the HIE was its random assignment of study participants to plans with varying levels of coinsurance.

The primary HIE findings with regard to utilization are displayed in Table 7-3. The levels of outpatient care, inpatient admissions, and total expenditures and the probabilities of medical care use all varied substantially by type of insurance plan (Manning et al., 1988). Higher

Table 7-3. Annual Use of Medical Services per Capita in the RAND Health Insurance Experiment, by Type of Plan

Plan	Outpatient Visits (no.)	Inpatient Admissions (no.)	Total Expenses (adjusted $)	Probability of Any Medical (%)	Probability of Any Inpatient (%)
Free	4.5	0.13	750	87	10
Coinsurance rate					
25%	3.3	0.11	617	79	8
50%	3.0	0.09	573	77	7
95%	2.7	0.10	504	68	8
Individual deductible[a]	3.0	0.12	630	72	10
p value for chi-square (df = 4)	< 0.001	0.02	0.002	< 0.001	< 0.001

Source: Manning et al., 1988, Table 4.1, p. 19.
[a] Individual deductible plan had 95 percent coinsurance on ambulatory care, free inpatient services, and individual deductibles of $150 to a maximum of $450 per family (Newhouse, 1991).

coinsurance led to lower use of services, including ambulatory care, hospitalizations, prescription drugs, and diagnostic tests. The pattern of findings held for both children and adults and for persons of all income groups (not shown) (Newhouse, 1991). The cost per person admitted to a hospital, a proxy for intensity, did not differ by plan, probably because of the similarity of the plans in the stop-loss provisions.

One of the questions pursued by the RAND researchers was whether or not inpatient care might be substituted under certain circumstances for outpatient care. The Individual Deductible plan had no cost-sharing for inpatient care and poor coverage for outpatient care (see note to Table 7-3). Compared to those in the free plan, participants in the individual deductible plan had fewer face-to-face ambulatory visits, but the number and probability of hospital admissions was about the same. As a consequence, total expenses were about 20 percent less than in the free plan. Thus, the researchers concluded that there was no real evidence to support the existence of substitution.

One particularly important issue is whether use of medical services declined across the board or whether declines were more evident in unnecessary or ineffective services. Lohr and colleagues categorized medical services by condition and according to their effectiveness in treating acute conditions. Coinsurance reduced use of effective and ineffective medical care comparably, although the reductions were greatest for poor adults and particularly poor children (Tables 7-4 and 7-5) (Lohr et al., 1986).

In another analysis of the RAND HIE, the symptoms of participants were classified as either serious or minor (requiring or not requiring

Table 7-4. Summary of the Significant Differences between RAND Health Insurance Experiment Plans in the Predicted Probability of an Episode of Highly and Rarely Effective Care

Effectiveness Category	Ratio of Cost-Sharing Plan to Free Care	Group Affected
Medical care was highly effective for acute conditions	0.59	Poor adults
	0.71	Nonpoor adults
	0.56	Poor children
Medical care was rarely effective (mainly acute conditions)	0.70	Poor adults
	0.78	Nonpoor adults
	0.54	Poor children
	0.76	Nonpoor children

Source: Lohr et al., 1986, p. 75.
Note: Nonsignificant results are not shown.

care by a physician in most instances) (Shapiro, Ware, and Sherbourne, 1986). The cost-sharing group saw a physician about one-third less often than the free-care group for minor symptoms ($p < .04$) and about 20 percent less often for serious symptoms ($p < .10$). Other studies based on HIE data found negative associations between cost-sharing and antibiotic use (Foxman et al., 1987), and emergency services (O'Grady et al., 1985). Cost-sharing was not significantly associated with the choice of generalists versus specialists (Wells et al., 1987), nor apparently was cost-sharing associated with the percentage of hospitalizations or days of hospitalization that were classified as inappropriate (Siu et al., 1986).

The HIE is surely a landmark study, and its methodology was carefully developed, yet it is important to note some of its limitations. Foremost for our purposes, no participants lacked insurance, and even those with very high coinsurance levels had maximum payment levels adjusted to their incomes. Thus, it is impossible to draw conclusions about the effect on utilization of being totally uninsured.

The sample for the HIE was drawn from the general population (i.e., mostly well-insured, healthy individuals). The thrust of the research was to look at average utilization. As a result, despite the study size (over 7,500 participants), there may have been insufficient statistical power to describe precisely patterns of care for certain vulnerable subgroups, including the very poor or the very sick with rare diseases (W. Glaser, personal communication, February 13, 1992). The HIE has also been criticized for other methodological issues (Haggerty, 1985; Welch et al., 1987). Newhouse (1993), in a book on the HIE, made the case that potential threats to internal and external validity, including attrition, Hawthorne effects (patients changing their behavior because they know they are in a study), and representativeness, were small or

Table 7-5. Summary of the Significant Differences between RAND Health Insurance Experiment Plans in the Predicted Probability of an Episode of Care for Preventive Services, Chronic Conditions, and Acute Conditions

Condition	Cost-Sharing Probability as a Percentage of Free Plan[a]	Group Affected by Cost-Sharing
General medical examination	54	Poor adults
	71	Nonpoor adults
	68	Poor children
	79	Nonpoor children
Vision examinations	58	Poor adults
	61[b]	Poor children
Hay fever	39	Poor adults
Obesity	49	Nonpoor adults
Acute upper respiratory infection	49	Poor children
	65	Nonpoor children
Acute pharyngitis	54	Poor adults
	68	Nonpoor adults
	56	Poor children
	82	Nonpoor children
Otitis media	45[b]	Poor adults
	69[b]	Poor children
Diarrhea and gastroenteritis	37	Poor children
Vaginitis and cervicitis	50	Poor women
	54	Nonpoor women
Skin rashes and other noninfectious skin diseases	57	Poor adults
	69	Nonpoor adults
	60[b]	Poor children
Lacerations, contusions, and abrasions	58	Poor adults
	72	Nonpoor adults
	46	Poor children
Acute sprains and strains	33	Poor children
Other injuries and adverse effects	72	Nonpoor adults
	44	Poor children

Source: Lohr et al., 1986, p. 74.
[a] Effect of cost-sharing significant at $p < .05$
[b] Significant at $p < .10$

inconsequential. While most of the charges made by critics of the HIE seem either minor or unavoidable given the scope and objectives of the study, there are limitations to our ability to extrapolate HIE findings to behavior by those who become uninsured. Readers may likewise take caution in accepting the findings which showed no effect on certain rare health outcomes due to the wide confidence intervals around the results.

Other studies have provided information that complements the HIE results (Table 7-2). Greene and Gunselman (1986), for example, found similar deficits in utilization among persons on a Blue Cross coinsurance plan compared with a control group. These reductions in utilization, by the way, led to savings for the employer at the expense of the employee. In other words, coinsurance can shift some of the financial burden of health care away from the employer and onto the employee, at least in the short-term.

Cost sharing in HMOs elicits similar changes in utilization. Office visits to physicians in an HMO declined 11 percent after imposition of a $5/visit fee, with control for age, sex, family size, and tenure in the HMO (Cherkin, Grothaus, and Wagner, 1989). The effect on health status was not assessed, nor was it noted whether the reductions were for appropriate or inappropriate use.

Scheffler (1984) and Roddy, Wallen, and Meyers (1986) each studied the effect of imposing dramatic cost-sharing provisions on the United Mine Workers Health Plan in 1977. In each study ambulatory visits and hospital admissions declined. Visits for preventive care or for conditions that were self-limiting stayed low two years after cost sharing was introduced, while visits for other, perhaps more serious conditions, returned to prior rates after two years (Roddy, Wallen, and Meyers, 1986). The authors concluded that cost-sharing had only short-term effects on essential care and longer-term effects on nonessential care. In a related study, Fahs (1992) studied what happens when physicians are faced with cost-sharing for some of their patients but not others. In this study, physicians in the group practice serving both UMW and other patients *increased* fees and utilization for the other patients to compensate for their lost revenue from UMW patients.[2]

The effect of cost sharing may vary with the patient's condition. Farley (1986) used 1977 data from NMCES to show that patients with hypertension who had comprehensive first-dollar coverage made 11 percent more visits to a physician ($p < .05$) for this problem than patients who faced a deductible, with control for income, and physician and hospital supply factors. This percentage increase amounted to about one-third of a visit, on average. First-dollar coverage was not associated with differential use for patients with heart problems, hernias, and serious gynecological problems. Farley also found that coinsurance was associated with fewer hospital admissions. Patients with 20 percent coinsurance rates had 8 percent lower admission rates than those who were fully insured.

The effect of coinsurance on utilization specifically by the poor has obvious implications for the design of government-funded health insurance. Soumerai et al. (1987) found that copayments adversely affected the use of necessary pharmaceuticals by a Medicaid population. In a study in Canada in the 1960s, the introduction of a copayment provision in the province of Saskatchewan significantly ($p < .05$) reduced the use of physicians' services by 18 percent by poor families compared with reductions of 6–7 percent by the nonpoor, with control for age and number of children in the family (Beck, 1973). As with the mine workers' studies, the utilization rates returned to near previous levels over time, despite the continued cost-sharing. However, this held true only for the nonpoor (Beck and Horne, 1978). Glaser (1991, p. 417) cites numerous other international examples where cost-sharing caused short-term disruption but did not achieve significant long-term reductions in utilization.

Finally, a well-known study by Roemer et al. (1975) of California's "copayment experiment" for Medicaid recipients went a step further. Utilization of ambulatory physician visits declined in the copayment cohort compared with that of a control group of Medicaid patients who were not subject to copayments. After a period of several months, hospitalization rates in the copayment group rose to levels higher than those for the control group, suggesting that the inhibiting effect of co-payment on the use of ambulatory care may have led to higher use of expensive inpatient services. The authors concluded that copayments for the poor are penny-wise and pound-foolish. As noted earlier, similar offsets were not noted in the RAND Health Insurance Experiment.

In summary, cost-sharing has a clear impact on ambulatory services. Although the evidence is inconsistent, cost-sharing may reduce hospital use as well. The ability of cost-sharing to reduce *inappropriate* hospital use is unclear, although several studies suggest that hospital use may increase due to inadequate access to ambulatory care. The impact of coinsurance appears to be blunt. It affects all sorts of care, including care characterized as effective or needed for the treatment of serious symptoms. Cost-sharing affects the poor more than the nonpoor, and some researchers question whether the effects are equal across disease classes and whether they remain stable in the long-term.

OUTCOME INDICATORS

There is relatively limited information on the association of cost-sharing with health status or health outcomes. The RAND HIE is the only source of information to our knowledge that examined these issues in a broad range of settings and income levels. One of the main findings of the RAND HIE is that there is little association between cost-sharing and general or overall health status or other health outcomes for the average person (Keeler et al., 1987; Brook et al., 1990). This lack of as-sociation occurred despite differences of about 25 percent in the use of services and expenditures between persons in the free-care plans and persons in the cost-sharing plans. The main findings are summa-rized in Table 7-6.

The RAND researchers recognized that their ability to detect differ-ences in overall health status among persons in good health would be limited. They therefore concentrated their analytic efforts on persons

Table 7-6. The association of Cost-Sharing with Health Care Outcomes, RAND Health Insurance Experiment Studies

Study	Effect on Outcome
Brook et al., 1983[a]	For persons with average health or income, the only significant difference was for corrected far vision; For poor persons with high blood pressure, blood pressure was lowered in the free plan; For persons with high risk of dying, persons in free plan did better; No other significant effects were found among eight measures and health habits.
Keeler et al., 1987	For twenty measures of health (e.g., chronic phlegm or hay fever), plus measures for pain and worry, results were mixed or minor.
Valdez et al., 1985	Small and nonsignificant differences occurred for parents' perceptions of children's health or in physiological measures; large but nonsignificant differences occurred for poor children with preexisting conditions.
Shapiro, Ware, and Sherbourne, 1986	The prevalence of serious symptoms in the sick poor declined more for persons in the free plan than in the cost-sharing plan.

Note: Differences, when noted, favored the free plan.

[a] Detail provided in Table 7-7.

who were initially in ill health (i.e., whose health status scores from the entry examinations fell in the sickest 20 percent of the distribution). To gauge differences between socioeconomic classes, they compared outcomes for those in the lowest and highest income brackets. Once again, cost-sharing had no significant effect on general health status (Brook et al., 1983), but it had significant adverse effects on specific physiologic measures (Tables 7-6 and 7-7). Among persons who had high blood pressure or poor eyesight or whose poor health status placed them at high risk of dying, participants in the free-care plan had better exit values (were in better health) than those in the cost-sharing plans (Table 7-7). These findings were significant ($p < .05$) for low-income persons in one of the elevated risk categories (risk of dying) and for all incomes combined in two of the risk categories (eyesight and risk of dying). Valdez et al. (1985) used a similar methodology to examine outcomes for children by measuring parents' perceptions of their children's overall health and specific physiologic conditions. Outcomes improved for free plan members, but a small sample size limited the power to detect statistically significant differences.

One of the challenges taken up by the RAND researchers was to establish a link between their findings on process and outcomes. With this in mind, another report based on the RAND HIE examined differences between the free-care and cost-sharing groups in outcome indi-

Table 7-7. Differences in Predicted Exit Values for Free-Care Minus Cost-Sharing Plans: Selected Physiological Measures in Elevated-Risk Groups by Income

Physiological Variable	Definition of Elevated Risk Group[a]	All Incomes (95% CI)	Low Income[b] (95% CI)	High Income[b] (95% CI)
High diastolic blood pressure[c]	> 83 mmHG or taking hypertension drugs at enrollment	−0.7 (−2.2,0.8)	−2.3[d] (−4.9,0.3)	0.1 (−2.0,2.2)
Poor functional far vision[e]	Line 3 (20/25) or worse for better eye	−0.2 (−0.3,−0.1)	−0.3 (−0.6,0.02)	−0.07 (−0.4,0.2)
High risk of dying[f]	Risk >1.42	−0.21 (−0.39,−0.04)	−0.30 (−0.60,−0.04)	−0.13 (−0.4,0.1)

Source: Adapted from Brook et al., 1984, Tables 7 and 8.
Note: All confidence intervals (CI) that do not include 0 are significant at p < .05. Negative values indicate better health outcomes (i.e., lower risks) for the free care plan.

[a] Elevated-risk groups are the least healthy 20 percent of the people as defined with respect to the individual health measure denoted in each row. For functional far vision, all persons with uncorrected natural vision worse than 20/20 are included.
[b] Low-income = twentieth percentile or below; high income = sixtieth percentile or above.
[c] Measured in millimeters of mercury (mmHg).
[d] p = .08.
[e] Measured in number of Snellen lines.
[f] The risk of dying relative to that of persons with average values on major risk factors (i.e., smoking, cholesterol, systolic blood pressure).

cators that were thought to be closely related to (i.e., were probably affected by) the process of care (Brook et al., 1990). The authors established two types of quality criteria based on outcomes. One type was based on whether specific physiologic levels (e.g., control of diabetics' blood sugar level) were achieved or maintained. The other type of outcome criteria were devoted to patient's perceptions as to whether their health care had an *impact* on concerns like pain, worry, or activity restrictions. Specific process criteria for achieving outcome targets (e.g., foot care instruction for diabetics) were also defined to reflect acceptable quality of care. Overall, 81 percent of both types of outcome criteria and 62 percent of process criteria were met. Because fewer process criteria were met relative to the proportion of outcome criteria, the authors suggested that overall improvements in the process of care could be made, but they might have little impact on outcomes. There were no significant differences in achieving outcome criteria between the free-care and cost-sharing plans, and only minor differences in achieving the process criteria.

The essential message, then, of the RAND HIE is that the health effects of cost-sharing were generally not dramatic, and in fact were limited primarily to the sickest and poorest members of society. There is perhaps a lesson here for health services researchers. The health of most segments of our population is generally good and is relatively insensitive to policy changes, such as cost-sharing, that are aimed at marginal consumption of services. Poor outcomes that really matter are often rare, and it can be difficult to link changes in process indicators to effects on outcomes (see, for example, Wise et al., 1988). The impacts of social experiments on health may be limited and are more likely to be evident among the vulnerable and disadvantaged. That is where evaluation efforts most often ought to be focused unless very large samples can be studied.

There have been a few other studies beside the HIE on the relation of cost-sharing to outcomes, but information is scant. Hubbell, Waitzkin, and Rodriguez (1990) examined the effect of financial barriers on access. Barriers were determined subjectively by physician coders who noted when insurance had failed to cover recommended care or when an uninsured patient could not afford recommended care. The cross-sectional study was performed on 188 patients with low incomes seen at a university-affiliated facility. Patients coded as having financial barriers scored significantly lower than control subjects on the psychological function and mental health component of the functional status questionnaire and tended to score lower on other functional status measures.

Cost-sharing can have a dampening effect on patients' willingness to seek care for socially sensitive conditions. In Los Angeles County, a $20 fee was imposed from 1986 to 1988 and then dropped in the public clinic for sexually transmitted disease (Richwald et al., 1991). Visits decreased by 17 percent after imposition of the fee and then increased by 14 percent (nearly back to original levels) after the fee was once again dropped a few months later following public outcry. Prompt treatment of sexually transmitted diseases is critical in controlling the transmission of infection to other parties. Reported cases of primary and secondary syphilis rose by 99 percent during the period of the fee and then decreased by 14 percent in the twelve-month period after the fee was dropped.

CHANGES IN OR LOSS OF INSURANCE

PROCESS INDICATORS

Involuntary loss of insurance, especially among the poor, has multiple repercussions for the way people seek and obtain health care. One natural experiment occurred as a result of the 1981 OBRA. OBRA instituted changes that effectively denied AFDC assistance and its associated Medicaid coverage to many families on welfare who had jobs (Rowland, Lyons, and Edwards, 1988). A survey of Medicaid patients in Hennepin County, Minnesota, tracked their insurance coverage and access following the passage of this legislation. Two years later most of the subjects had private insurance, but the private policies were not as comprehensive as Medicaid. Fifteen percent of the subjects reported that their new private policies did not cover prescription medications, 6 percent had coverage that did not include physician services, and 1 percent did not cover inpatient admissions. Compared with their responses before they lost Medicaid, three times as many persons reported that they did not have enough money to pay their doctors. As a consequence, they delayed seeking medical care or went without it (Moscovice and Davidson, 1987).

In 1982 California transferred responsibility for the medically indigent adult (MIA) population away from Medicaid to the counties and reduced the state subsidy. This plan effectively eliminated Medicaid insurance for this group of patients. At least three investigations have examined the effects of this change. MIAs at the UCLA Medical Center were compared with other Medicaid patients who did not lose their eligibility. There were two- to threefold differences in the proportion who were able to identify a usual source of care, who were satisfied with their care, or who agreed with the statement, "I can get medical care whenever I need it" (Lurie et al., 1984). In a second study of MIAs in Orange County, Akin et al. (1989) followed persons who applied for Medicaid but were found ineligible and assessed the clinical importance of the patients' conditions according to a five-point scale (where 1 represented the least severe conditions and 5 represented conditions that would most likely lead to long-term disability). Of the patients with more serious problems (levels 3, 4, and 5), 76 percent had not received treatment four weeks later. A third study by Brown and Cousineau (1991) compared the actual or "observed" number of inpatient days and outpatient visits for the medically indigent in two counties after the loss of Medicaid eligibility, with an "expected" number based on patterns of care during the time when MIAs were covered by Medicaid. The results indicated that loss of Medicaid coverage led to approximately 19 percent fewer inpatient discharges and 78 percent fewer visits than expected. The authors concluded that access was significantly reduced by loss of Medicaid.

When a budget shortfall occurred in 1983, the VA Medical Centers withdrew eligibility for outpatient care for certain "medically stable" patients. Seventeen months after discharge from the program at one of the VA Centers, a sample of 157 patients was compared with a control group who retained their eligibility. The discharged former VA patients were more likely to claim they lacked necessary access to care (58 percent versus 5 percent, $p < .001$) and to have reduced or eliminated their prescribed medications (47 percent versus 25 percent, $p = .002$). Of the discharged patients who had reduced or stopped their medications, 71 percent had done so because of cost. The drugs affected by the change included antihypertensives/diuretics, potassium, antiar-rhythmics, and anti-inflammatory agents (Fihn and Wicher, 1988). All of these medications are potentially clinically important.

OUTCOME INDICATORS

In addition to having a dampening effect on utilization, involuntary loss or change in insurance can have unforeseen consequences on health status. Negative consequences of loss of insurance have impor-tant policy implications in the debate over universal health insurance, since a national plan might obviate discontinuities in coverage.

In the study described earlier, medically indigent adults who lost Medicaid coverage in California experienced a significant decrease in overall health status and a clinically meaningful increase in blood pres-sure among hypertensive subjects, compared with the control group who kept their coverage. A small number of excess deaths was also noted in the group that was dropped from Medicaid (Lurie et al., 1986).

The termination of VA benefits had similar health effects. Seven-teen months after the study began, 41 percent of "stable" VA patients whose outpatient benefits were discontinued reported that their health status was "much worse," compared with 8 percent of those whose eligibility was retained (Fihn and Wicher, 1988). Furthermore, the percentage of dropped patients whose blood pressure was deemed by clinicians to be "out of control" rose from 5 to 41 percent over the seventeen-month period, compared with a rise of only 9 to 17 percent among the comparison group. Meuleman and Mounts (1985) also measured the effect of the VA policy and found that 44 percent of vet-erans who lost their eligibility reported that their health had worsened nine months later.

MEDICAID AND MANAGED CARE

The history of Medicaid and managed care offers an important per-spective on the potential for reductions in access and quality of care (see, generally, Hurley, Freund, and Paul, 1993). Under legislation passed early in Medicaid's history, states were able to incorporate man-aged care into programs for Medicaid beneficiaries, but only on a vol-untary basis. In the 1970s a series of scandals occurred involving Medicaid contracts with HMOs in California. Former Governor Ronald Reagan had encouraged the development of competitive contracts with HMOs for Medicaid while simultaneously sponsoring cutbacks in funding for the fee-for-service program. The goal was to save money by inducing persons to enroll voluntarily in managed care plans. How-ever, unrealistically low bids were accepted from organizations having little experience in the provision of capitated services, followed by charges of misleading marketing practices, underservice, and poor quality of care. These events eventually led to more stringent regulations and a precipitous decline nationwide in the number of Medicaid programs with managed care components (Enthoven, 1980; Spitz, 1987; Luft and Morrison, 1991).

The 1981 OBRA conferred upon state Medicaid programs the freedom to experiment with cost containment approaches under a special waiver program that allowed mandatory assignment of beneficiaries to managed care. The theoretical effect of mandatory assignment to managed care on patient access is arguable. For example, low provider reimbursement, high red tape, and other factors have led to a long history of less than optimal participation by physicians in the Medicaid program; ipso facto, Medicaid recipients have less choice of providers than privately insured persons. Add to this the episodic and potentially redundant care offered in hospital emergency rooms and outpatient clinics, and one might easily conjecture that the institution of managed care, with an identifiable primary care case manager, could improve the lot of the publicly insured. Theoretically, the provision of managed care can augment information on availability of community services and improve continuity of care, as well.

The counterargument is made by advocates and policy analysts who focus on the gate-keeping role of primary care managers and the absence of alternatives within a closed system of care (Spitz and Abramson, 1987). Although persons with private insurance may have financial disincentives to use out-of-plan care, they presumably have incomes high enough to allow them to do so if they feel strongly enough about it. Medicaid recipients do not have this option. Furthermore, the potential for conflict of interest is present whenever providers are placed at risk and stand to gain financially if their patients underuse services.

Despite continuing controversy, the 1981 OBRA legislation catalyzed the growth of Medicaid managed care, and by 1986 over 650,000 persons in nineteen states were enrolled in managed care programs (Spitz, 1987).[3] By 1991 the numbers increased to 3.6 million Medicaid enrollees in 235 different plans (Hurley, Freund, and Paul, 1993). The evidence reviewed in this section pertains principally to two experiments that occurred in the last decade—the Medicaid Competition Demonstrations and the Arizona Health Care Cost-Containment System.

To encourage experimentation and evaluation, six states were originally funded in the early 1980s to embark on what was known as the Medicaid Competition Demonstrations (Freund and Hurley, 1987). The guiding principle was the use of managed care for utilization and cost control. Seven sites were funded with the idea of testing slightly different models of care, including competitive HMOs (Florida, Minnesota, Missouri, New York), partially capitated case management (Missouri and New Jersey), and health insuring organizations (HIOs) that require a risk-assuming fiscal intermediary (Monterey and Santa Barbara Counties, California, and Minnesota) (see Anderson and Fox, 1987, for a fuller description). Sites without managed care programs were also followed as quasi-experimental controls.

An evaluation component was built into the demonstrations, with the goal of assessing access, utilization, quality of care, satisfaction, and a host of operational issues. Data sources included consumer surveys and claims, and administrative records. Access to care was indicated by subjective measures (e.g., the perception of enrollees as to whether off-hours care was available) and objective measures (e.g., waiting and travel times). Information on the process of care for a number of tracer conditions was gleaned from medical charts.

PROCESS INDICATORS

Freund et al. (1989a) reported the major findings of the Medicaid Competition Demonstration evaluation. Although some of the demonstration sites enrolled Medicaid beneficiaries voluntarily there was no evidence of selection bias. Use of managed care also apparently did not disrupt access. Multivariate analyses controlling for health status and demographic variables showed no significant differences between managed care and control sites in objective measures of access (e.g., travel and waiting times) and a slight advantage for the managed care plans in terms of subjective measures (e.g., having convenient office hours) (Freund et al., 1989a).

Certain sorts of service utilization were markedly affected by the switch to managed care. Freund et al. (1989b) examined utilization before and after the experiment began and compared changes over time at the demonstration sites with corresponding changes over time at the control sites. The researchers found significant reductions at the demonstration sites in the use of inpatient services (32–43 percent fewer hospital stays), physician services (13–34 percent fewer visits), and use of specialists (32–67 percent fewer referrals). The appearance and magnitude of these effects varied across sites and age groups (children and adults). There were no apparent differences in the use of preventive services including childhood immunizations, Pap smears, and breast examination (Carey, Weiss, and Homer, 1990). The use of primary care physicians increased, at least for adults (Hurley, Paul, and Freund, 1989), but this result can be expected directly from the substitution of gatekeeper care for a more open system.

Because the emergency department is frequently used as a source of care by the Medicaid population, its use was considered an important study outcome. Hurley, Paul, and Freund (1989) found up to a 55 percent drop in use in the demonstration sites in terms of the proportion of persons with an emergency department visit and up to a 60 percent reduction in the number of emergency department visits per 100 beneficiaries. With control for demographic characteristics, Hurley, Freund, and Taylor (1989a,b) used multivariate models to examine the proportion of persons with at least one emergency department visit and found reductions of 27–37 percent for children and 30–45 percent for adults. Differences in the number of visits for persons with at least one visit were not significant.[4]

The Arizona Health Care Cost-Containment System (AHCCS) is the other major social experiment of managed care for Medicaid beneficiaries. Before AHCCS was implemented in 1982, Arizona did not participate in the Medicaid program and instead delegated care of the poor to county health departments. AHCCS was initiated as an alternative to a full-scale Medicaid program and is the only one of its kind among the states. Eligible persons select a single provider who holds a competitively bid contract with the state. Contractors are obligated to provide a comprehensive set of services to patients under a capitated system. The early implementation of AHCCS was plagued by operational difficulties, including the failure of a "private administrator concept," problems with eligibility determination, and delays in the institution of quality assurance procedures (McCall et al., 1985; Iglehart and White, 1987). Some policy experts have also suggested that the establishment of AHCCS resulted in the undermining of the stability of the county system, thereby compromising access and quality of care for the noneligible poor (Freeman and Kirkman-Liff, 1985; Anderson and Fox, 1987).

Two published articles have examined the impact of AHCCS's implementation on access to care and found either improvements or no difference for AHCCS participants. Freeman and Kirkman-Liff (1985) surveyed comparable samples of poor persons before and after the implementation of AHCCS. Access to care increased for AHCCS enrollees in 1984 relative to poor persons who received their care from counties in 1982. Compared with disadvantaged county patients in 1982, there was: (1) a 25–45 percent reduction in the proportion of respondents without a usual source of care, the figure varying with the date of enrollment and tenure in the program; and (2) a 56 percent reduction in the proportion of those who had no physician visit in the last year.

McCall, Jay, and West (1989) also surveyed the AHCCS population and compared the results with those of a group of Medicaid beneficiaries in a neighboring state. The survey of over 500 persons in each site included questions on perceived access to emergency and urgent care, travel and waiting times, ambulatory care, and satisfaction concerning a number of different parameters. The authors found few significant differences between the two groups.

A number of other Medicaid managed care programs have been evaluated, and the findings suggest they have met with mixed success

(Table 7-8). In at least one instance, total costs increased, driven by the use of specialists and prescription drugs (Hurley, Freund, and Paul, 1993).

The evaluations of Medicaid-managed care exhibit certain short-comings. In none of the studies reported here was an experimental control group established that could assure internal validity of the results. In the Hurley, Freund, and Paul (1993) book on Medicaid managed care, the authors described other limitations that they and others faced. For example, it was difficult to attribute changes in behavior or cost-savings to the managed care element as opposed to other con-founding state or federal temporal changes that may have been taking place. The selection of nonequivalent control groups may have ampli-fied the effects of the demonstration program; and of course, the spon-sors of the programs (usually state governments) wanted the results to appear in the best light. Hurley and colleagues judged that only about half of the evaluations they reviewed in their book had used rigorous methodology.

In summary, the use of managed care in Medicaid programs has been increasing rapidly. The explicit goal generally has been cost con-tainment with the hope that access is not threatened. Studies of the Medicaid Competition Demonstrations have documented decreased use of physician services and emergency rooms. However, together with studies of the AHCCCS there is no compelling evidence of a major deleterious impact on access in terms of process of care.

OUTCOME INDICATORS

Satisfaction with care was measured in two reports on the Competition Demonstrations (Freund et al., 1989a; Temkin-Greener and Winchell, 1991). These reports analyzed different sites and had somewhat con-flicting results. In both studies, enrollees in the demonstration sites ex-pressed high levels of satisfaction with their care; more than 80 percent reported general satisfaction. Nevertheless, Freund et al. reported that these rates were significantly lower than in the comparison sites, where 90 percent or more of the patients reported that they were satisfied. However, in the Temkin-Greener study, there were no significant dif-ferences in general satisfaction between the fee-for-service and HMO samples; moreover, demonstration patients (i.e., those enrolled in managed care) scored higher on certain components of satisfaction such as "humaneness of doctors."

Satisfaction with AHCCCS also was studied by McCall, Jay, and West (1989). Medicaid patients in the AHCCCS HMOs were generally satis-fied with their care, but the level of satisfaction was slightly higher in the comparison sites.

Evidence of the effect of Medicaid-managed care on perinatal out-comes is also mixed. Studies of managed care programs operating un-

Table 7-8. Summary of the effects of Medicaid Managed Care on Cost and Use in Twelve Programs

	Increase	Decrease	Mixed/ No Change	Unknown
Physician visits	3 (25%)	5 (42%)	4 (33%)	0 (0%)
Emergency department use	0 (0)	9 (75)	0 (0)	3 (25)
Ancillary services	1 (8)	7 (58)	1 (8)	3 (25)
Prescription drug use	1 (8)	5 (42)	1 (8)	5 (42)
Inpatient use	1 (8)	4 (33)	5 (42)	2 (17)
Costs	2 (17)	7 (58)	2 (17)	1 (8)

Source: Hurley, Freund, and Paul, 1993, p. 89.
Note: Numbers indicate the number of programs; percentages (shown parenthetically) are a percentage of all programs in that category. Percentages might not add up to 100 due to rounding.

der the Medicaid Competition Demonstration found no link to birth outcomes. For example, birth outcomes and complications of pregnancy were analyzed for more than 2,000 women at two of the demonstration sites and two comparison counties (Carey, Weis, and Homer, 1991). There were no significant differences among sites. Goldfarb et al. (1991) also investigated the outcome of managed care in Philadelphia's HealthPASS program, a Medicaid-managed care program that was not in the demonstration. Birth outcomes including birth weight, gestational age, and mortality were compared for a total of 434 women enrolled in HealthPASS and a matched sample of Medicaid fee-for-service patients. There were no significant differences between the groups. No difference in birth outcomes was also reported in a small ($N = 98$) study by Reis (1990).

Managed care programs are designed as gatekeeper systems, and even though overall care might be better coordinated, the programs are generally not directed at improving care specifically for pregnant women. Some of these programs, however, were combined with special efforts to improve prenatal care. The "case management" approach to prenatal care is a term that carries a particular meaning in this context. It refers to targeted interventions with special emphasis on outreach, comprehensiveness and education.

Evaluations of "case management" efforts found improved outcomes for managed care recipients. Three studies in three different sites found that coordinated case management led to increases in birth weight for low-income women, using Medicaid women in fee-for-service settings as control groups (Sokol et al., 1980; Korenbrot, 1984; Buescher et al., 1987). These results are interesting because they suggest that it is not simply financial barriers that affect outcomes, but also the style or organization of care.

Almost no other evidence on health outcomes in Medicaid-managed care programs exists. A single study of the chronically mentally ill in Minnesota found no consistent evidence of deleterious effects due to managed care (Lurie et al., 1992). Although this study was restricted to the chronically mentally ill, the authors employed a broad range of outcome measures including general health status, physical functioning, social functioning, and psychiatric symptoms. It would be clearly advantageous, of course, if these results could be replicated in other states and other managed care settings.

8

INSURANCE, ACCESS, AND
HEALTH CARE REFORM:
SUMMARY AND POLICY IMPLICATIONS

It is now certain that one of the big questions before the American people during the next few years will be public health. . . . The issues in the debate are momentous. . . . The truth is that some portion of the American people—no one knows exactly the number—can and do get the best medical care in the world. But another portion get this kind of care only when they are lucky, or if they make a tremendous financial sacrifice; while still a third portion do not get it at all.

R. W. Davenport, "Health Insurance Is Next," Fortune, *1950*

The sentiment captured in the epigraph for this chapter could easily have appeared in any recent editorial in any major U.S. newspaper or magazine. Because the remarks were taken from an appraisal of options presented to the public in 1950, they offer stark evidence that problems with health insurance are not new, nor will they easily go away.

Why the resurgence of interest in the health insurance system? Part of the answer is that, for most Americans, lack of insurance has become a "we" problem rather than a "they" problem. Since the 1980s, the number of uninsured persons has risen steadily. Thirty-six million nonelderly Americans lacked health insurance in 1991, and at least another 21 million had inadequate coverage. The number of uninsured persons has been growing even as Medicaid caseloads are expanding. Perhaps more important, one out of four people—or 63 million persons—will lose their health insurance for some time during a two-year period (Himmelstein and Woolhandler, 1992).

The economics are also important. Our current health expenditures exceed 14 percent of the gross domestic product; under current policies, they will reach 18.6 percent, or $14,000 for each family, by the year 2000. U.S. health care costs are substantially higher than those of our international competitors: approximately 50 percent higher than Canada's, 75 percent higher than those of Germany and France, and nearly threefold those of England (Schieber, Poullier, and Greenwald, 1993). Private payers and especially big business have been subsidizing providers for the care of the Medicaid population, the uninsured, and even Medicare beneficiaries (Prospective Payment Assessment Commission, 1993). In today's competitive environment, cost-shifting of this sort can no longer take place without consequence. The effect on the national deficit is also substantial. Without a change in existing policy, federal spending for Medicare will increase from $144 billion to $291 billion between now and the end of the decade; federal spending for Medicaid will increase from $72 billion to $164 billion.

The current insurance market seems to work poorly. Insurance companies have strong incentives to compete by selecting good risks rather than concentrating on managing care efficiently. Small businesses in particular are now faced with extremely high administrative costs. With a growing number of insurers using exclusions for preexisting conditions, arbitrary cancellations, and hidden limitations on benefits, consumers have restricted options for affordable policies that provide adequate protection.

Finally, the fabric of the safety net is not as tightly woven as one might like. Hospitals, even some publicly owned, turn away indigent people not in dire need of care (Weissman and Solish, 1989). Many rural areas and inner cities are underserved, while physicians tend to locate their practices in wealthy suburbs where patients can pay for care. Clinics that serve poor people are sparsely located, lack continuity, and have long waiting times.

A multitude of studies have tested whether these deficiencies of the system have had any discernable effects on access to medical care and patients' health outcomes. In the remainder of this chapter we summarize our findings and then briefly review the history of national health insurance reform in the United States and the general options for reform that we now face. We also discuss a number of key questions concerning access that must be addressed in reform. We conclude by identifying potentially productive avenues for the next generation of research on health insurance status and access to care.

WHAT HAVE WE LEARNED ABOUT ACCESS AND INSURANCE STATUS?

The relationships between payer status and health status are complicated. All three of the key comparison groups—the privately insured, those insured by Medicaid, and the uninsured—are heterogeneous in terms of their health status. For example, the uninsured no doubt include some individuals so healthy that they feel that the likelihood they will need costly health care, and thus health insurance, is very small. Other uninsured individuals are so ill that they are uninsurable. It is therefore not surprising that measures of disease prevalence and severity of illness vary across payer groups in ways that are not fully consistent. Persons who lack insurance tend to have lower perceived health status after age adjustment but fewer chronic conditions. These differences in health status between and within insurance groups make suspect any conclusions from studies that fail to adjust properly for initial health status. They also raise concerns that a comparison of payment groups in their entirety rather than subgroups defined by health or other characteristics will fail to illuminate other factors that may account for noted differences.

Despite these and other methodologic limitations, the voluminous literature on health care process indicates clearly that the source of payment has a substantial effect on the amount, location, and even quality of care received in the U.S. health care system. Many of the differences appear in primary care. Patients who are uninsured are less likely to have a regular doctor and more likely to receive care from emergency departments or hospital outpatient clinics. Data on waiting times suggest that their care is also less convenient. Perhaps as a result, uninsured persons tend to receive fewer preventive health services. There are also marked disparities in the total number of ambulatory visits, with the uninsured receiving many fewer on average than the other two insurance groups.

The evidence on the content of secondary care in hospitals provides a complementary picture. People who lack insurance delay care, and there is evidence to suggest that they come into the hospital more severely ill. They may also be hospitalized more frequently for conditions that could have been treated on an ambulatory basis. Even after admission to the hospital, the care provided to uninsured persons is different; their lengths of stay are shorter and they often use fewer discretionary, high-cost procedures. There is also emerging evidence that the quality of their care may be compromised, although these data are preliminary.

The literature demonstrating differences in outcomes of care by insurance status is also substantial, albeit less dramatic and less broad than the research findings on the process of care. For example, in the RAND HIE (see Appendix A), patients who had to pay for their health care and who were poor and initially in ill health or who had chronic disease (e.g., hypertension) had worse health outcomes at the end of the experiment; Lurie et al. (1984, 1986) found that poor patients who lose their insurance and have chronic disease are likely to suffer decrements in health status; Braveman et al. (1989) showed that uninsured persons have worse perinatal outcomes; Ayanian et al. (1993) showed that women without insurance or covered by Medicaid who are diagnosed with breast cancer had shorter life expectancies; and several recent studies suggested that uninsured people have higher rates of hospital mortality (Hadley, Steinberg, and Feder, 1991; Yergan et al., 1988; Young and Cohen, 1991) and avoidable hospitalizations (Billings et al., 1993; Weissman et al., 1992).

If there is a disparity in the number and strength of findings between studies on the process of health care and studies examining health outcomes, it should not be surprising. First, health outcomes are affected by multiple factors other than health services, including smoking, poor nutrition, environment and genetics, so correlating outcomes with specific causal factors is problematic. Second, it is difficult to study outcomes because events of interest may be rare or may take a long time to appear, nor are many outcomes routinely recorded in large computerized databases (because providers are reimbursed for providing services, not for improving outcomes). Third, interest in studying outcomes has only recently expanded, whereas interest in process measures is long-standing. Finally, many researchers believe that we are practicing on the "flat of the curve," where additional input of health services has only a minimal effect. These factors may explain why the provision of health insurance to poor uninsured pregnant women has not been shown to be associated with improvements in birth outcomes in the two intervention studies (Piper et al., 1990; Haas et al., 1993) reviewed here. Nevertheless, other studies showing that persons who are poor, sick, *and* uninsured seem to have relatively worse outcomes suggest that policy interventions should be focused on the most vulnerable groups.

The RAND HIE and related studies have provided information on the impact of cost-sharing. Cost-sharing results in reduced utilization and cost of health care, although other studies suggest that these effects are mitigated for certain diseases, for children, or in the long term. As one might expect, the effect of cost-sharing on health is most prominent among those with low income. Low-income persons who are more severely ill to begin with seem to suffer more under cost-sharing plans in terms of poor health outcomes. These data suggest that the incorporation of cost-sharing into future policy interventions might best be done with a sliding scale or other income adjustment.

It seems clear that the adoption of Medicaid has led to improvements in the process of care for its beneficiaries, although problems in access persist. There are still many gaps in our understanding of the behavioral aspects of supply and demand for Medicaid services. We know little, for example, about whether evidence of lower access for Medicaid beneficiaries is due more to their socioeconomic position or to Medicaid's poor reimbursement rates. We therefore do not know whether additional resources could best be utilized to expand eligibility or to increase fee levels.

One important issue that has been investigated only in limited circumstances is the possibility that certain restrictions on access, implemented with the goal of saving money, may sometimes backfire, at least partially. The RAND HIE and others (e.g., Scheffler, 1984) provide evidence that higher cost-sharing results in lower utilization of ambulatory services without an overall increase in hospitalization. These results are consistent with survey data showing that uninsured persons have lower utilization of both ambulatory and hospital services. Nevertheless, the studies by Roemer et al. (1975) looking at the Medi-Cal experiment, by Weissman et al. (1992) showing increased numbers of avoidable hospitalizations for groups that have limitations in ambulatory care, and by Soumerai et al. (1991) showing increased nursing home use when numbers of medications provided to Medicaid beneficiaries were capped, all indicate that there may sometimes be offsetting costs related to an increased use of specific clinical services. Because health policy is viewed by some as a subset of budget policy, inquiries like these are particularly important. These studies need to be verified and expanded.

A BRIEF HISTORY OF NATIONAL HEALTH INSURANCE REFORM IN THE UNITED STATES

Do we need health system reform? The election of President Bill Clinton galvanized an uneasy coalition that is embarked on an unprecedented debate on the need for comprehensive health reform and the merits of various approaches. With both Republicans and Democrats calling for reform, it may be sobering to review our past efforts. The repeated attempts we have made to achieve national health reform bespeak the difficulty in the task.

Young people would no doubt be shocked to hear that national health insurance very nearly passed during the Nixon administration. Their parents may be surprised to hear of President Truman's strong push in this direction. Even their grandparents may be unaware that labor organizations worked hand in hand with the American Medical Association in the early part of this century toward the enactment of national health insurance. A brief history is in order.[1]

The earliest efforts to provide government-sponsored health insurance can be traced to the worker's compensation laws, supported by Theodore Roosevelt in his Bull Moose campaign of 1912 and passed by several states between 1910 and 1916, as a result of activity by the American Association for Labor Legislation (AALL). Rather than paying for health service *per se,* early worker's compensation laws replaced lost wages. Health insurance was the next logical step. An AALL Committee on Social Insurance was formed from the association membership, and a model health insurance bill was written and introduced in several state legislatures. The AMA supported the general idea of the proposal and in fact offered to help with the medical sections. The AALL fully expected compulsory national health insurance (NHI) to be enacted by 1918. However, by 1920 the AMA reversed its position, and opposition by the medical industry (e.g., physicians and pharmaceutical companies) and even other labor groups distrustful of governmental monopolies, doomed the legislation.

Although essentially a private nonprofit effort, the development of the Blue Cross plans during the 1930s provided a model for spreading the cost of medical care among the working population. It is interesting that the motivation for these plans emanated largely from providers' concerns that hospitalized patients could not afford to pay their bills.

Although health insurance was certainly on the minds of many who built the New Deal during Roosevelt's administration, comprehensive medical benefits were not included in the Social Security Act. The AMA generated significant opposition within the profession to any bill that in their view smacked of socialism, which set the tone for their public policy stances for many years to come. The rapid spread of private health insurance also no doubt alleviated the concerns of the middle class over threats to their economic security in the event of illness.

Not until the election of President Truman did another major thrust for NHI come. Truman embraced the notion of NHI in 1945 and made it a pillar of his campaign against Dewey in 1948. Truman's election assured the place of NHI on the national agenda. The plan called for national compulsory insurance run by the federal government via a National Health Insurance Board. It was to be financed by a 3 percent federal payroll tax. Benefits included medical, surgical, and hospital services, plus home nursing and dental care. The progressive Republican plan, offered as the main alternative, embraced a more conservative approach. The Republican plan called for regional health authorities to establish voluntary, nonprofit health insurance plans that must be approved by the federal government. The premiums would be set as a sliding scale according to families' incomes, with the federal and state governments paying the difference. (This was the major concession to the progressives in the party.) However, the Republican plan fell short of making insurance compulsory and did not restrict what insurers could offer in terms of benefits (Davenport, 1950.)

Rashi Fein (1986) attributed the failure of Truman's proposal to at least five reasons: (1) a strong grass-roots campaign against major health reform legislation by the AMA, (2) the fact that most middle-income Americans already had health insurance and were happy with the postwar economic boom, (3) an inability to reach a compromise between the fundamentally different Democratic and Republican positions, (4) a schism in the liberal wing between those wanting broad universal coverage for all and those willing to settle for means-tested benefits targeted at poor people, and (5) the traditional ambivalence of Americans toward any strong government program.

The passage of Medicare and Medicaid in the 1960s relieved much of the pressure for NHI. Elderly and poor persons were the most vulnerable segments of the population, and it seemed to most as if their needs were met via these programs. Nevertheless, Senator Edward Kennedy first proposed his Health Security Act in 1969 and, during the last three decades, offered a number of revisions.

During the Nixon administration, the Department of Health, Education, and Welfare (DHEW)[2] was very active in devising health care legislation. Several of its top analysts busily crafted a formal plan for NHI. The Nixon plan was a limited attempt to fill the gaps in the safety net by proposing two central pieces: the Family Health Insurance Plan (FHIP) would cover low-income families, while the National Health Insurance Standards Act would require employers to provide comprehensive insurance to employees. Cost-sharing would be required for all but the poorest families. Medicare and Medicaid would be combined. The FHIP would be financed by general revenues. The promotion of HMOs was a prominent feature of the proposals. Senator Kennedy's bill provided a clear alternative, since it would have abolished Medicare and Medicaid and assured full coverage for all citizens, as opposed to the subsidy approach taken by the Republicans.

Despite these differences, the Kennedy and Nixon camps were able to work out a compromise. First, in 1974 Nixon replaced his previous plan with a much more comprehensive one called the Comprehensive Health Insurance Program (CHIP). Then, together with Congressman Wilbur Mills, the powerful chairman of the House Ways and Means Committee, Kennedy offered a new proposal that took CHIP as its starting point. The Kennedy–Mills proposal limited the maximum liability that a family would pay, geared premiums to income, and reinforced the provisions for universal coverage. Given this activity, in 1974 the passage of NHI seemed almost certain. Although there was substantial optimism, the legislation was still opposed by both conservatives and liberals, each unwilling to accept a second-best solution, and President Nixon was more absorbed in international than domestic policy. The bill, therefore, was never reported out of committee, and the concept of comprehensive NHI languished for many years.

According to Fein (1986), "Proponents of NHI did not know it at the time, but the summer of 1974 marked a watershed."[3] Attention turned to controlling hospital costs. Joseph A. Califano, the secretary of DHEW and architect of the Hospital Cost Containment Act of 1977, referred to the hospital industry as "obese." Only after considerable political energy was expended on this bill did the Carter administration propose an NHI plan in 1979.

Termed "middle-of-the-road" (Anderson, 1985), Carter's Healthcare Plan took an incremental approach to health care reform. The package called for universal coverage with phase-in of covered services beginning in 1983, near the end of what would have been Carter's second term. The proposal began with continued coverage of poor, elderly, and disabled people, and added a federally sponsored public back-up program modeled after Medicare that would be available to persons unable to obtain coverage through their employers (to compete with, not replace, private insurance). Employers would be mandated to provide a minimum set of benefits that would cover catastrophically high health costs for employees. Yet once again a complex legislative process and lack of strong, focused leadership by the president led to the plan's eventual demise. In the Carter administration, health reform ran at least third place behind energy issues and welfare reform. The proposal ultimately died quietly in the Senate Finance Committee in 1980, with little attention from the media. The Reagan years completed the transformation of concern over access to concern over cost, and the issue of NHI was all but buried. This stance was more or less continued by President Bush.

The Clinton election imparted a signal change. Clinton ran strongly on a program to develop comprehensive health reform, and at least a few observers claimed that some of the reason for President Bush's defeat was his do-nothing stance on health system reform. As this book goes to press, the country is locked in a debate over far-reaching changes to the health care system of a scope and potential impact that have not been seen since the Truman presidency.

OPTIONS FOR HEALTH CARE REFORM

Over the past fifty years, hundreds of NHI proposals have been developed and introduced to Congress. Although a description of the specifics of the various bills is beyond our scope, it seems appropriate to provide a general orientation to the more recent incarnations.

The proposals for health reform fall into four broad categories: (1) all-government, universal coverage; (2) compulsory, private universal coverage; (3) incremental public strategies; and (4) incremental private strategies. We present this framework as a way of thinking about reform.[4]

ALL-GOVERNMENT SYSTEMS

There are two basic types of all-government universal systems. One is modeled on the United Kingdom's National Health Service (NHS), in which the government owns the means of production and is the provider of health care or at least employs the providers. The NHS is financed from general revenues, and all services are free at the point of use. (The Veteran's Affairs system in the United States is a variant of this approach.) This option is not usually given much of a political chance in the United States.

The second major all-government option is often referred to as Canadian-style health care. In Canada, the government is the sole source of insurance. The provinces each run their own plans, but must meet national standards. Care is offered virtually without charge. Technology, rates of payment to providers, and capital expenditures are closely controlled. Although some feel that the restriction on price increases and the availability of certain services has hampered quality, public opinion polls exhibit strong national support and a high degree of satisfaction with the system.

The single-payer insurance approach has had strong backing from the liberal wings in this country. The cardinal feature is that the government pays the providers of care directly. As with all the plans reviewed in this discussion, the "devil is in the details"—in other words, the concept of single payer can cover a multitude of plans. For example, a single-payer plan could be financed through general (progressive) tax revenues, payroll taxes, or premiums based on consumers' ability to pay; it can be a single national plan or a series of state-run (or regional) plans; it may come with or without cost-sharing and with or without budget caps. In addition to fee-for-service payment, it can involve the use of prepaid health plans, including HMOs and networks that provide for out-of-network fee-for-service use.

COMPULSORY, PRIVATE SYSTEMS

Compulsory private systems involve employer and/or individual mandates. Compulsory employer-based systems or individual mandates would retain the current health insurance structure to some degree, but would rely on a regulatory mandate to ensure universal coverage. Because not everyone is employed, employer mandates must be coupled with another source of insurance to ensure universal coverage.

The most popular version of the employer mandate before the 1992 presidential election was the "play or pay" plan. Under play or pay, employers are required to provide private insurance ("play") or pay an equivalent tax, with government insuring nonworkers and poor people. This middle road worried both sides of the ideological aisle. A "pay" option set too high would be a burden on small employers; yet if the level was set too low, it would induce many employers to pay the tax and the system would revert to a de facto all-government health system.

The preservation of the employer link to the financing and delivery of health care has some drawbacks. The burdens of finance would fall heavily on those businesses that currently do not provide insurance. For the majority of patients who obtain insurance through their employer, a change in employment status can still lead to a disruption in care. Finally, absent additional reform, the problems in the health insurance market for small businesses and others that were described in chapter 2 will persist.

Individual mandates can be implemented with or without an employer mandate to achieve universal coverage. Most proposals couple this approach with substantial subsidies to the poor. From a theoretical perspective, health economists tend to favor individual mandates, since they force individuals to make tradeoffs between the type of insurance coverage they buy and other purchases. Because employers are now the dominant source of coverage, an individual mandate without an accompanying employer mandate might lead to substantial disruption in existing patterns of payment. There would be an incentive for many businesses that now provide insurance to low-income workers to discontinue this practice, since federal subsidies would provide a "windfall" that could be split between the business and the employee. The ultimate result would be substantially increased federal liability.

The Health Security Act (HSA) proposed by the Clinton administration in 1993 assures universal coverage through both an employer mandate and an individual mandate. All employers pay for coverage but most do not provide it directly. Under the HSA, each state creates one or more regional alliances that organize a menu of health plans, negotiate premiums, and enroll individuals in plans. The health plans provide a guaranteed set of comprehensive benefits and make the choice of delivering them through fee-for-service networks, preferred provider organizations, and HMOs. The HSA prohibits health plans from denying or canceling coverage to any person on the basis of preexisting medical conditions or other characteristics. Health plans must offer community rates to patients (although alliances will risk-adjust payments to the health plan on the basis of patient characteristics) and assure the portability of coverage (i.e., persons must be able to keep the same insurance when they change jobs). Under the HSA, employers pay 80 percent of the weighted-average premium, and individuals are responsible for the remainder. This amount is often termed the "20 percent share," although it will vary, depending on the cost of the health plan chosen by the individual. An individual will pay more than 20 percent for a high-cost plan and less for a low-cost plan. Unemployed individuals who have no unearned income are responsible for only the 20 percent share of the premium; they receive a subsidy if their incomes fall below 150 percent of poverty. Unemployed individuals who have unearned income are responsible for the other 80 percent of the premium, in addition, although persons with incomes up to 250 percent of poverty pay on a sliding scale.

Employer payments will be capped at 7.9 percent of their payroll (the national average is 9 percent for firms that provide insurance for their employees), except for small businesses (75 employees or fewer), whose caps may go as low as 3.5 percent, depending on the workers' average wage level and employer size. Individual payments for the 20 percent share are capped at 3.9 percent of income. Large firms with greater than 5,000 employees are permitted to opt out of the regional alliances and provide insurance directly through a "corporate alliance." The Medicare program remains intact, and in 1996, beneficiaries are scheduled to receive a new benefit covering outpatient prescription drugs. New long-term care programs also expand access to home and community-based care. Medicaid recipients may join any eligible health plan, just like the rest of the population.

INCREMENTAL PUBLIC STRATEGIES

The United States already has two incremental public programs of national health insurance: Medicare and Medicaid. One set of proposals would merely extend Medicare to a larger subset of Americans. Because the problem of the uninsured is often viewed as a problem of the poor and unemployed, another often-mentioned option is to expand Medicaid. In fact, this expansion has been taking place slowly over the last decade, as Congress has added mandated coverage for poor pregnant women and their children. Under health reform proposals, the Medicaid option often comes with a provision to offer subsidized "buy-ins" for poor families not meeting the income and categorical eligibility criteria.

The advantage of Medicaid expansion is that it can provide a lot of people with comprehensive benefits. A state-based administrative structure is already in place, and the Medicaid bureaucracy tends to be filled with workers committed to human services who are sensitive to disadvantaged client groups. It clearly permits coverage that is not tied to employment and has successfully piloted cost-containment schemes, including managed care, case management, and selective contracting. The disadvantages also are substantial. Medicaid has a history of paying below-market rates, and to extend the program would concretize the existing two-tiered system. The stigma of the welfare link would continue. On a practical level, it would be very difficult to set the buy-in subsidy at a workable level. If set too low, few would take advantage of it; if set too high, it would encourage employers who now offer private coverage to drop their own coverage and buy into Medicaid.

The emphasis of the current system reform movement clearly stresses the demand side of health insurance by either providing incentives or mandating the purchase of insurance coverage by individuals. Let us not forget, however, that a major incremental public strategy of the 1970s and 1980s was to expand the supply side. Federal, state, and local governments have enacted countless schemes to improve reimbursement for the providers of care to uninsured patients as an indirect means of improving access. To make services directly available, they have funded or established dedicated "safety net" providers. One option for health care reform would be to improve or expand some of these strategies. For example, all-payer rate-setting systems[5] and disproportionate share adjustments try to shore up the ability of hospitals to shift costs to meet public needs. Statewide uncompensated care pools explicitly fund hospital care for poor uninsured people by essentially taxing hospital services to pay for free care and bad debts. Legislators in some states have found it easier to impose "taxes" on specific users of services than to pass broad-based income or sales taxes.

The supply-side approach has been criticized for "insuring" institutions rather than individuals. Rather than giving the consumer the purchasing power of insurance, each provider acts as an independent welfare agency. Variations in patients' eligibility, in documentation of financial need, or in the commitment of specific institutions to serving poor people can often result in variable access to care.

INCREMENTAL PRIVATE STRATEGIES

Rather than a complete overhaul of the current system, a number of private, voluntary, incremental strategies have been proposed to try to make things work better as they are now. These strategies may take many different shapes and can be used in various combinations. They may be categorical (apply to only selected populations) or broad based. Some reform proposals use incentives to reform the health insurance system to encourage access to coverage or simply provide coverage to selected groups. Most private strategies rely heavily on trying to increase the competitiveness in the system, and all assume that government will continue to care for the worst-off individuals.

Catastrophic Coverage. Because the major fear of so many Americans is that a serious illness will ruin them financially, the idea of expanded catastrophic coverage has appeal for many Americans. The idea is to force (mandate) employers to offer, at a minimum, coverage with a large deductible. In some versions the state is the payer of last resort for catastrophic events and/or subsidizes the premium for low-income and unemployed individuals. Although in a sense this strategy could be listed as one that provides universal coverage, the extent of benefits is so limited that it is rarely viewed as a realistic solution. Most services would still have to be covered by voluntary insurance. This approach is unlikely to encourage appropriate ambulatory or preventive care and would encourage heavier use of secondary and tertiary services because funding is essentially unlimited once the deductible is met.

Subsidized Insurance for Unemployed People. Under the provisions of the COBRA of 1985 (P.L. 99–272), employees who lose their jobs are allowed to continue to purchase health insurance from their former employers at group rates plus a small administrative charge. The continuation provision, as it is called, is effective for eighteen months following the last date of employment. This program has limitations. For example, many employees (when they still have their jobs) receive large subsidies from their employers toward the purchase of insurance, but COBRA does not mandate that the subsidies continue once employment is terminated. When a person loses employment, it may be unlikely that he or she will be able to afford to purchase insurance at unsubsidized rates. Also, statistics show that only a small proportion of uninsured people have recently lost their jobs. The reform proposals aim to expand and liberalize this program.

Industry Pooling Mechanisms. The idea here is that self-employed persons and small businesses would buy insurance if they could get it at group rates. Government would establish industrywide risk pools and treat all individual employers as a single large group. Community rating (with appropriate adjustment for risk factors), the elimination of exclusions due to preexisting conditions, and mandatory renewal are additional features sometimes included in these sorts of reform. Critics claim that the pools would have to be very heavily subsidized to have a major impact on the rate at which previously uninsured individuals would purchase insurance (Aaron, 1991).

Risk Pools for Individuals. A number of states have established statewide risk pools for individuals considered "uninsurable" due to preexisting conditions. This will never work to any large degree. The central problem is that this approach is not *insur*ance, it is *assur*ance, because costs are *assur*ed of occurring when sick people enroll in the plan. There is no risk to spread. Governments can help to make sure that the insurance is available, but they cannot make it affordable.

Tax Credits. Tax credits are considered a universal option under the private sector strategy because they apply to everyone (although people who do not earn enough to pay taxes would obviously not be able to take advantage of tax credits.) These sorts of reforms are meant to address inequities and inefficiencies in the tax code. It is argued that the historical exclusion for company-based insurance plans benefits people with high incomes (and higher marginal tax rates) more than it benefits people with low incomes, and that the employer subsidy leads to health care inflation.

The tax credit approach would replace existing exclusions for employer-based health insurance and tax deductions for other health care costs with a refundable tax credit set at a fixed percentage of the cost of the premium. The goal is to equalize the subsidy to different individuals with the same income regardless of whether an employer provides coverage. Some variations on this theme would make purchase of insurance mandatory; others would offer vouchers for the poor.

Other Insurance and Private Option Reforms. Reformers have proposed myriad other strategies aimed at making peripheral improvements to the health insurance system. These include laws that would require the coverage of certain benefits (e.g., prenatal and well-child care) to be provided by employers, prohibit extended waiting periods, or allow tax deductions for persons who do not itemize their tax returns; others would provide a tax-deductible pool of money (a "medical I.R.A." option available to all persons) that can be used by individuals for medical expenditures or alternatively saved.

KEY QUESTIONS CONCERNING ACCESS FOR HEALTH REFORMERS

The health system we have five years from now will not be the same as the one we have today. President Clinton has made health care reform a cornerstone of his domestic policy. Powerful interests have lined up in favor of some action. In light of the research reviewed in this book, it is appropriate to ask how health system reform will change the status quo for persons who face barriers to access, especially those emanating from the type of insurance they carry or the lack of insurance altogether.

In addressing this issue, we note that health system reform has multiple objectives, including cost control and quality improvement. It can certainly be argued that these objectives indirectly affect access. For example, everyone's access will be threatened if the health care system is allowed to swallow up a larger and larger proportion of the economy in an uncontrolled fashion. An increasing number of the middle class may find that they cannot afford health insurance premiums, or may end up buying insurance with inadequate coverage. The pressure to cut back on publicly funded programs like Medicaid and even Medicare will grow even stronger. Nevertheless, given the focus of this book, we have limited our questions to those affecting access directly.

"WILL COVERAGE REALLY BE UNIVERSAL?"

The concept of *universality* is slippery. Plans that sound like they cover everyone sometimes do not upon close inspection. In a matrix of reform proposals published in the *Journal of the American Medical Association*, nearly all of the plans were deemed to have "universal" coverage

(Blendon and Edwards, 1991). This term was applied to Canadian-style single-payer plans as well as to the plan supported by the conservative Heritage Foundation, which recommended providing tax credits for the purchase of private insurance. The use of tax credits applies to all citizens. (The same can be said of tax deductions for home mortgages, but this has not solved the growing problem of the homeless.) If health insurance is not compulsory or if it is expensive, many low-income families will not be able to afford it and will not purchase it. Some proposals offer subsidies only to persons below poverty, others to 150 percent of poverty, others to 200 percent. What happens to the family that is just getting by at 201 percent? How much of a burden will cost-sharing impose on low-income families? Also, most proposals are budgeted for current economic trends. Is there a guarantee that the subsidy level will be maintained in the future? A downturn in the economy can have a serious impact on federal subsidy outlays. More important, without effective cost containment, rapidly escalating health care expenditures can make existing subsidy levels inadequate. Finally, most proposals do not cover noncitizens and undocumented aliens. Knowing who is specifically included, who is excluded, and who is merely invited are important but often difficult details to determine.

"WILL ACCESS TO HEALTH CARE IMPROVE?"

Providing previously uninsured persons with insurance will almost certainly increase the number of contacts they have with the medical care system. The early experience with Medicaid is proof of that. In fact, in the early stages, pent-up demand could translate into very high usage rates by people who were previously uninsured. Likewise, the number of people who are denied care or who forego needed care for serious symptoms is likely to drop.

Other indicators of access may not be so greatly influenced by the mere provision of insurance. We know that patients with Medicaid tend to use emergency rooms and outpatient clinics more than others, even though they have insurance and can identify a usual source of care more often than uninsured persons. The studies of health outcomes give similarly mixed messages. Research on the rates of avoidable hospital conditions among Medicaid recipients or the effects on birth and maternal outcomes occurring after Medicaid expansion suggests that the provision of insurance to previously uninsured individuals does not always guarantee better health care outcomes.

The importance of public health infrastructure for disadvantaged populations has long been recognized (Lewin, 1993). We need to preserve our networks of essential community providers while bolstering our investment in public health services. This is especially true during the transition, when both the increased cost and the positive expectations associated with the provision of universal coverage may lead to an erosion of support for existing public health structures.

"WILL IT PROLONG THE TWO-TIERED HEALTH CARE SYSTEM?"

There have always been two medical care systems in this country: one for poor people and another for the rest of the country. There are several reasons for this. One is the stigma associated with being a recipient of a public program. A second has to do with financing. Examine the two major health reforms of the 1960s—Medicare and Medicaid. The contrast is striking between the funding levels for Medicare, which is a broad-based "universal" program for all workers, and for Medicaid, which serves the disenfranchised. As a result, provider reimbursement levels for Medicaid recipients are often very low. Any program that can be identified with the poor ("them") is a likely candidate for budget cuts in times of fiscal problems. Poor patients may also have trouble finding care because there is prejudice against people in lower socioeconomic conditions, because of hidden racism (most physicians are white, lots of poor people are not), or because physicians tend not to practice in low-income areas.

Even programs that provide universal coverage may raise concerns about the perpetuation of two-tiered care. Both the expansion of Medicaid and "play or pay" options threaten to establish a government-based system that would serve primarily poor people. Even if care is provided through the private market, there will likely be concern about two classes of care. As long as there are multiple options and financial costs for individuals that may restrict those with low income to less attractive plans, access can suffer.

"HOW WILL MINORITIES AND OTHER SOCIODEMOGRAPHIC OR CLINICAL SUBGROUPS BE AFFECTED?"

Health reform that relies on the employment sector may be biased against minorities, the poor, and the disabled. These groups are less likely to be employed full time. If reforms are employer-based and incremental rather than universal, disadvantaged groups may be less likely to receive coverage. Even if universal coverage is enacted, these groups may be restricted to lower-quality options if price is a big factor and if subsidies fail to counteract inequalities in income.

The methods we use to pay providers may also have an adverse impact on access to care for certain subgroups of patients. Capitation will provide incentives for providers to indulge in market skimming. Whenever adverse selection is possible, competitive health plans will try to avoid enrolling persons with chronic diseases or other characteristics (e.g., elderly) associated with higher utilization. Risk adjustment can reduce these untoward incentives, although the state-of-the-art is far from perfect and our technical ability to adjust for all the factors that lead to increased utilization is limited.

"WILL THERE BE SPECIAL EFFORTS TO IMPROVE ACCESS IN UNDERSERVED AREAS?"

Almost 60 million people live in federally designated health-shortage areas, the majority in rural America. These areas tend to have fragile economies, their populations tend to have lower incomes, and higher percentages of patients are uninsured or covered by Medicaid. However, the problems extend beyond poverty and a lack of insurance coverage. Higher workloads, professional isolation, and reduced educational and cultural opportunities for health care providers and their families make it less likely that physicians will settle and stay in rural areas. As a result, rural areas have far fewer practicing physicians per capita than urban areas. Rural areas often have special needs that will not be met by improving financial access to care and increasing the number of health care practitioners. For example, many rural poor people do not have a car of their own and must rely on friends and family for transportation.

Will reform meet the special needs of underserved areas? Are there incentives for providers to move into underserved areas and remain there? Are there provisions to combat the professional isolation that can leave rural practitioners overexposed and without appropriate specialty backup? Finally, are there supports for the network of community health centers, migrant health centers, and local health departments that are a major source of care for large segments of the population in these communities?

"IS THE BENEFIT PLAN ADEQUATE?"

The issue of benefit design has a number of important aspects that lead to several related questions. Is cost-sharing high? Will the plan encourage the use of prevention and primary care? Is coverage for dental care, drugs, mental health care, or long-term care services included?

Access is not a binary concept. Underinsurance is not just a problem for persons who lack coverage for preexisting conditions. Access to bare-bones, "basic" health insurance plans may be barely access at all. If multiple options are offered and financial aid is low, many persons with low incomes may buy basic coverage that comes with high deductibles and coinsurance. Even today, most of the patients whose costs are written off to bad debt and free care in hospitals *have* insurance. If low-income families still face high cost-sharing when a member falls ill, the access promised by universal coverage will not have been achieved.

The generosity, or comprehensiveness, of the benefit package is often a point of controversy. On one hand are people who believe that a federal guarantee should be minimal and not force people to purchase health care coverage that they do not intend to use. On the other hand are those who insist that comprehensive coverage, including an emphasis on preventive medicine, is necessary to rearrange priorities so that we as a nation will be promoting health instead of merely treating disease.

"WILL ACCESS TO CARE MEAN ACCESS TO HIGH-QUALITY CARE?"

Even if universal coverage and comprehensive benefits are provided, one may still ask questions about the quality of care. Today we lack standard information on the quality of our care and how it varies by health plan, institutional provider, and practitioner. Patients lack the information they need to choose wisely, and providers lack information to guide their efforts in quality improvement. There is concern that existing programs in quality assurance rely too much on inspection, retrospective judgment, and punishment. Providers are bombarded by a confusing array of information and contradictory advice about the necessity for various treatments and the appropriate interval for providing them. Often there is a long time lag before research findings that can best guide clinical practice are appropriately disseminated. Providers also often misgauge how well their behavior conforms to the best clinical practice. With no information on how poorly they perform, there is little incentive for providers to change. Equally disturbing is the evidence presented in earlier chapters that suggests that the quality of care varies by patients' social and economic status.

Will reform reduce these problems? Will access to care mean access to high-quality care? Support for the development and dissemination of information on the effectiveness of different treatments can reduce providers' confusion concerning the most appropriate practice. Clinical practice guidelines can be helpful, but there is controversy about the way they should be developed and implemented. Information on the quality of care provided to consumers may facilitate their informed choice of provider and treatment. Likewise, constructive feedback offered to providers will perhaps allow them to guide their own efforts to improve the quality of care.

"WHAT HAPPENS DURING THE TRANSITION?"

Nearly all of the health reform proposals have some sort of phase-in plan for adding benefits or expanding covered populations. The details may be important. Are there provisions for preserving the existing safety net for patients during a transition? Do patterns of institutional support change drastically? If system-wide incentives are changed, it may be wise to include support for safety net providers so that disruption during the transition is reduced.

Equally important is the task of monitoring the expansion of insurance. In some proposals, universal coverage is mandated only once costs are under control. How committed is the reform to making the transition to universal coverage a reality?

"WHO ARE THE HIDDEN WINNERS AND LOSERS, AND HOW MIGHT THEIR EXPERIENCES AFFECT ACCESS?"

Winners and losers can be groups of individuals, institutions, or society at large. Poor persons who are otherwise unable to obtain good health insurance coverage are the obvious winners in health care reform. Are there other winners or losers? The answers can often be found in the fine print of "pass-through" provisions (e.g., Medicare support for hospitals that care for a disproportionate share of the poor) and "set asides" (the Health Security Act will provide more than $9 billion to academic health centers), or in simply thinking through the benefits and burdens of social change.

Public hospitals (the communities that support them) and other institutional providers that offer substantial amounts of uncompensated care under the current system could be winners. Their patient mix will suddenly become much better payers. Bad debt and free care could be reduced substantially, depending on the adequacy of the standard benefit package for low-income families. However, public facilities could also be big losers. Current institutional support for the care of poor patients or for teaching may be restricted. In addition, once someone has insurance, he or she may be more likely to seek care in another institution, especially if the municipal facility is perceived as having poor-quality care. Public hospitals must reposition themselves in the market to maintain their market share or else they may be forced to close. A system without safety net providers could be ideal in the long run if we are able to provide equitable services in their absence, but it may be a frightening prospect in the short run for poor populations that have relied on them until now.

Physicians will also be affected by reform. Those who write off substantial amounts of charity care under the present system will gain financially when more people are insured. Physician incomes also might grow as a result of increased demand for medical services by patients who would otherwise be uninsured. Many physicians would win under these scenarios, unless cost-containment provisions that accompany reform reduce physician income.

Reform may also have noneconomic impacts on physicians. If forms for payment and utilization management are standardized, the burdens of paperwork and administration may be reduced. On the other hand, physicians worry that an increased federal role may mean further encroachment on their autonomy.

Under most models of reform, big businesses win. Their insurance premiums have been subsidizing the small businesses that do not provide insurance by paying charge rates that are higher than average costs so that hospitals can "cost-shift" to cover the expenses of treating uninsured and underinsured patients. Under employer mandates, many analysts believe that small businesses will lose, although many of those providing insurance now are likely to see their rates go down.

The public wins if health care becomes more efficient and cost effective as a result of improvements in access. After all, there are adverse economic consequences to a lack of access that we all bear indirectly if not directly. There are costs that occur from the overuse of emergency rooms and outpatient departments instead of private physicians. Patients in clinics may have repetitive diagnostic work-ups because of a lack of continuity and available records. A lack of regular sources of care can lead to doctor-shopping, at least among Medicaid recipients, which can result in unnecessary physician visits. Better access can also reduce visits to the emergency room when patients are able to call their physician for over-the-phone assurance or instructions for minor problems (Hurley, Freund, and Paul, 1993). Prompt access to high-quality care may prevent certain conditions from getting worse and requiring more expensive care later. Of course society can lose if costs are not controlled, if quality or choice is diminished, or if broad-based rationing occurs.

"WHAT ROLE SHOULD RESEARCH CONTINUE TO PLAY REGARDING ACCESS AND HEALTH CARE REFORM?"

The current debate on comprehensive health reform may result in legislation that will substantially change existing patterns of insurance status and payer. Under certain strategies, differences among payers will be eliminated. Does that mean that the kind of research represented by this book will become obsolete? That is doubtful. No matter what course the country takes, barriers to access will likely remain, and there will still be an important role for research. Indeed, it will be research that will ultimately tell us whether reform succeeded or failed.

Unless we adopt a publicly run, compulsory system, we are still likely to have important segments of the population using different payers. Even the Clinton administration's HSA would leave certain segments of the population covered by Medicare or in corporate rather than regional alliances, which will lead to natural questions about differences in access, patterns of care, and health outcomes.

Although differences in access by payer may become less important, there will still be a whole spectrum of new questions on access related to the functioning of any reform. One important set of questions will concern the impact of insurance for newly enfranchised groups. We know a little about what happens to people when they lose insurance (from studies of cutbacks in the California and Minnesota Medicaid programs, and the Veterans Affairs system), but we have almost no information about the converse situation. What happens as the pool of insured persons is expanded? Is there pent-up demand, and what is its magnitude?

Uninsured patients have traditionally sought care from a network of community based, publicly supported providers. Do these patterns persist or are these patients gradually mainstreamed? What is the role of institutions like municipal hospitals that "specialize" in caring for poor people? We should also not forget the burden of uncompensated care that often falls unevenly on safety net providers. Under many health reform strategies, some poor patients will still not be insured (illegal aliens are the most obvious) and others may have inadequate policies. We need to track the magnitude and distribution of uncompensated care in the new environment. Legal and ethical questions regarding the responsibilities of charitable institutions operating in competitive systems must be addressed.

As coverage is expanded to some or all who are currently uninsured, how important are barriers to access associated with cultural, geographical, or other economic factors (see Lewin, 1993)? The research by Haas et al. (1993) raised disturbing questions about the value of insuring a poor population when their connection to the health care system is weak. How will the use of services and outcomes change and how will those patterns differ for different groups of patients?

The provision of uniform coverage will likely lead us to focus more on the fine details of the delivery system. How will Medicaid patients and those who might otherwise have been without insurance fare in structured (i.e., managed care) environments? Are certain skills in "working the system" necessary for patients to obtain good-quality care from HMOs, and do poor people possess them?

In short, no matter what course the country takes in reforming our health care system, numerous questions about access to care will remain. Interest in providing NHI has waxed and waned for nearly eighty years. The prominence of health care in our economy and the increasing numbers of Americans who lose coverage annually have brought this issue again to the front pages of our newspapers and to the top of our legislative agenda. Among industrialized Western nations, the United States is unique in that it does not have universal coverage through a national system of health care. What services patients get and how well they do depend in part on how they pay for their care. The centrality of insurance coverage to one's ability to obtain equitable access to care is surely no longer questioned. It is just as certain, however, that other social and nonmedical factors play a part. We need to understand better the social and economic costs of muddling forth as we do now and contrast them with the costs associated with different options for reform. Doing nothing is not a viable alternative.

APPENDIX A

NATIONAL SURVEYS AND MAJOR STUDIES ON ACCESS INCLUDED IN THIS BOOK

This appendix offers brief descriptions and key references associated with major surveys used to describe the insurance status of U.S. residents and their access to medical care. These surveys were selected because in most cases they are national in scope and repeated periodically. The RAND Health Insurance Experiment is an obvious exception to these selection criteria. It is included because it is one of the most-cited studies of the effects of cost sharing on utilization and outcomes and in fact was responsible for developing many of the methods used in the field today.

SURVEYS ON ACCESS SPONSORED BY THE ROBERT WOOD JOHNSON FOUNDATION

Between 1978 and 1986 the Robert Wood Johnson Foundation sponsored three national access surveys that have been reported in a variety of sources (Robert Wood Johnson Foundation, 1978, 1983, 1987; also see Aday, Andersen, and Fleming, 1980; Aday, Fleming, and Andersen, 1984; Andersen et al., 1987; Freeman et al., 1987).[1] Because the primary focus of these surveys was on access and not on differences by payment source, some of the reports compared the uninsured to the insured, but they did not differentiate between Medicaid and privately insured persons, nor did they always separate out results for persons under and over age sixty-five. The article by Freeman et al. (1987) separates out some of the analyses for nonelderly by insurance class.

THE RAND HEALTH INSURANCE EXPERIMENT

The RAND HIE was a controlled trial in health care financing funded by the U.S. Department of Health and Human Services. It had the objective of shedding light on how the design of insurance benefits might affect medical care utilization, expense, and health status. Analyses were designed to assess how these effects varied by income group. The HIE was one of the largest health care research projects ever ventured. Beginning in 1974, RAND assigned families representing nearly 6,000 individuals from six sites in the United States to one of fourteen different fee-for-service (FFS) insurance plans, with various levels of cost-sharing, and to one prepaid group practice HMO. The wealthiest 3 percent of the population and persons over age sixty-two were excluded. The FFS plans had coinsurance rates of 0 (free-care), 25, 50, and 95 percent. A maximum of $1,000 in expenditures was set for any family, although this was lowered for low-income families. In addition, a subset of the 95 percent cost-sharing families were assigned to the "individual deductible" plan, which had high deductibles for outpatient care, but free inpatient care. The purpose of comparing this latter plan with the free-care plan was to see whether more comprehensive coverage of outpatient care would save money by reducing the frequency of avoidable hospitalizations (Newhouse, 1991).

NATIONAL MEDICAL CARE UTILIZATION AND EXPENDITURE SURVEY

The National Medical Care Utilization and Expenditure Survey (NMCUES), performed in 1980, was jointly sponsored by the Health Care Financing Administration (HCFA) and the National Center for Health Statistics (NCHS). NMCUES was a national probability survey that gathered information on health insurance coverage, health care utilization, and expenditures through five survey rounds during a one-year period (NCHS, 1983). The respondents comprised about 6,600 households consisting of 17,900 persons and were representative of the civilian, noninstitutionalized U.S. population. A series of descriptive reports were published, some of which pertained to access (see, e.g., Leicher et al., 1985; Kasper, 1986; Howell, 1988).

NATIONAL MEDICAL CARE EXPENDITURE SURVEY AND NATIONAL MEDICAL EXPENDITURE SURVEY

The National Medical Care Expenditure Survey (NMCES) provided information on the civilian noninstitutionalized population regarding use of health services, health expenditures, and health insurance in 1977. The survey was funded and administered by the National Center for Health Services Research (NCHSR, now know as the Agency for Health Care Policy Research, AHCPR) and NCHS. The national sample comprised about 14,000 households representing 40,000 individuals. This cohort was interviewed five times during the span of twelve months.

Another series of studies, initiated in the 1980s, also involved a major data collection effort—the 1987 NMES. Like its predecessor, NMES provides information about the noninstitutionalized population. The survey included extensive information on health expenditures by or on behalf of American families and individuals, the financing of these expenditures, and each person's use of services. The NMES was a research project of the Center for General Health Services Intramural Research, AHCPR. In addition, and in contrast to the earlier studies, NMES also provided extensive information on the population residing in or admitted to nursing homes and facilities for the mentally retarded. Together, the major components of NMES contained information that permitted national estimates of health status, use of health services, insurance coverage, expenditures, and sources of payment for the civilian population of the United States during the period from January 1 to December 31, 1987. Oversampling of population groups of special interest makes possible in-depth studies of these groups.

CURRENT POPULATION SURVEY

The main purpose of the CPS is to collect monthly statistics on employment for the nation and individual states. Administered by the Bureau of the Census, recent samples are on the order of 60,000 households representing over 150,000 individuals. Each year the March supplement includes questions on family income, work experience, and health insurance coverage for each adult family member. Although the CPS is used routinely for estimates of the number of uninsured and their work force participation, recent changes in the wording of the insurance questions has made comparisons over time unreliable (Moyer, 1989).

NATIONAL HEALTH INTERVIEW SURVEY

The NHIS is a survey conducted by the NCHS, focussing on the civilian noninstitutionalized population in the United States. The 1986 NHIS included a special section on insurance status and collected information on approximately 24,000 households containing 60,000 persons. The detailed information on the use of physicians by type and location is based principally on questions referring to the two-week period preceding the interview.

SURVEY OF INCOME AND PROGRAM PARTICIPATION

The SIPP[2] is a longitudinal survey, conducted by the U.S. Bureau of the Census, which consists of a nationally representative sample of more than 10,000 households. The purpose of SIPP is to collect detailed sociodemographic information on income, wealth, and poverty to gauge the effect of federal and state programs on the economic well-being of families and individuals. The SIPP is composed of overlapping panels of subjects, one beginning each year since 1984. The SIPP generates information on month-to-month fluctuations in household and individual income; labor force status; participation in government-funded programs such as AFDC, Food Stamps, and Medicaid; and health insurance coverage. Sampled households are interviewed every four months over a period of about two and one-half years. The reference period consists of the four months preceding each interview, and information is collected for both the individual and the individual's household (including children under age fifteen). The SIPP has been useful in studies addressing gaps in health care coverage because it provides an opportunity to observe lack of or changes in health insurance over an extended period.

APPENDIX B

METHODS USED IN CHAPTER 3–7

The literature review of the impact of insurance status on access was performed with a combination of techniques that included searching computerized databases, scanning the bibliographies of key articles, collecting reports generated from major health care utilization surveys published by the government and other sources, and polling experts in the field. The list of articles was updated via the use of current tables-of-contents services[1] from area universities.

The principal computerized search was performed on Paperchase, a system that indexes all health and medical care publications included in both the MEDLINE database and the entire Health Planning and Administration database. We included all English-language articles published since 1980. The keywords of *uninsured, medical indigency, Medicaid, uncompensated care, managed care, deductibles,* and *coinsurance* were "crossed" with *delivery of health services, health care rationing, personal health services, hospitalization, length of stay, quality of health care, consumer satisfaction, health services accessibility, hospital use, pharmaceutical use, primary care, preventive care, process and outcomes of care,* and several others, to produce a list of approximately 1,200 references, which were then reviewed by the authors for inclusion in this review. The list of references belonging to each selected reference was scanned. In some cases, a reference before 1980 was included if it represented particularly important work or if current research on that topic was sparse. A supplementary search was performed with a similar strategy by the Group Health Association of America's Library Reference Service. Finally, earlier versions of the bibliography were reviewed by the U.S. Office of Technology Assessment and a number of known and anonymous reviewers, all of whom suggested gaps in the literature.

NOTES

CHAPTER 1 INTRODUCTION: A FRAMEWORK FOR THINKING ABOUT INSURANCE STATUS AND ACCESS TO CARE

1. One will occasionally see South Africa listed as the other industrialized country without a national health system. However, South Africa is not industrialized in the way that other European and Western-oriented countries are. Aside from an urban industrial sector, much of the country is characterized by a subsistence economy and basic agriculture. Also, South Africa is not one of the OECD countries included in Table 1–1.

2. Estimates of the uninsured population are controversial. Changes in the wording of questionnaires and contrasts in estimates of being uninsured at a point in time versus being uninsured all year have led to different figures. For more information, see Chapter 2.

3. For historical and sociological discussions of the development of health insurance, see Law (1976), Starr (1982), and Glaser (1991).

4. A recent report provided a similar definition of access as, "the timely use of personal health services to achieve the best possible health outcomes" (Institute of Medicine, 1993).

5. Nevertheless, the "enabling" concept has application in the sociological disciplines. Models of health-seeking behavior such as the health beliefs model view insurance as an enabler. This means that insurance helps to remove financial barriers between people's need or want for health care and their effective demand for or use of health care. It also implies only indirect links to outcomes, mediated by the use of services.

6. Andersen et al. (1987) referred to these and other population characteristics as "dimensions of policy vulnerability" because their access may be especially vulnerable to the design of health programs. Of course, some characteristics can be altered by other social programs, such as income redistribution or public education programs.

7. Federal poverty status considers both the size of a family and the total family income. The poverty threshold for a family of four in 1986 was $11,203 (Congressional Research Service, 1988a, p. 102). Most authors refer to the poor as at or below the poverty threshold. "Near-poor" is usually anywhere from 150 to 200 percent of poverty.

8. Wilensky and Berk examined all age groups.

9. For basic history and program descriptions, from among a plethora of articles and books on the Medicaid program, try Gornick et al. (1985), Rowland et al. (1988), Friedman (1990), Waid (1990), and the Medicaid Source Book put out by the Congressional Research Service (1988b).

10. In 1988 the maximum allowable income limits for a family of three ranged from a high of 77 percent of federal poverty in California to a low of 14 percent in Alabama (Congressional Research Service, 1988, pp. 286–87). Federal poverty guidelines were set at $9,690 for a family of three. Some states exceeded the poverty level due to income disregards.

11. One might refer to this more correctly as being sporadically insured.

12. There are some data on persons whose medical expenses became catastrophic (Wyszewianski, 1986) or who were insured and poor (Freeman et al., 1990), but there is no reason to believe that all of these persons had inadequate insurance.

13. Medicaid-managed care can take many forms (Hurley and Freund, 1988b). Further description is found in the chapter on special cases. See also Wilensky and Rossiter (1991).

14. The RAND HIE has the closest resemblance to a controlled trial, yet still has detractors (see Chapter 7 and Appendix).

CHAPTER 2 WHO ARE THE UNINSURED AND HOW DID THEY GET THAT WAY?

1. This section of the chapter is based on reports and analyses performed by U.S. Congress, Office of Technology Assessment (1992), Lewin/ICF (Needleman et al., 1990), Congressional Research Service (1988), and Pepper Commission (1990).

2. This figure is apparently controversial. Other estimates put the percentage of uninsured Hawaiians at a little more than half this figure (Miike, 1993).

3. We will refrain from the obvious temptation to use OOPEs as an acronym for Out-of-Pocket Expenditures.

CHAPTER 3 HEALTH STATUS

1. There is a third reason, as well. Insurance companies are very interested in the health status of the uninsured. If a public program were to mandate universal health insurance, insurers would have a strong incentive to claim that the uninsured are sicker than most Americans, and therefore must have higher premiums, paid for or subsidized by government. For similar reasons, insurance companies seek data on the health status of covered populations to segment the market. "Skimming" is one of the disadvantageous results of an unregulated insurance market, and could continue under national health insurance, as well.

2. The authors developed an index of self-reported health based on five separate questions.

3. However, results from the Robert Wood Johnson Foundation (1987) included all age groups, which may be a serious source of confounding.

4. The data presented in this chapter are limited, since we restricted ourselves to comparisons of health status across payer groups. Other studies use different *controls* for health status, but since they fail to report baseline differences across groups, we are unable to report on their analyses here. For example, some of the RAND HIE analyses of health care utilization are restricted to persons with an array of symptoms, acute conditions, specific complaints (e.g., chronic phlegm or hay fever) or measures of pain or worry, but these measures are not used to describe the epidemiological distribution in the population. The RWJF reports routinely ask about needed care that is not obtained, but we do not know the type and frequency of needed care and how it is distributed by insurance status.

CHAPTER 4 INTERMEDIATE PROCESS INDICATORS

1. Although providers may certainly be nonphysicians, we restrict ourselves primarily to contacts between patients and physicians, in part to conserve space, but also because it is what most researchers study.

2. There is some debate over the direction of causality. It may be that persons who are high utilizers of care are more likely to obtain a regular source of care.

3. One exception is Rosenbach (1985), who, using NMCUES, found no significant differences by payer in the proportions of low-income children whose regular source was a physician.

4. More than three-quarters of patients studied were uninsured, and about 8–10 percent were on Medicaid.

5. Uncompensated care comprises free care and bad debts, both of which are strongly associated with caring for the uninsured. Free care represents a subsidy for both the poor uninsured and the poor insured who cannot pay all or part of their hospital bill (Weissman et al., 1992). The source of bad debts may be attributed either to those with inadequate insurance or simply to people who can afford to pay their bills but do not.

CHAPTER 5 THE QUANTITY AND QUALITY OF CARE

1. This is by no means a proven concept. In fact, Chapter 7 contains evidence that suggests that lower ambulatory utilization is associated with *fewer* hospitalizations, on average. Thus, perhaps it is more accurate to say that hospitalizations for *selected* conditions could be avoided if ambulatory care is targeted and improved.

2. Medicare, Medicaid, CHAMPUS/CHAMPVA, or other public insurance.

3. Their case would have been stronger, still, had they compared utilization among higher-income young people, as well.

4. Wilensky and Berk examined all age groups.

5. Within 150 percent of poverty.

6. Persons aged seventeen to forty-four with Medicaid may have had more visits than nonpoor persons due to higher fertility rates and the associated use of prenatal visits.

7. Patients awarded free care will obviously also have "unpaid" bills.

8. Wilensky and Berk examined all age groups.

9. Wilensky and Berk examined all age groups.

10. Discretionary conditions are those for which consensus among physicians is lacking as to whether hospital care or ambulatory care is superior. Contrast this with low-discretion conditions, such as heart attacks, for which there is consensus that nearly all patients need to be hospitalized.

11. Indigent services are presumably for medically indigent adults, not eligible for Medicaid, who are seen primarily in municipal hospitals.

12. Wilensky and Berk examined all age groups.

13. In addition to the material reviewed here, problems with obtaining prenatal care are presented in a later section.

14. As with all access problems for uninsured persons and Medicaid recipients, this is not meant to imply that other social and cultural factors do not play a part. Strong family structures, the availability of nurse midwives, familiarity by the provider with the language and customs of the community, and good public education and outreach may address some of these problems of access in poor communities.

CHAPTER 6 OUTCOMES OF CARE

1. It may be that birth-giving women enrolling near the end of their pregnancy may also have a predisposition toward poor outcomes or some other unmeasured risk factor, but the study design was unable to assess this.

2. The proportion of patients who had Medicaid or were uninsured was 62 percent in Shasta County and 53 percent in San Luis Obispo County.

3. Seventy-two percent of patients were uninsured.

4. Ninety percent had Medicaid or were uninsured.

CHAPTER 7 SPECIAL CASES: COST-SHARING, CHANGES IN OR LOSS OF INSURANCE, AND PREPAID MANAGED CARE

1. See also Newhouse (1981) for a review of the cost-sharing literature from the late 1970s.

2. Some of this effect may be due to a small hospital sample or the particular use of medical price indexes for the period of the study. See Newhouse (1993, footnote 55).

3. Another estimate by the National Governors' Association identified 59 programs in twenty-eight states (Freund and Hurley, 1987); and Anderson and Fox (1987) identified 135 HMO plans in twenty-five states.

4. Some analysts are concerned that restrictions on the use of emergency departments in managed care plans may have deleterious effects. Shaw et al. (1990), for example, examined care for children at nondemonstration sites and suggested that some patients with urgent problems were not able to obtain appropriate care after being denied treatment at emergency departments.

CHAPTER 8 INSURANCE, ACCESS, AND HEALTH CARE REFORM: SUMMARY AND POLICY IMPLICATIONS

1. This section was drawn from Law (1976), Wimberly (1980), Anderson (1985), Fein (1986), and Fawley (1992).

2. Now known, without the educational component, as the Department of Health and Human Services (DHHS).

3. Some observers felt that the Democratic leadership was overly optimistic regarding the mood of the country, and the compromise position failed to appease still-powerful conservative elements.

4. For other frameworks and summaries, see Congressional Research Service (1988a), Aaron (1991), and Blendon and Edwards (1991).

5. Rate-setting systems set charge structures that all payers must follow and that often include funding for uncompensated care.

APPENDIX A NATIONAL SURVEYS AND MAJOR STUDIES ON ACCESS INCLUDED IN THIS BOOK

1. The 1986 survey is the seventh in a series of access surveys. Previous surveys were conducted by the Center for Health Administration Studies of the University of Chicago.

2. Information on SIPP taken from Swartz, Marcotte, and McBride (1993) and Monheit and Schur (1988). For more information, see: U.S. Bureau of the Census, survey of income and program participation, information booklet for the 1984 panel, waves 1–9. Form SIPP-4020 (7-16-86) (1986).

APPENDIX B METHODS USED IN CHAPTERS 3–7

1. A practice of academic librarians to supply researchers with the tables of contents of key journals on a regular basis (e.g., once a month).

REFERENCES

Aaron, H. J. 1991. *Serious and Unstable Condition*. Washington, D.C.: Brookings Institution.

Aday, L. A., and Andersen, R. 1975. *Development of Indices of Access to Medical Care*. Ann Arbor, Mich.: Health Administration Press.

———. 1984. The national profile of access to medical care: where do we stand? *American Journal of Public Health* 74:1331–39.

Aday, L. A., Andersen, R., and Fleming, G. V. 1980. *Health Care in the U.S.: Equitable for Whom?* Beverly Hills, Calif.: Sage Publications.

Aday, L. A., Fleming, G. V., and Andersen, R. 1984. *Access to Medical Care in the U.S.: Who Has It, Who Doesn't*. Chicago: University of Chicago Press.

Adler, K., and Emmerich, M. 1990. Late prenatal care for the uninsured in Eau Clair. *Wisconsin Medical Journal* 89(1) (January):21–3.

Akin, B. V., Rucker, L., Hubbell, F. A., Cygan, R. W., and Waitzkin, H. 1989. Access to medical care in a medically indigent population. *Journal of General Internal Medicine* 4:216–20.

Altman, S. H., Brecher, C., Henderson, M. G., and Thorpe, K. E. 1989. *Competition and Compassion: Conflicting Roles for Public Hospitals*. Ann Arbor, Mich.: Health Administration Press.

Andersen, R. M., Aday, L. A., Lyttle, C. S., Cornelius, L. J., and Chen, M. S. 1987. *Ambulatory Care and Insurance Coverage in an Era of Constraint*. Center for Health Administration Studies. Continuing Research Series No. 35. Chicago: Pluribus Press.

Andersen, R. M., McCutcheon, A., Aday, L. A., Chiu, G. Y., and Bell, R. 1983. Exploring dimensions of access to medical care. *Health Services Research* 18:50–74.

Anderson, G., Brook, R., and Williams, A. 1991. A comparison of cost-sharing versus free care in children: effects on the demand for office-based medical care. *Medical Care* 29:890–98.

Anderson, M. D., and Fox, P. D. 1987. Lessons learned from Medicaid managed care approaches. *Health Affairs* 6(1) (Spring):71–86.

Anderson, O. W. 1985. *Health Services in the United States: A Growth Enterprise since 1875*. Ann Arbor, Mich.: Health Administration Press.

Andrews, R., Herz, E., Dodds, S., and Ruther, M. 1991. Access to hospital care for California and Michigan Medicaid recipients. *Health Care Financing Review* 12:99–104.

Andrulis, D. P., and Gage, L. S. 1986. *Patient Transfers to Public Hospitals: A National Assessment*. Washington, D.C.: National Association of Public Hospitals.

Ansell, D. A., and Schiff, R. L. 1987. Patient dumping: status, implications, and policy recommendations. *JAMA* 257:1500–1502.

Astrachan, B. M., and Scherl, D. J. 1991. On the care of the poor and the uninsured. *Archives of General Psychiatry* 48:481.

Aved, B. M., and Harp, V. 1983. Assessing the impact of copayment on family planning services: a preliminary analysis in California. *American Journal of Public Health* 73:763–65.

Ayanian, J. Z., Kohler, B. A., Abe, T., and Epstein, A. M. 1993. The relation between health insurance coverage and clinical outcomes among women with breast cancer. *New England Journal of Medicine* 329:326–31.

Baker, D. W., Stevens, C. D., and Brook, R. H. 1991. Patients who leave a public hospital emergency department without being seen by a physician. *JAMA* 266:1085–90.

Ball, J. K. 1985. Preventive medical care for the poor: the impact of Medicaid on utilization. Unpublished, pp. 1–24.

Bazzoli, G. J. 1986. Health care for the indigent: overview of critical issues. *Health Services Research* 21:353.

Beauregard, K. 1991. *Persons Denied Private Health Insurance due to Poor Health.* Pub. No. 92–0016. Rockville, Md.: Agency for Health Care Policy and Research.

Beck, R. G. 1973. The effects of co-payment on the poor. *Journal of Human Resources* 9:129–42.

Beck, R. G., and Horne, J. M. 1978. *An Analytical Overview of the Saskatchewan Copayment Experiment in the Hospital and Ambulatory Settings.* Toronto: Ontario Council of Health.

Becker, E. R., and Sloan, F. A. 1983. Utilization of hospital services: the roles of teaching, case mix, and reimbursement. *Inquiry* 20:248–57.

Berg, J. W., Ross, R., and Latourette, H. B. 1977. Economic status and survival of cancer patients. *Cancer* 39:467–77.

Berki, S. E. 1986. A look at catastrophic medical expenses and the poor. *Health Affairs* 9(4) (Winter):139–45.

Berki, S. E., and Ashcraft, M. L. 1979. On the analysis of ambulatory utilization: an investigation of the roles of need, access and price as predictors of illness and preventive visits. *Medical Care* 17:1163–81.

Berliner, H. S. 1988. Patient dumping: no one wins and we all lose. *American Journal of Public Health* 78:1279–80.

Berwick, D. M., and Hiatt, H. H. 1989. Who pays? *New England Journal of Medicine* 321:541–42.

Billings, J., and Teicholz, N. 1990. Uninsured patients in District of Columbia hospitals. *Health Affairs* 9(4) (Winter):158–65.

Billings, J., Zeitel, J., Lukomnik, J., Carey, T. S., Balnk, A. E., and Newman, L. 1993. Impact of socioeconomic status on hospital use in New York City. *Health Affairs* 12(1) (Spring):162–73.

Bindman, A. B., Keane, D., and Lurie, N. 1990. A public hospital closes. *JAMA* 264:2899–2904.

Bindman, A. B., Grumbach, K., Keane, D., Rauch, L., and Luce, J. M. 1991. Consequences of queuing for care at a public hospital emergency department. *JAMA* 266:1091–96.

Blane, D. 1985. An assessment of the Black Report's explanation of health inequities. *Sociology of Health and Illness* 7:423–45.

Blendon, R. J. 1988. *Do all Americans have access to needed health care regardless of their ability to pay?* Testimony before the U.S. Senate Finance Committee, Washington, D.C., July 25.

Blendon, R. J., and Donelan, K. 1990. The public and the emerging debate over national health insurance. *New England Journal of Medicine* 323:208–12.

Blendon, R. J., Aiken, L. H., Freeman, H. E., Kirkman-Liff, B. L., and Murphy, J. W. 1986. Uncompensated care by hospitals or public insurance for the poor: does it make a difference? *New England Journal of Medicine* 31:1160–63.

Blendon, R. J., Donelan, K., Lukas, C. V., Thorpe, K. E., Frankel, M., Bass, R., and Taylor, H. 1992. Caring for the uninsured and underinsured: the uninsured and the debate over the repeal of the Massachusetts universal health care law. *JAMA* 267:1113–17.

Blendon, R. J., and Edwards, W. S. 1991. Caring for the uninsured choices for reform. *JAMA* 266(17):2376.

Bloom, B. 1990. Health insurance and medical care: health of our nation's children, United States, 1988. *Advance Data from Vital and Health Statistics.* Pub. No. 188. Hyattsville, Md.: National Center for Health Statistics.

Blumenthal, D., and Rizzo, J. A. 1991. Who cares for uninsured persons?: a study of physicians and their patients who lack health insurance. *Medical Care* 29:502–20.

Bodenheimer, T. 1992. Underinsurance in America. *New England Journal of Medicine* 327(4):274–78.

Bonham, G. S., and Corder, L. S. 1981. *NMCES Household Interview Instruments.* Pub. No. 81–3280. Rockville, Md.: National Center for Health Services Research.

Boston Globe. 1991. A national health plan—now. *Boston Globe* November 17, p. 82.

Bradbury, R. C., Golec, J. H., and Stearns, F. E. 1991. Comparing hospital length of stay in independent practice association HMOs and traditional insurance programs. *Inquiry* 28:87–93.

Braveman, P., Egerter, S., Bennett, T., and Showstack, J. 1991. Differences in hospital resource allocation among sick newborns according to insurance coverage. *JAMA* 266:3300–3308.

Braveman, P., Oliva, G., Grisham, Miller, M., Reiter, R., and Egerter, S. 1989. Adverse outcomes and lack of health insurance among newborns in an eight-county area of California, 1982–1986. *New England Journal of Medicine* 321:508–12.

Brook, R. H. 1991. Health, health insurance, and the uninsured. *JAMA* 265:2998–3002.

Brook, R. H., Kamber, C. J., Lohr, K. N., Goldberg, G. A., Keeler, E. B., and Newhouse, J. P. 1990. Quality of ambulatory care: epidemiology and comparison by insurance status and income. *Medical Care* 28:392–433.

Brook, R. H., Ware, J. E., Rogers, W. H., Keeler, E. B., Davies, A. R., Sherbourne, C. A., Goldberg, G. A., Lohr, K. N., Camp, P., and Newhouse, J. P. 1984. The effect of co-insurance on the health of adults: results from the RAND Insurance Experiment. R-3055-HHS. Santa Monica, Calif.: RAND Corp.

Brook, R. H., Ware, J. E., Rogers, W. H., Keeler, E. B., Davies, A. R., Donald, C. A., Goldberg, G. A., Lohr, K. N., Masthay, P. C., and Newhouse, J. P. 1983. Does free care improve adults' health?: results from a randomized controlled trial. *New England Journal of Medicine* 309:1426–34.

Brown, E. R. 1989. Access to health insurance in the United States. *Medical Care Review* 46:349–85.

Brown, E. R., and Cousineau, M. R. 1991. Loss of Medicaid and access to health services. *Health Care Financing Review* 12:17–26.

Buczko, W. 1986. Physician utilization and expenditures in a Medicaid population. *Health Care Financing Review* 8:17–26.

———. 1989. Hospital utilization and expenditures in a Medicaid population. *Health Care Financing Review* 11:35–47.

Buescher, P. A., Smith, C., Holliday, J. L., and Levine, R. H. 1987. Source of prenatal care and infant birth weight: the case of a North Carolina county. *American Journal of Obstetrics and Gynecology* 156:204–10.

Bullough, B. 1972. Poverty, ethnic identity and preventive health care. *Journal of Health and Social Behavior* 13:347–59.

Bunker, J. P., Gomby, D. S., and Kehrer, B. H., eds. 1989. *Pathways to Health: The Role of Social Factors.* Menlo Park, Calif.: Henry J. Kaiser Family Foundation.

Burstin, H. R., Lipsitz, S. R., and Brennan, T. A. 1992. Socioeconomic status and risk for substandard medical care. *JAMA* 268:2383–87.

Campbell, D. T., and Stanley, J. C. 1966. *Experimental and Quasi-experimental Designs for Research.* Chicago: Rand McNally.

Carey, T., Weis, K., and Homer, C. 1990. Prepaid vs. traditional Medicaid plans: effects on preventive health care. *Journal of Clinical Epidemiology* 43:1213–20.

———. 1991. Prepaid vs traditional Medicaid plans: Lack of effect on pregnancy outcomes and prenatal care. *Health Services Research* 26:165–81.

Chen, M., and Lyttle, C. S. 1987. Multivariate analysis of access to care. In Andersen, R. M., Aday, L. A., Lyttle, C. S., Cornelius, L. J., and Chen, M. S., eds., *Ambulatory Care and Insurance Coverage in an Era of Constraint.* Center for Health Administration Studies, Continuing Research Series No. 35. Chicago: Pluribus Press.

Cherkin, D. C., Grothaus, L., and Wagner, E. H. 1989. The effect of office visit copayments on utilization in a health maintenance organization. *Medical Care* 27:1036–45.

Coffey, R. M. 1983. *Patients in Public Hospitals: Who Pays, How Sick?* Research note 2. Rockville, MD: National Center for Health Services Research.

Cohen, J. W. 1989. Medicaid policy and the substitution of hospital outpatient care for physician care. *Health Services Research* 24:33–66.

Congressional Research Service, Library of Congress. 1988a. *Health Insurance and the Uninsured: Background Data and Analysis.* Pub. no. 85–568. Washington, D.C.: U.S. Government Printing Office.

———. 1988b. *Medicaid Source Book: Background Data and Analysis.* A report prepared for the Subcommittee on Health and the Environment of the Committee on Energy and Commerce, U.S. House of Representatives. Washington, D.C.: U.S. Government Printing Office.

———. 1990. *Insuring the Uninsured: Options and Analysis.* A report prepared for the Subcommittee on Health and the Environment of the Committee on Energy and Commerce, U.S. House of Representatives. Pub. no. 90–441. Washington, D.C.: U.S. Government Printing Office.

Cook, T. D., and Campbell, D. T., eds. 1979. *Quasi-experimentation: Design and Analysis Issues for Field Settings.* Boston, Mass.: Houghton Mifflin Co.

Cornelius, L. J. 1991. Access to medical care for black Americans with an episode of illness. *Journal of the National Medical Association* 83:617–26.

Cornelius, L. J., Beauregard, K., and Cohen, J. 1991. *Usual Sources of Medical Care and Their Characteristics.* National Medical Expenditure Survey, Research Findings 11, Pub. No. 91–0042. Rockville, Md.: Agency for Health Care Policy and Research.

Craddick, J. W. 1979. The medical management analysis system. *Quality Review Bulletin* 5:2–8.

Cromwell, J., and Mitchell, J. B. 1984. An economic model of large Medicaid practices. *Health Services Research* 19:197–218.

Cunningham, P. J., and Monheit, A. C. 1990. Insuring the children: a decade of change. *Health Affairs* 9(4) (Winter):76–90.

Dallek, G. 1985. Six myths of American medical care: what the poor really get. *Health/PAC Bulletin* 16:9–17.

Damiano, P., Brown, E. R., Johnson, J., and Scheetz, J. P. 1990. Access to dental care for Medi-Cal Recipients. Presented at American Public Health Association, New York City.

Davenport, R. W. 1950. Health insurance is next. *Fortune* 41:62–152.

Davis, K. 1976. Achievements and problems of medicaid. *Public Health Reports* 91:309–16.

Davis, K., and Rowland, D. 1983. Uninsured and underserved: inequities in health care in the United States. *Milbank Memorial Fund Quarterly* 61:149–76.

Davis, K., Gold, M., and Makuc, D. 1981. Access to health care for the poor: does the gap remain? *Annual Review of Public Health* 2:159–82.

Department of Health and Social Security. 1980. *Inequalities in Health: Report of a Research Working Group* (The Black Report). London: Department of Health and Social Security.

Dicker, M., and Sunshine, J. H. 1988. *Determinants of Financially Burdensome Family Health Expenses, United States, 1980.* National Medical Care Utilization and Expenditure Survey. Series C, Analytical Report No. 6, Pub. No. 88–20406. Washington, D.C.: U.S. Government Printing Office.

Dickhudt, J. S., Gjerdingen, D. K., and Asp, D. S. 1987. Emergency room use and abuse: how it varies with payment mechanism. *Minnesota Medicine* 70:571–74.

Diehr, P., Yergan, J., Chu, J., Feigl, P., Glaefke, G., Moe, R., and Bergner M. 1989. Rodenbaugh. Treatment modality and quality differences for black and white breast-cancer patients treated in community hospitals. *Medical Care*, 27(10):942–58.

Donabedian, A. 1976. Effects of Medicare and Medicaid on access to and quality of health care. *Public Health Reports* 91:322.

Dowd, B. E., Johnson, A., and Madson, R. 1986. Inpatient length of stay in Twin Cities health plans. *Medical Care* 24:694.

Duncan, R. P., and Kilpatrick, K. E. 1987. Unresolved hospital charges in Florida. *Health Affairs* 6(1) (Spring):157–66.

Dunham, N. C., Dunham, M. H., Kindig, D. A., Lastiri, S., and Vanderburg, J. A. 1989. Wisconsin: the impact of an HMO-based health plan for indigent adults. *Advances in Health Econ Health Service Reg* 10:201–19.

Dunlop, B. D., Wells, J. A., and Wilensky, G. R. 1989. The influence of source of insurance coverage on the health care utilization patterns of the elderly. *Journal of Health and Human Resources Administration* 11:285–311.

Dutton, D. 1986. Financial, organizational and professional factors affecting health care utilization. *Social Science and Medicine* 23:721–35.

Dutton, D. B. 1978. Explaining the low use of health services by the poor: costs, attitudes or delivery systems. *American Sociological Review* 43:348–68.

Eckholm, E. 1993. The uninsured: 37 million and growing. *New York Times* July 11, p. 5.

Edwards, W. S., and Berlin, M. 1989. *Questionnaires and Data Collection Methods for the Household Survey and the Survey of American Indians and Alaska Natives.* National Medical Expenditure Survey Methods 2, Pub. No. 89–3540. Rockville, Md.: National Center for Health Services Research.

Egbert, L. D., and Rothman, I. L. 1977. Relation between the race and economic status of patients and who performs their surgery. *New England Journal of Medicine* 297:9091.

Eisenberg, J. M. 1979. Sociologic influences on decision-making by clinicians. *Ann Int Medicine* 90(6):957–64.

Enthoven, A. C. 1980. *Health Plan: The Only Practical Solution to the Soaring Cost of Medical Care.* Reading, Mass.: Addison-Wesley.

Epstein, A. M., Stern, R. S., and Weissman, J. S. 1990. Do the poor cost more?: a multihospital study of patients' socioeconomic status and use of hospital resources. *New England Journal of Medicine* 322:1122–28.

Fahs, M. C. 1992. Physician response to the United Mine Workers' cost-sharing program: the other side of the coin. *Health Services Research* 27:25–45.

Farley, P. J. 1985. Who are the underinsured? *Milbank Memorial Fund Quarterly/Health and Society* 63:476–503.

———. 1986. Hospital and ambulatory services for selected illnesses. *Health Services Research* 21:5587–616.

Faulkner, and Gray. 1991. Dumping doctor decision raises anxiety. *Medicine and Health: Perspectives* July 29.

———. 1992. Briefly this week. *Medicine and Health* 46.

Fawley, I. L. 1992. A historical perspective on health reform. *MGM Journal* March/April:44–49.

Fein, R. 1986. *Medical Care, Medical Costs: The Search for a Health Insurance Policy.* Cambridge, Mass.: Harvard University Press.

Feldman, R., and Sloan, F. 1988. Competition among physicians, revisited. *Journal of Health Politics, Policy and Law* 13:239–61.

Fihn, S. D., and Wicher, J. B. 1988. Withdrawing routine outpatient medical services: effects on access and health. *Journal of General Internal Medicine* 3:356–62.

Foley, J. D. 1991. *Uninsured in the United States: The Nonelderly Population without Health Insurance: Analysis of the March 1990 Current Population Survey.* Washington, D.C.: Employee Benefit Research Institute.

———. 1993. *Sources of Health Insurance and Characteristics of the Uninsured: Analysis of the March 1992 Current Population Survey.* SR-16, Issue Brief No. 133. Washington, D.C.: Employee Benefit Research Institute.

Ford, E., Cooper, R., Castaner, A., Simmons, B., and Mar, M. 1989. Coronary arteriography and coronary bypass survey among whites and other racial groups relative to hospital-based incidence rates for coronary artery disease: Findings from NHDS. *American Journal of Public Health* 79:437–40.

Fossett, J. W., Perloff, J. D., Kletke, P. R., and Peterson, J. A. 1991. Medicaid patients' access to office-based obstetricians. *Journal of Health Care for the Poor and Underserved* 1:405–21.

Foxman, B., Valdez, R. B., Lohr, K. N., Goldberg, G. A., Newhouse, J. P., and Brook, R. H. 1987. The effect of cost sharing on the use of antibiotics in ambulatory care: results from a population-based randomized controlled trial. *Journal of Chronic Disease* 40:429–37.

Frank, R. G., Salkever, D. S., and Mullann, F. 1990. Hospital ownership and the care of uninsured and Medicaid patients: findings from the National Hospital Discharge Survey. *Health Policy* 14:1–11.

Freeman, H. E., Aiken, L. H., Blendon, R. J., and Corey, C. R. 1990. Uninsured working-age adults: characteristics and consequences. *Health Services Research* 24(6):811–23.

Freeman, H. E., and Kirkman-Liff, B. L. 1985. Health care under AHCCCS: an examination of Arizona's alternative to Medicaid. *Health Services Research* 20:245–66.

Freeman, H. E., Aiken, L. H., Blendon, R. J., and Corey, C. R. 1990. Uninsured working-age adults: characteristics and consequences. *Health Services Research* 24:811–23.

Freeman, H. E., Blendon, R. J., Aiken, L. H., Subman, S., Mullinix, C. F., and Corey, C. R. 1987. Americans report on their access to health care. *Health Affairs* 6(1) (Spring):6–18.

Freund, D. A., and Hurley, R. E. 1987. Managed care in Medicaid: selected issues in program origins, design, and research. *Annual Review of Public Health* 8:137–63.

Freund, D. A., Hurley, R. E., Adamache, K. W., and Mauskopf, J. 1990. The performance of urban and public hospitals and NHCs (neighborhood health centers) under Medicaid capitation programs. *Hospital and Health Service Administration* 35:525–46.

Freund, D. A., Hurley, R. E., Paul, J., Grubb, C., Rossiter, L. F., and Adamache, K. W. 1989a. Interim findings from the Medicaid competition demonstrations. *Advances in Health Economics and Health Services Research* 10:153–81.

Freund, D. A., Rossiter, L. F., Fox, P. D., Meyer, J. A., Hurley, R. E., Carey, T. S., and Paul, J. E. 1989b. Evaluation of the Medicaid competition demonstration. *Health Care Financing Review* 11:81–110.

Friedman, B., Parker, P., and Lipworth, L. 1973. The influence of Medicaid and private health insurance on the early diagnosis of breast cancer. *Medical Care* 11:485–90.

Friedman, E. 1987. Problems plaguing public hospitals: uninsured patient transfers, tight funds, mismanagement and misperception. *JAMA* 257:1850–57.

———. 1990. Medicare and Medicaid at 25. *Hospitals* 64:38–54.

———. 1991. The uninsured: from dilemma to crisis. *JAMA* 265:2491–95.

Friedman, G. 1982. Access to care: serving the poor and elderly in tough times. *Hospitals* 56:83–90.

Garfinkel, S., Corder, L., and Dobson, A. 1986. *Health Services Utilization in the U.S. Population by Health Insurance Coverage.* National Medical Care Utilization and Expenditure Survey. Series B, Descriptive Report No. 13, Pub. No. 20213. Washington, D.C.: U.S. Government Printing Office.

Garrison, L. P. 1990. Medicaid, the uninsured, and national health spending: Federal policy implications. *Health Care Financing Review* (Annual Suppl.): 167–70.

Ginsburg, P. B., and Manheim, L. M. 1973. Insurance, copayment and health services utilization: A critical review. *Journal of Econ and Business* 25:142–53.

Gittelsohn, A. M., Halpern, J., Sanchez, R. L. 1991. Income, race, and surgery in Maryland. *Am J Public Health* 81(11):1435–41.

Glaser, W. 1991. *Health Insurance in Practice: International Variations in Financing, Benefits, and Problems.* San Francisco: Jossey-Bass.

Goldfarb, N. I., Hillman, A. L., Eisenberg, J. M., Kelley, M. A., Cohen, A. V., and Dellheim, M. 1991. Impact of a mandatory Medicaid case management program on prenatal care and birth outcomes. *Medical Care* 29:64–71.

Goldfield, N. 1992. The Nixon years: failed national health reform from both parties. *Physician Executive* 18:20–26.

Gonnella, J. S., Hornbrook, M., and Louis, D. Z. 1984. Staging of disease: A case mix measurement. *JAMA* 251:637.

Gornick, M., Greenberg, J., Eggers, P., and Dobson, A. 1985. Twenty years of Medicare and Medicaid: covered populations, use of benefits, and program expenditures. *Health Care Financing Review* (Annual Suppl.):13–59.

Gortmaker, S. L. 1981. Medicaid and the health care of children in poverty and near poverty: Some successes and failures. *Medical Care* 19:567–82.

Grabowski, H. 1988. Medicaid patients' access to new drugs. *Health Affairs* 7(5) (Winter):102–14.

Gravdal, J. A., Krohm, C., and Glasser, M. 1991. Payment mechanism and patterns of use of medical services: the example of hypertension. *Journal of Family Practice* 32:66–70.

Greenberg, E. R., Chute, C. G., Stukel, T., Baron, J. A., Freeman, D. H., Yates, J., and Korson, R. 1988. Social and economic factors in the choice of lung cancer treatment: a population based study in two rural states. *New England Journal of Medicine* 318:612–17.

Greene, S. B., and Gunselman, D. L. 1986. Cost sharing and its effects on hospital utilization: The Blue Cross and Blue Shield of North Carolina experience. *Medical Care* 24:711–20.

Grumet, G. W. 1989. Health care rationing through inconvenience: the third party's secret weapon. *New England Journal of Medicine* 321:607–11.

Guendelman, S., and Schwalbe, J. 1986. Medical care utilization by Hispanic children: how does it differ from black and white peers? *Medical Care* 24:925–40.

Guttmacher, S. 1984. Poor people, poor care. *Health PAC Bulletin* 15:15–17.

Haas, J. S., Udvarhelyi, I. S., and Epstein, A. M. 1993. The effect of health coverage for uninsured pregnant women on maternal health and the use of cesarean section. *JAMA* 270:61–64.

Haas, J. S., Udvarhelyi, I. S., Morris, C. N., and Epstein, A. M. 1993. The effect of providing health coverage to poor uninsured pregnant women in Massachusetts. *JAMA* 269:87–91.

Hadley, J., Steinberg, E. P., and Feder, J. 1991. Comparison of uninsured and privately insured hospital patients: condition on admission, resource use and outcome. *JAMA* 265:374–79.

Hafner-Eaton, C. 1993. Physician utilization disparities between the uninsured and insured: comparisons of the chronically ill, acutely ill, and well nonelderly populations. *JAMA* 269:787–92.

Haggerty, R. J. 1985. The RAND Health Insurance Experiment for children. *Pediatrics* 75:969–71.

Hahn, B., and Flood, A. B. 1993a. *Modeling the Relationship between Insurance and General Health for Adults.* Rockville, Md.: Agency for Health Care Policy and Research.

———. 1993b. *No Insurance, Public Insurance, and Private Insurance: Do These Options Contribute to Differences in General Health?* Rockville, Md.: Agency for Health Care Policy and Research.

Hand, R., Sener, S., Imperato, J., Chmiel, J. S., Sylvester, J., and Fremgen, A. 1991. Hospital variables associated with the quality of care for breast cancer patients. *JAMA* 266:3429–32.

Hayward, R. A., Bernard, A. M., Freeman, H. E., and Corey, C. R. 1991. Regular source of ambulatory care and access to health services. *American Journal of Public Health* 81:434–38.

Hayward, R. A., Shapiro, M. F., Freeman, H. E., and Corey, C. R. 1988a. Inequities in health services among insured Americans: do working-age adults have less access to medical care than the elderly? *New England Journal of Medicine* 318:1507–12.

———. 1988b. Who gets screened for cervical and breast cancer?: results from a new national survey. *Archives of Internal Medicine* 148:1177–81.

Health Insurance Association of America. 1990. *Source Book of Health Insurance Data.* Washington, D.C.: HIAA.

Heinen, L., Fox, P. D., and Anderson, M. D. 1990. Findings from the Medicaid competition demonstrations: a guide for the states. *Health Care Financing Review* 11:55–67.

Held, P. J., Pauly, M. V., Bovbjerg, J. D., Newmann, J., and Salvatierra, O. Jr. 1988. Access to kidney transplantation: has the United States eliminated income and racial differences? *Archives of Internal Medicine* 748:2594–2600.

Hiatt, H. M. 1989. A study of medical injury and medical malpractice. *New England Journal of Medicine* 321:480–84.

Himmelstein, D. U., Woolhandler, S., Harnly, M., Bader, M. B., Silber, R., Backer, H. D., and Jones, A. A. 1984. Patient transfers: medical practice as social triage. *American Journal of Public Health* 74:494–97.

Himmelstein, D. U., and Woolhandler, S. 1992. *The National Health Program Chartbook.* Cambridge: The Center for National Health Program Studies. p. 5.

Hohlen, M. M., Manheim, L. M., Fleming, G. V., Davidson, S. M., Yudkowsky, B. K., Werner, S. M., and Wheatley, G.M. 1990. Access to office-based physicians under capitation reimbursement and Medicaid case management: findings from the Children's Medicaid program. *Medical Care* 28:59–68.

Holahan, J., and Cohen, J. 1986. *Medicaid: The Trade-off between Cost Containment and Access to Care.* Washington, D.C.: Urban Institute.

Holahan, J., and Zedlewski, S. 1991. Expanding Medicaid to cover uninsured Americans. *Health Affairs* 10:45–61.

Hornbrook, M. C., and Goldfarb, M. G. 1983. A partial test of a hospital behavioral model. *Social Science and Medicine* 17:667–80.

Howell, E., Corder, L., and Dobson, A. 1985. *Out-of-Pocket Health Expenses for Medicaid Recipients and Other Low Income Persons, 1980.* National Medical Care Utilization and Expenditure Survey. Series B, Descriptive Report No. (4) 1–52.

Howell, E., Herz, E., Brown, G., and Wang, R. 1989. *Outcomes and Costs of Obstetrical Care in California: A Comparison of Medicaid and Non-Medicaid Deliveries in October of 1983.* Contract no. 500–86–0016. Prepared for Health Care Financing Administration. Washington, D.C.: McGraw-Hill.

Howell, E. M. 1988. Low-income persons' access to health care: NMCUES Medicaid data. *Public Health Reports* 103:507–14.

Howell, E. M., and Brown, G. A. 1989. Prenatal, delivery, and infant care under Medicaid in three states. *Health Care Financing Review* 10:1–15.

Howell, E. M., Baugh, D. K., and Pine, P. L. 1988. Patterns of Medicaid utilization and expenditures in selected states, 1980–84. *Health Care Financing Review* 10:1–16.

Howell, E. M., Herz, E. J., Wang, R., and Hirsch, M. B. 1991. A comparison of Medicaid and non-Medicaid obstetrical care in California. *Health Care Financing Review* 12:1–16.

Hubbell, F. A., Waitzkin, H., and Rodriguez, F. I. 1990. Functional status and financial barriers to medical care among the poor. *Southern Medical Journal* 83:548–50.

Hubbell, F. A., Waitzkin, H., Mishra, S. I., and Dombrink, J. 1989a. Evaluating health-care needs of the poor: A community oriented approach. *American Journal of Medicine* 87:127–31.

Hubbell, F. A., Waitzkin, H., Rucker, L., Akin, B. V., and Heide, M. G. 1989b. Financial barriers to medical care: a prospective study in a university-affiliated community clinic. *American Journal of the Medical Sciences* 297:158–62.

Hurley, R. E., and Freund, D. A. 1988a. Determinants of provider selection or assignment in a mandatory case management program and their implications for utilization. *Inquiry* 25:402–10.

———. 1988b. A typology of Medicaid managed care. *Medical Care* 26:764–74.

Hurley, R. E., Freund, D. A., and Paul, J. E. 1993. *Managed Care in Medicaid: Lessons for Policy and Program Design.* Ann Arbor, Mich.: Health Administration Press.

Hurley, R. E., Freund, D. A., and Taylor, D. E. 1989a. Emergency room use and primary care case management: evidence from four Medicaid demonstration programs. *American Journal of Public Health* 79:843–46.

————. 1989b. Gatekeeping the emergency department: impact of a Medicaid primary care case management program. *Health Care Management Review* 14:63–71.

Hurley, R. E., Paul, J. E., and Freund, D. A. 1989. Going into gatekeeping: an empirical assessment. *Quarterly Review of Biology* October:306–14.

Iglehart, J. K., and White, J. K. 1987. Perspectives on health policy: experiments with Medicaid: Cost containment vs. access. *Health Progress* September:26–29.

Institute of Medicine, M. Millman, ed. 1993. *Access to Health Care in America.* Washington, D.C.: National Academy Press.

Jencks, S. F., and Benedict, M. B. 1990. Accessibility and effectiveness of care under Medicaid. *Health Care Financing Review* Spec. No:47–56.

Jensen, G. A. 1992. The dynamics of health insurance among the near elderly. *Medical Care* 30:598–614.

Joe, T., Meltzer, J., and Yu, P. 1985. Arbitrary access to care: the case for reforming Medicaid. *Health Affairs* 4(1):59–74.

Johns, L., and Adler, G.S. 1989. Evaluation of recent changes in Medicaid. *Health Affairs* Spring:171–81.

Jonasson, O., and Barrett, J. A. 1987. Transfer of unstable patients: Dumping or duty? *JAMA* 257:1519.

Kasper, J. D. and McMillan, A. 1986. *Perspectives on health care: United States, 1980.* National Medical Care Utilization and Expenditure Survey, Series B, Descriptive Report 14, Pub. No. 86–20214. Washington, D.C.: 1–43.

Keeler, E. B., and Rolph, J. E. 1983. How cost sharing reduced medical spending of participants in the health insurance experiment. *JAMA* 249:2220–22.

Keeler, E. B., Sloss, E. M., Brook, R. H., Operskalski, B. H., Goldberg, G. A., and Newhouse, J. P. 1987. Effects of cost sharing on physiological health, health practices, and worry. *Health Services Research* 22:279–306.

Keirn, W., and Metter, G. 1985. Survival of cancer patients by economic status in a free care setting. *Cancer* 55:1552–55.

Kellerman, A. L., and Ackerman, T. F. 1988. Interhospital patient transfer: the case for informed consent. *New England Journal of Medicine* 319:643.

Kellerman, A. L., and Hackman, B. B. 1988. Emergency department patient "dumping": an analysis of interhospital transfers to the Regional Medical Center at Memphis, Tennessee. *American Journal of Public Health* 78:1287–92.

————. 1990. Patient "dumping" post-COBRA. *American Journal of Public Health* 80:864–67.

Kelly, J. V. 1985. Provision of charity care by urban voluntary hospitals. In Rogers, S. J., Rousseau, A. M., and Nesbitt, S. W., eds., *Hospitals and the Uninsured Poor: Measuring and Paying for Uncompensated Care.* New York: United Hospital Fund of New York.

Kinzer, D. M. 1984. Care of the poor revisited. *Inquiry* 21:5–16.

Kjellstrand, C. V. 1988. Age, sex and race inequality in renal transplantation. *Archives of Internal Medicine* 148:1305–9.

Kohut, A., Toth, R. C., Bowman, C. 1993. *The Public, Their Doctors, and Health Care Reform.* New York: Times-Mirror Center for the People and the Press.

Korenbrot, C. C. 1984. Risk reduction in pregnancies of low-income women: Comprehensive prenatal care through the OB access project. *Mobius* 4:34–43.

Krieger, J. W., Connell, F. A., and LoGerfo, J. P. 1992. Medicaid prenatal care: a comparison of use and outcomes in fee-for-service and managed care. *American Journal of Public Health* 82:185–90.

Ku, L., Ellwood, M. R., and Klemm, J. 1990. Deciphering Medicaid data: Issues and needs. *Health Care Financing Review* Annual Suppl.

Laufenburg, H. F. 1989. Medicaid patients' use of HMO services. *Wisconsin Medical Journal* 88:19–21.

Lave, J., and Leinhardt, S. 1976. The cost and length of a hospital stay. *Inquiry* 13:327.

Lave, J. R., and Frank, R. G. 1988. Factors affecting Medicaid patients' length of stay in psychiatric units. *Health Care Financing Review* 10:57–66.

Law, S. A. 1976. *Blue Cross: What Went Wrong?* 2nd edition. New Haven: Yale University Press.

Lefkowitz, D. C., and Monheit, A. C. 1991. *Health Insurance, Use of Health Services, and Health Care Expenditures.* National Medical Expenditure Survey, Research Finding 12. Rockville, Md.: Agency for Health Care Policy and Research. (Prepublication review draft, August 11.)

LeGrand, J. 1978. The distribution of public expenditure: the case of health care. *Economica* 45:125–42.

Leibowitz, A., Manning, W. G., Keeler, E. B., Duan, N., Lohr, K. N., and Newhouse, J. P. 1985a. Effect of cost-sharing on the use of medical services by children: interim results from a randomized controlled trial. *Pediatrics* 75:942–951.

——. 1985b. *The Effect of Cost Sharing on the Use of Medical Services by Children.* R-3287-HHS. Santa Monica, Calif.: RAND Corp.

Leicher, E. S., Howell, E. M., Corder, L., and LaVange, L. M. 1985. *Access to Medical Care in 1980.* National Medical Care Utilization and Expenditure Survey. Series B, Descriptive Report No. 12. Rockville, Md.: National Center for Health Statistics.

Letsch, S. W., Lazenby, H. C., Levit, K. R., and Cowan, C. A. 1992. National health expenditures, 1991. *Health Care Financing Review* 14(2): 1–30.

Levit, K. R., Olin, G. L., and Letsch, S. W. 1992. Americans' health insurance coverage, 1980–91. *Health Care Financing Review* 14: 31–57.

Lewin, M. E. 1993. Barriers to health care access: beyond insurance. In Meyer, J. A., and Carrol, S. S., eds. *Building Blocks for Change: How Health Care Reform Affects Our Future.* Washington, D.C.: Economic and Social Research Institute.

Lewin, T. 1991. U.S. law on hospital care of poor faces test. *New York Times,* March 23.

Lindberg, G. L., Lurie, N., Bannick-Mohrland, S., Sherman, R. E., and Farseth, P. A. 1989. Health care cost containment measures and mortality in Hennepin County's Medicaid elderly and all elderly. *American Journal of Public Health* 79:1481–85.

Lindsey, P. A., and Newhouse, J. P. 1990. The cost and value of second surgical opinion programs: a critical review of the literature. *Journal of Health Politics, Policy and Law* 15:543–70.

Link, C. R., Long, S. H., and Settle, R. F. 1980. Cost sharing, supplementary insurance, and health services utilization among the Medicare elderly. *Health Care Financing Review* 2:25–31.

——. 1982. Access to medical care under Medicaid: Differentials by race. *Journal of Health Politics, Policy and Law* 7:345–65.

Lohr, K.N., and Brook, R.H. 1980. Quality of care in episodes of respiratory illness among Medicaid patients in New Mexico. *Annals of Internal Medicine* 92:99–106.

Lohr, K. N., Brook, R. H., Kamberg, C. J., Goldberg, G. A., Leibowitz, A., Keesey, J., Reboussin, D., and Newhouse, J. P. 1986. *Use of medical care in the RAND health insurance experiment: Diagnosis- and service-specific analyses in a randomized controlled trial.* RAND Health Insurance Experiment Series R-3469-HHS. Santa Monica, Calif.: RAND Corp.

Long, S. H., and Rodgers, J. 1989. The effects of being uninsured on health care service use: estimates from the survey of income and program participation. Paper presented at the annual meeting of the Allied Social Science Association, Atlanta, Ga.

Long, S. H., and Settle, R. F. 1985. Cutbacks in Medicaid eligibility under the omnibus budget reconciliation act of 1981: implications for access to health care services among the newly ineligible. Unpublished report prepared for Health Care Financing Administration, Contract No. 500–83–0058.

———. 1988. An evaluation of Utah's primary care case management program for medicaid recipients. *Medical Care* 26:1021–32.

Long, S. H., Settle, R. F., and Stuart, B. C. 1986. Reimbursement and access to physicians' services under Medicaid. *Journal of Health Economics* 5:236–51.

Luft, H. S. 1978. How do HMO achieve their savings? *New England Journal of Medicine* 298:1336–43.

———. 1981. Can HMOs serve the poor? In Luft, H. S., ed., *Health Maintenance Organizations: Dimensions of Performance.* New York: Wiley-Interscience, pp. 320–31.

Luft, H. S., and Morrison, E. M. 1991. Alternative delivery systems. In Ginzberg, E., ed., *Health Services Research: Accomplishments and Potential.* Cambridge, Mass.: Harvard University Press, pp. 195–233.

Lurie, N., Ward, N. B., Shapiro, M. F., and Brook, R. 1984. Termination from Medi-Cal: does it affect health? *New England Journal of Medicine* 311:480–84.

Lurie, N., Kamberg, C. J., Brook, R. H., Keeler, E. B., and Newhouse, J. P. 1989. How free care improved vision in the health insurance experiment. *American Journal of Public Health* 79:640–42.

Lurie, N., Moscovice, I. S., Finch, M., Christianson, J. B., and Popkin, M. K. 1992. Does capitation affect the health of the chronically mentally ill? *JAMA* 267:3300–3304.

Lurie, N., Manning, W. G., Peterson, C., Goldberg, G. A., Phelps, C. A., and Lillard, L. 1987. Preventive care: do we practice what we preach. *American Journal of Public Health* 77:801–4.

Lurie, N., Ward, N. B., Shapiro, M. F., Gallego, C., Vaghaiwalla, R., and Brook, R. H. 1986. Termination of Medi-Cal benefits: a follow-up study one year later. *New England Journal of Medicine* 314:1266–68.

Lyons, J. S., Hammer, J. S., Larson, D. B., Visotsky, H. M., and Burns, B. J. 1987. The impact of a prospective payment system on psychosocial service delivery in the general hospital. *Medical Care* 25:140–47.

McCall, N., Jay, E. D., and West, R. 1989. Access and satisfaction in the Arizona health care cost containment system. *Health Care Financing Review* 11:63–77.

McCall, N., Rice, T., Boismier, J., and West, R. 1991. Private health insurance and medical care utilization: evidence from the Medicare population. *Inquiry* 28:276–87.

McCall, N., Henton, D., Crane, M., Haber, S., Freund, D., and Wrightson, W. 1985. Evaluation of the Arizona health care cost-containment system. *Health Care Financing Review* 7:77–88.

McKinlay, J. B. 1972. Some approaches and problems in the study of the use of services—an overview. *Journal of Health Sociology Behavior.* 13(2):115–52.

Manning, W. G., Leibowitz, A., Goldberg, G. A. 1984. A controlled trial of the effect of a prepaid group practice on use of services. *New England Journal of Medicine* 310:1501–10.

Manning, W. G., Newhouse, J. P., Duan Naihua, Keeler, E., Benjamin, B., Leibowitz, A., Marquis, M. S., and Swanziger, J. 1988. *Health Insurance and the Demand for Medical Care: Evidence from a Randomized Experiment.* R-3476HHS. Santa Monica, Calif.: RAND Corp.

Marquis, M. S. 1984. *Cost-Sharing and the Patient's Choice of Provider.* 4–3126-HHS. Santa Monica, Calif.: RAND Corporation.

Martin, S. G., Frick, A. P., and Shwartz, M. 1984. An analysis of hospital case mix, cost and payment differences for Medicare, Medicaid, and Blue Cross Plan patients using DRGs. *Inquiry* 21:369–79.

Mayer, J. P., Johnson, C. D., Blakely, C. H., and Taylor, J. R. 1989. Pregnant women eligible under Medicaid expansion of maternity services: implications for outreach. *Evaluation and the Health Professions* 12:424–36.

Mayer, W., and McWhorter, W. 1989. Black/white differences in nontreatment of bladder cancer patients and implications for survival. *American Journal of Public Health* 79:772–75.

Maynard, C., Fisher, L. D., Passamani, E. R., and Pullum, T. 1986. Blacks in the coronary artery surgery study: risk factors and coronary artery disease. *Circulation* 74:64–71.

Mechanic, D. 1979. Correlates of physician utilization: why do major multivariate studies of physician utilization find trivial psychosocial and organizational effects? *Journal of Health and Social Behavior* 20:387–96.

Melnick, G. A., and Mann, J. M. 1989. Are Medicaid patients more expensive?: a review and analysis. *Medical Care Review* 46:229–53.

Meuleman, J., and Mounts, M. 1985. Health status of veterans found ineligible for ongoing outpatient care. *Journal of Community Health* 10:108–14.

Miike, L. 1993. *Health insurance: The Hawaii Experience.* Prepared under contract to the Office of Technology Assessment. Washington, D.C.: Office of Technology Assessment.

Monheit, A. C., and Schur, C. L. 1988. The dynamics of health insurance loss: a tale of two cohorts. *Inquiry* 25:315–27.

Monheit, A. C., Hagan, M. M., Berk, M. L., and Farley, P. J. 1985. The employed uninsured and the role of public policy. *Inquiry* 22:348–64.

Morey, R. C. 1980. A performance measure for the Medicaid program. *Inquiry* 17:18–24.

Mort, E. A., Wessman, J. S., and Epstein, A. M. 1994. Physician discretion and racial variation in the use of surgical procedures. *Arch Int Med.* In press.

Moscovice, I., and Davidson, G. 1987. Health care and insurance loss of working AFDC recipients. *Medical Care* 25:413–25.

Moyer, M. E. 1989. A revised look at the number of uninsured Americans. *Health Affairs* 8:102–10.

Muller, C. 1986. Review of twenty years of research on medical care utilization. *Health Services Research* 21:129–44.

Mundinger, M. O. 1985. Health service funding cuts and the declining health of the poor. *New England Journal of Medicine* 313:44–37.

National Center for Health Statistics, Bonham, G. S. 1983. *Procedures and Questionnaires of the National Medical Care Utilization and Expenditure Survey.* National Medical Care Utilization and Expenditure Survey. Series A, Methodological Report 1, Pub. No. 83–20001. Washington, D.C.: U.S. Government Printing Office.

Needleman, J., Arnold, J., Sheila, J., and Lewin, L. S. 1990. *The Health Care Financing System and the Uninsured.* Final report, HCFA Contract No. 500–89–0023. Washington D.C.: Lewin/ICF.

Newacheck, P. W. 1988. Access to ambulatory care for poor persons. *Health Services Research* 23:401–19.

———. 1989. Improving access to health services for adolescents from economically disadvantaged families. *Pediatrics* 84:1056–63.

Newacheck, P. W., and Halfon, N. 1988. Preventive care use by school-aged children: Differences by socioeconomic status. *Pediatrics* 82:462–68.

Newhouse, J. P. 1978. *The Economics of Medical Care.* Reading, Mass.: Addison-Wesley.

————. 1981. The demand for medical care services: a retrospect and prospect. In Van der Gaag, J., and Perlman, M. *Health, Economics, and Health Economics.* New York: North Holland Publishing Co.

————. 1989. Do unprofitable patients face access problems? *Health Care Financing Review* 11:33–43.

————. 1991. Controlled experimentation as research policy. In Ginzberg, E., ed., *Health Services Research: Accomplishments and Potential.* Cambridge, Mass.: Harvard University Press, pp. 161–94.

Newhouse, J. P., and the Insurance Experiment Group. 1993. Central findings and policy implications. In Newhouse, J. P., and the Insurance Experiment Group. *Free for All?: Lessons from the RAND Health Insurance Experiment.* Cambridge, Mass.: Harvard University Press.

Newhouse, J. P., Manning, W. G., Morris, C. N., Orr, L. L., Duan, N., Keeler, E. B., Leibowitz, A., Morris, C. N., Orr, L. L., Duan, N., Keeler, E. B., Lebowitz, A., Marquis, K. H., Marquis, M. S., Phelps, C. E., and Brook, R. H. 1981. Some interim results from a controlled trial of cost sharing in health insurance. *New England Journal of Medicine* 305:1501–7.

Norris, F. D., and Williams, R. L. 1984. Perinatal outcomes among Medicaid recipients in California. *American Journal of Public Health* 74:1112–17.

Oberg, C. N. 1990. Medically uninsured children in the United States: a challenge to public policy. *Pediatrics* 85:824–38.

Oberg, C. N., Hoagberg, B. L., Skovholt, C., Hodkinson, E., and Vanman, R. 1991. Prenatal care use and health insurance status. *Journal of Health Care for the Poor and Underserved* 2:270–91.

Oberg, C. N., Lia-Hoagberg, B., Hodkinson, E., Skovhold, C., and Vanman, R. 1990. Prenatal care comparisons among privately insured, uninsured, and Medicaid-enrolled women. *Public Health Reports* 105:533–35.

O'Grady, K. F., Manning, W. G., Newhouse, J. P., and Brook, R. H. 1985. The impact of cost sharing on emergency department use. *New England Journal of Medicine* 313:484–90.

O'Kane, M. E. 1989. Strategy for assessing the quality of care in the Medicare program. Unpublished background paper, Institute of Medicine, Washington, D.C.

Orr, S. T., and Miller, C. A. 1981. Utilization of health services by poor children since advent of Medicaid. *Medical Care* 19:583–90.

Orr, S. T., Charney, E., and Straus, J. 1988. Use of health services by black children according to payment mechanism. *Medical Care* 26:939–47.

Orr, S. T., Charney, E., Straus, J., and Bloom, B. 1991. Emergency room use by low income children with a regular source of health care. *Medical Care* 29:283–86.

Page, W. F., and Kuntz, A. J. 1980. Racial and socioeconomic factors in cancer survival. *Cancer* 45:1029–40.

Paringer, L., and McCall, N. 1991. How competitive is competitive bidding? *Health Affairs* 10(4) (Winter):220–30.

Pauly, M. 1978. Is medical care different?. In, Greenberg, W., ed., *Competition in the Health Care Sector.* Rockville, Md.: Aspen Systems.

Pepper Commission. 1990. A call for action: final report of the Pepper Commission on Comprehensive Health Care. Washington, D.C.: Government printing office, 1990. (28–860.)

Perloff, J. D., Kletke, P. R., and Neckerman, K. M. 1987. Physicians' decisions to limit Medicaid participation: determinants and policy implications. *Journal of Health Politics, Policy and Law* 12:221–35.

Perrin, J. M. 1986. High technology and uncompensated care. In Sloan, F., Blumstein, J., and Perrin, J., eds., *Uncompensated Hospital Care: Rights and Responsibilities.* Baltimore, Md.: Johns Hopkins University Press, pp. 54–71.

Piper, J. M., Baum, C., and Kennedy, D. L. 1987. Prescription drug use before and during pregnancy in a Medicaid population. *American Journal of Obstetrics and Gynecology* 157:148–56.

Piper, J. M., Ray, W. A., and Griffin, M. R. 1990. Effects of Medicaid eligibility expansion on prenatal care and pregnancy outcome in Tennessee. *JAMA* 264:2219–23.

Plough, A. L., Korda, H., and Delbanco, T. 1985. *Boston at Risk.* Boston, Mass.: Boston Foundation Primary Health Care Seminar.

Prospective Payment Assessment Commission. 1993. *Medicare and the American Health Care System: Report to Congress.* Washington, D.C.: Prospective Payment Assessment Commission.

Reinhardt, U. E. 1989. Comments. *Health Care Financing Review* (annual supplement):101.

Reis, J. 1990. Medicaid maternal and child health care: prepaid plans vs. private fee-for-service. *Res Nurs Health* 13:163–71.

Relman, A. S. 1983. The RAND health insurance study: is cost-sharing dangerous to your health? *New England Journal of Medicine* 309:1453.

———. 1986. Texas eliminates dumping: a start toward equity in hospital care. *New England Journal of Medicine* 314:578–79.

Restuccia, J. D., Payne, S. M. C., and Tracey, L. V. 1989. Framework for the definition and measurement of underutilization. *Medical Care Review* 46:255–70.

Rice, T., Brown, E. R., and Wyn, R. 1993. Holes in the Jackson hole approach to health care reform. *JAMA* 270:1357–62.

Rice, T. H., and Labelle, R. J. 1989. Do physicians induce demand for medical services? *Journal of Health Politics, Policy and Law* 14:587–600.

Richwald, G. A., Rederer, H., Gavin, V., Hoffman, V., Nelson, A., and Bartholomew, R. L. 1991. Are patient fees a barrier to STD clinic attendance?: the Los Angeles County experience. Presented at the annual meeting of the American Public Health Association, Atlanta, Ga.

Riley, G., Lubitz, J., and Rabey, E. 1991. Enrollee health status under Medicare risk contracts: An analysis of mortality rates. *Health Services Research* 26:137–63.

Rizzo, J. 1990. *Financially Distressed Hospitals: A Profile of Behavior before and after PPS.* Hospital Studies Research Note 14. Rockville, Md.: Agency for Health Care Policy and Research.

Robert Wood Johnson Foundation. 1978. *A New Survey on Access to Medical Care.* Special report no. 1. Princeton, N.J.: RWJF.

———. 1983. *Updated Report on Access to Health Care.* Special report no. 1. Princeton, N.J.: RWJF.

———. 1987. *Access to Health Care in the United States: Results of a 1986 Survey.* Special report no. 2. Princeton, N.J.: RWJF.

Roddy, P. C., Wallen, J., and Meyers, S. M. 1986. Cost sharing and use of health services: The United Mine Workers of America Health Plan. *Medical Care* 24:873–76.

Roemer, M. I., Hopkins, C. E., Carr, L., and Gartside, F. 1975. Copayments for ambulatory care: penny-wise and pound-foolish. *Medical Care* 13:457–66.

Rogers, D. E., and Blendon, R. J. 1977. The changing American health scene: sometimes things get better. *JAMA* 237:1710–14.

Roos, N. P., and Roos, L. L. 1982. Surgical rate variations: do they reflect the health or socioeconomic characteristics of the population? *Medical Care* 20(9):945–58.

Rosenbach, M. 1986. The impact of Medicaid on physician use by low-income children. *American Journal of Public Health* 79:1220–26.

Rosenbach, M. L. 1985. *Insurance Coverage and Ambulatory Medical Care of Low-Income Children: United States, 1980.* Series C, Analytical Report No. 1, Pub. No. 85–20401. Washington, D.C.: U.S. Government Printing Office.

Rosenbaum, S., Hughes, D., Butler, E., and Howard, D. 1989. Incantations in the dark: Medicaid, managed care, and maternity care. *Milbank Quarterly* 66:661–93.

Rowland, D., and Lyons, B. 1989. Triple jeopardy: Rural, poor, and uninsured. *Health Services Research* 23:975–1004.

Rowland, D., Lyons, B., and Edwards, J. 1988. Medicaid: health care for the poor in the Reagan era. *Annual Review of Public Health* 9:427–50.

Rundall, T., Gordon, N., Parker, L., and Perkins, C. 1991. California residents with and without health insurance. Presented at 119th Annual Meeting, APHA, Atlanta, GA.

Rutstein, D. D., Berenberg, W., Chalmers, T. C., Child, C. G., Fishman, A. P., and Perrin, E. B. 1976. Measuring the quality of medical care: a clinical method. *New England Journal of Medicine* 294:582–88.

Schaller, D. F., Bostrom, A. W., and Rafferty, J. 1986. Quality of care review: recent experience in Arizona. *Health Care Financing Review* (Spec. No.): 65–74.

Scheffler, R. M. 1984. The United Mine Workers' Health Plan: an analysis of the cost-sharing program. *Medical Care* 22:247.

Schieber, G. J., Poullier, J. P., and Greenwald, L. M. 1993. Health spending, delivery, and outcomes in OECD countries. *Health Affairs* 12(2) (Summer):120–29.

Schiff, R. L., Ansell, D., Scholosser, J. E., Idris, A. H., Morrison, A., and Whitman, S. 1986. Transfers to a public hospital: a prospective study of 467 patients. *New England Journal of Medicine* 314:552–57.

Schlesinger, M., Bentkover, J., Blumenthal, D., Musacchio, R., and Willer, J. 1987. The privatization of health care and physicians' perceptions of access to hospital services. *Milbank Quarterly* 65:25–58.

Schramm, W. F. 1985. WIC prenatal participation and its relationship to newborn Medicaid costs in Missouri: a cost/benefit analysis. *American Journal of Public Health* 75:851–57.

Schur, C. L., and Taylor, A. K. 1991. Choice of health insurance and the two-worker household. *Health Affairs* 10(1) (Spring):155–63.

Schwethelm, B., Margolis, L. H., Miller, C., and Smith, S. 1989. Risk status and pregnancy outcome among Medicaid recipients. *American Journal of Preventive Medicine* 5:157–63.

Shapiro, M. F., Ware, J. E., and Sherbourne, C. D. 1986. Effects of cost sharing on seeking care for serious and minor symptoms: results of a randomized controlled trail. *Annals of Internal Medicine* 104:246–51.

Shaw, K. N., Slebst, S. M., and Gill, F. M. 1990. Indigent children who are denied care in the emergency department. *Annals of Emergency Medicine* 19:59–62.

Shea, S., Misra, D., Erhlich, M. H., Field, L., and Francis, C. K. 1992. Predisposing factors for severe, uncontrolled hypertension in an inner-city minority population. *New England Journal of Medicine* 327:776–81.

Shearer, M. 1989. Health care for the uninsured: the statistics are staggering. *Michigan Medicine* 88:14–15.

Short, P. E., Cornelius, L. J., and Goldstone, D. E. 1990. Health insurance status of minorities in the United States. *Journal of Health Care for the Poor and Underserved* 1(1):9–24, discussions 28–30.

Short, P. F., and Lefkowitz, D. 1991. Encouraging preventive services for low-income children: The effect of expanding Medicaid. Presented at the annual meeting of the Association for Health Services Research.

Short, P. F., Cantor, J. C., and Monheit, A. C. 1988. The dynamics of Medicaid enrollment. *Inquiry* 25:504–16.

Short, P. F., Monheit, A., and Beauregard, K. 1988. Uninsured Americans: A 1987 profile. Presented at the annual meeting of the American Public Health Association, Boston, Mass.

Siemetiyacki, J., Richardson, L., and Ples, I. B. 1980. Equality in medical care under National Health Insurance in Montreal. *New England Journal of Medicine* 303(1):10–15.

Singer, J., Sulvetta, Wallack, S., Solish, M., and Beatrice, D. 1985. Uncompensated care: Issues and options. HCFA report Agreement 18-C-98526/1–01.

Singh, S., Forrest, J. D., and Torres, A. 1989. Prenatal care in the United States: a state and county inventory. New York: The Alan Guttmacher Institute.

Siu, A. L., Sonnenberg, F. A., Manning, W. G., Goldberg, G. A., Bloomfield, E. S., Newhouse, J. P., and Brook, R. H. 1986. Inappropriate use of hospitals in a randomized trial of health insurance plans. *New England Journal of Medicine* 315:1259–66.

Sloan, F. A., Morrisey, M. A., and Valvona, J. 1988. Hospital care for the "self-pay" patient. *Journal of Health Politics, Policy and Law* 13:83–103.

Sloan, F. A., Valvona, J., and Hickson, G. B. 1985. Analysis of health care options in Tennessee: uncompensated care. Final report, Contract FA0649 with the Tennessee Dept. of Health and Environment.

Sloan, F. S., Valvona, J., and Mullner, R. 1986. Identifying the issues: a statistical profile. In Sloan, F., Blumstein, J., and Perrin, J., eds., *Uncompensated Hospital Care: Rights and Responsibilities.* Baltimore, Md.: Johns Hopkins University Press.

Sloss, E. M., Keeler, E. B., Brook, R. H., Operskalski, B. H., Goldberg, G. A., and Newhouse, J. P. 1987. Effect of a health maintenance organization on physiologic health. *Annals of Internal Medicine* 107:130–38.

Sofaer, S. 1990. Restrictive reimbursement policies and uncompensated care in California hospitals, 1981–1986. *Hospital and Health Services Administration* 35:189–206.

Sokol, R. J., Woolf, R. B., Rosen, M. G., and Weingarden, K. 1980. Risk, antepartum care, and outcome: impact of a maternity and infant care project. *Obstetrics and Gynecology* 56:150–56.

Solberg, L.I., Peterson, K. E., Ellis, R. W., Romness, K., Rohrenbach, E., Thell, T., Smith, A., Routier, A., Stillmank, M. W., and Zak, S. 1990. The Minnesota project: a focused approach to ambulatory quality assessment. *Inquiry* 27:359–67.

Soumerai, S. B., Avorn, J., Ross-Degan, D., and Gortmaker, S. 1987. Payment restrictions for prescription drugs under Medicaid: Effects on therapy, cost, and equity. *New England Journal of Medicine* 317:550–56.

Soumerai, S. B., Avorn, J., McLaughlin, T. J., and Choodnovskiy, I. 1991. Effects of Medicaid drug-payment limits on admission to hospitals and nursing homes. *New England Journal of Medicine* 325:1072–77.

Spillman, B. C. 1992. The impact of being uninsured on utilization of basic health care services. *Inquiry* 29:457–66.

Spitz, A. M., Rubin, G. L., McCarthy, B. J., Marks, J., Burton, A. H., and Berrier, E. 1983. The impact of publicly funded perinatal care programs on neonatal outcome. *American Journal of Obstetrics and Gynecology* 147:295–300.

Spitz, B. 1985. Medicaid case management: Lessons for business. *Business and Health* 2:16–20.

————. 1987. A national survey of Medicaid case-management programs. *Health Affairs* 6(1) (Spring):61–70.

Spitz, B., and Abramson, J. 1987. Competition, capitation, and case management: barriers to strategic reform. *Milbank Quarterly* 65:348–70.

St. Clair, P. A., Smeriglio, V. L., Alexander, C. S., Connell, F. A., and Niebyl, J. R. 1990. Situational and financial barriers to prenatal care in a sample of low-income, inner-city women. *Public Health Reports* 105:264–66.

St. Peter, R. F., Newacheck, P. W., and Halfon, N. 1992. Access to care for poor children: separate and unequal? *JAMA* 267:2760–64.

Stafford, R. S. 1990. Cesarean section use and source of payment: an analysis of California hospital discharge abstracts. *American Journal of Public Health* 80:313–15.

————. 1991. The impact of nonclinical factors on repeat cesarean section. *JAMA* 265:59–63.

Starkenburg, R. J. 1990. Patient "dumping." *Medical Benefits* 7:8.

Starr, P. 1982. *The Social Transformation of American Medicine.* New York: Basic Books.

Stern, R. S., Weissman, J. S., and Epstein, A. M. 1991. The emergency department as a pathway to admission for poor and high-cost patients. *JAMA* 266:2238–43.

Sullivan, C. B., and Rice, T. 1991. The health insurance picture in 1990. *Health Affairs* 10(2) (Summer):104–15.

Sulvetta, M. B., and Swartz, K. 1986. *The Uninsured and Uncompensated Care: A Chartbook.* Washington, D.C.: National Health Policy Forum, George Washington University.

Swartz, K. 1984. *How Different Are Four Surveys' Estimates of the Number of Americans without Health Insurance?* Washington, D.C.: Urban Institute.

Swartz, K., and McBride, T. D. 1990. Spells without health insurance: Distributions of durations and their link to point-in-time estimates of the uninsured. *Inquiry* 27:281–88.

Swartz, K., and Purcell, P. 1989. Letter: uninsured Americans. *Health Affairs* 8:193–97.

Swartz, K., Marcotte, J., and McBride, T. D. 1993a. Personal characteristics and spells without health insurance. *Inquiry* 30:64–76.

————. 1993b. Spells without health insurance: the distribution of durations when left-censored spells are included. *Inquiry* 30:77–83.

Taube, C. A., and Rupp, A. 1986. The effect of Medicaid on access to ambulatory mental health care for the poor and near-poor under 65. *Medical Care* 24:677–86.

Temkin-Greener, H. 1986. Medicaid families under managed care: anticipated behavior. *Med Care* 24:721–32.

Temkin-Greener, H., and Winchell, M. 1991. Medicaid beneficiaries under managed care: provider choice and satisfaction. *Health Services Research* 26:509–29.

Thorpe, K. E., and Brecher, C. 1987. Improved access to care for the uninsured poor in large cities: do public hospitals make a difference? *Journal of Health Politics, Policy and Law* 12:313–24.

Thorpe, K. E., Siegel, J. E., and Dailey, T. 1989. Including the poor: The fiscal impacts of Medicaid expansion. *JAMA* 261:1003–7.

Torres, A., and Kenney, A. M. 1989. Expanding Medicaid coverage for pregnant women: estimates of the impact and cost. *Family Planning Perspectives* 21:19–24.

Traska, M. R. 1988. Medicaid fails many poor: Study. *Hospitals* 62:38.

Trevino, F. M., Moyer, M. E., Valdez, R. B., and Stroup-Benham, C. A. 1991. Health insurance coverage and utilization of health services by Mexican Americans, Mainland Puerto Ricans, and Cuban Americans. *JAMA* 265:233–37.

U.S. Bureau of the Census. 1992. *The Current Population Survey, March 1991: Technical Documentation.* Prepared by Data Users Services for the Bureau of the Census. Washington, D.C.: The Bureau, 1991.

U.S. Congress, Office of Technology Assessment. 1992. *Does Health Insurance Make a Difference?: Background Paper.* Pub. No. OTA-BP-H-99. Washington, D.C.: U.S. Government Printing Office.

U.S. Department of Labor, Bureau of Labor Statistics. 1990. *Employee Benefits in Medium and Large Firms, 1989.* Bulletin 2363. Washington, D.C.: U.S. Government Printing Office.

U.S. General Accounting Office. 1987. *Prenatal Care: Medicaid Recipients and Uninsured Women Obtain Insufficient Care.* Report to the Chairman, Subcommittee on Human Resources and Intergovernmental Relations, Committee on Government Operations, House of Representatives. Pub No. GAO/HRD-87-137. Washington, D.C.: U.S. Government Printing Office.

Valdez, R. B., Brook, R. H., Rogers, W. H., Ware, J. E., Keeler, E. B., Sherbourne, C.A., Lohr, K. N., Goldberg, G. A., Camp, P., and Newhouse, J. P. 1985. Consequences of cost-sharing for children's health. *Pediatrics* 75:952–61.

Valdez, R. B., Morgenstern, H., Brown, E. R., Wyn, R., Wang, C., and Cumberland, W. 1993. Insuring Latinos against the costs of illness. *JAMA* 269:889–94.

Vladeck, B. C. 1981. Equity, access, and the costs of health services. *Medical Care* 19 (suppl.):69–80.

Wagner, E. H., and Bledsoe, T. 1990. The RAND Health Insurance Experiment and HMOs. *Medical Care* 28:191–200.

Waid, M. O. 1990. Addendum: a brief summary of the Medicaid program. *Health Care Financing Review* (suppl): Spec. No: 171–2.

Waitzkin, H. 1984. Two-class medicine returns to the United States: Impact of Medi-Cal reform. *Lancet* 2(8412) 144–46.

Ware, J. E., Brook, R. H., Rogers, W. H., Keeler, E. B., Davies, A. R., Sherbourne, C. D., Goldberg, G. A., Camp, P., and Newhouse, J. B. 1986. Comparison of health outcomes at a health maintenance organization with those of fee-for-service care. *Lancet* 1017–22.

Weiner, J. P., Lyles, A., Steinwachs, D. M., and Hall, K. C. 1991. Impact of managed care on prescription drug use. *Health Affairs* Spring:10(1) 140–154.

Weissert, W. G., and Scanlon, W. J. 1985. Determinants of nursing home discharge status. *Medical Care* 23:333–43.

Weissman, J., and Epstein, A. M. 1989. Case mix and resource utilization by uninsured hospital patients in the Boston metropolitan area. *JAMA* 261:3572–76.

Weissman, J., Crane, S., and Sager, A. 1987. Controlling the gateway: managing access to care through hospital admissions and accounts offices. Presented at American Public Health Association Annual Meeting, New Orleans, October 18–22.

Weissman, J. and Solish, M. 1989. Hillsborough County Hospital Authority. In: Altman, S., Brescher, C., Henderson, M., and Thorpe K., eds. *Competition and Compassion: Conflicting Roles for Public Hospitals.* Ann Arbor, MI: Health Administration Press.

Weissman, J. S. 1987. Who cares?: Case mix and resource utilization by uninsured hospital patients in the Boston metropolitan area. Ph.D. dissertation. Waltham, Mass.: Brandeis University.

Weissman, J. S., and Epstein, A. M. 1993. The insurance gap: does it make a difference? *Annual Review in Public Health* 14:243–70.

Weissman, J. S., Gatsonis, C., and Epstein, A. M. 1992. Rates of avoidable hospitalizations by insurance status in Massachusetts and Maryland. *JAMA* 268:2388–94.

Weissman, J. S., Fielding, S. L., Stern, R. S., and Epstein, A. M. 1991. Delayed access to health care: Risk factors, reasons, and consequences. *Annals of Internal Medicine* 114:325–31.

Weissman, J. S., Van Deusen Lukas, C., and Epstein, A. M. 1992. Bad debt and free care in Massachusetts hospitals: the role of uninsured and underinsured patients. *Health Affairs* 11(2) (Summer):148–61.

Welch, B. L., Hay, J. W., Miller, D. S., Olsen, R. J., Rippey, R. M., and Welch, A. S. 1987. The RAND health insurance study: A summary critique. *Medical Care* 25:148–696.

Wells, K. B., Manning, W. G., Jr., Duan, N., Newhouse, J. P., and Ware, J. E., Jr. 1987. Cost-sharing and the use of general medical physicians for outpatient mental health care. *Health Services Research* 22:1–17.

Wenneker, M. B., Weissman, J. S., and Epstein, A. M. 1990. The association of payer with utilization of cardiac procedures in Massachusetts. *JAMA* 264:1255–60.

Wilensky, G. R. 1988. Filling the gaps in health insurance: impact on competition. *Health Affairs* 7(3) (Summer):133–49.

Wilensky, G. R., and Berk, M. L. 1982. Health care, the poor, and the role of medicaid. *Health Affairs* 1:93–100.

———. 1985. The poor, sick, uninsured and the role of Medicaid. In Rogers, S. J., Rousseau, A. M., and Nesbitt, S. W., eds., *Hospitals and the Uninsured Poor: Measuring and Paying for Uncompensated Care.* New York: United Hospital Fund of New York.

Wilensky, G.R., and Rossiter, L.F. 1991. Coordinated care and public programs. *Health Affairs* Winter 10(4):62–77.

Wilson, P. A., Griffith, J. R., and Tedeschi, P. J. 1985. Does race affect hospital use. *American Journal of Public Health* 75:263.

Wimberley, T. 1980. Toward national health insurance in the United States: an historical outline, 1910–1979. *Social Science and Medicine* 14:13–25.

Wise, P. H., First, L. R., Lamb, G. A., Kotelchuck, M., Chen, D. W., Ewing, A., Hersee, H., and Rideout, J. 1988. Infant mortality increase despite high access to tertiary care: an evolving relationship among infant mortality, health care, and socioeconomic change. *Pediatrics* 81(4):542–48.

Wissow, L. S., Gittelsohn, A. M., Szklo, M., Starfield, B., and Mussman, M. 1988. Poverty, race and hospitalization for childhood asthma. *American Journal of Public Health* 78:777–82.

Wolfe, S. M. 1989. Doctor who dumped poor patient loses case. *Public Citizen Health Research Group Health Letter* 5:11.

Woolhandler, S., and Himmelstein, D. U. 1988. Reverse targeting of preventive care due to lack of health insurance. *JAMA* 259:2872–74.

Wyszewianski, L. 1986. Financially catastrophic and high-cost cases: Definitions, distinctions, and their implications for policy formulation. *Inquiry* 23 (Winter):382–94.

Yelin, E. H., Kramer, J. S., and Epstein, W. 1983. Is health care use equivalent across social groups?: a diagnosis-based study. *American Journal of Public Health* 73:563–71.

Yergan, J., Flood, A. B., Diehr, P., and LoGerfo, J. P. 1988. Relationship between patient source of payment and the intensity of hospital services. *Medical Care* 26:1111–14.

Young, G. J., and Cohen, B. B. 1991. Inequities in hospital care, the Massachusetts experience. *Inquiry* 28:255–62.

Zollinger, T. W., Saywell, R. M., and Chu, D. K. 1991. Uncompensated hospital care for pregnancy and childbirth cases. *American Journal of Public Health* 81:1017–22.

INDEX

Page numbers in italics indicate figures; numbers followed by n *indicate notes; numbers followed by* t *indicate tables.*

AALL. *See* American Association for Labor Legislation
Access to care
  barriers to, 5–6, 124
  defining and measuring, 6–7, 8t, 9, 160n
  hospital admissions and, 101–102
    avoidable, 103
  improvements in, reform and, 147–148
  insurance status and, 1–16, 2t, 134–137,
    152–153
  problems with, 1–2, 87–88, 89t–90t, 90–91
  questions of, 146–153
  special cases of, 113–132
    changes in or loss of insurance, 124–126
    cost-sharing, 113–124
    Medicaid and managed care, 126–132
  surveys and studies on, 155–158
  framework for, 3–9
  limitations in, 15–16
Adults
  insurance status of, 36–37, 39t
  use of preventive care by, 94–95, 95t, 96t
AFDC. *See* Aid to Families with Dependent Children
African Americans
  adverse patient outcomes for, 110
  health risk of, 39–40, 41t
  See also Race
Age
  effect on physician visits, 70, 70t
  hospitalizations and, 76–77
  insurance status and, 36–37, 39t
  perceived health status and, 50

Agency for Health Care Policy and Research
  (AHCPR), 28, 156, 157
AHCCCS. *See* Arizona Health Care Cost-Containment System
AHCPR. *See* Agency for Health Care Policy and Research
AHCs. *See* Avoidable hospital conditions
Aid to Families with Dependent Children
  (AFDC), 23, 38
  effects of OBRA on, 124
  Medicaid and, 41
All-government systems for reform, 140–141
All-payer rate-setting systems, 144, 163n
AMA. *See* American Medical Association
Ambulatory care
  hospitalizations and, 102–103
    avoidable, 104
  utilization of, 65, 74, 162n
American Association for Labor Legislation
  (AALL), 137–138
American Medical Association (AMA), 137, 138
Application process for Medicaid, 24
Arizona Health Care Cost-Containment System
  (AHCCCS), 127, 129, 130
Avoidable hospital conditions (AHCs), 103–106,
  105t

Barriers to care
  avoidable hospital admissions and, 104–105
  nonfinancial, 5–6
Biased selection, 15
Blue Cross, 22, 138
  history of, 18–19
  study of coinsurance plan, 116t, 119–120
Blue Shield, 19, 22
Bureau of the Census, 157
Bush, George, 140

Califano, Joseph A., 139–140
Canadian insurance system, 141, 147
  contrasted with U.S. systems, 26, 27t
Cancer
  delays in seeking care and, 90
  diagnostic stage and survival rates, 108–109
Carter, James Earl, 140
"Case management" approach to prenatal care,
  131
Catastrophic coverage, 144
Catastrophic expenses, 45
Center for General Health Services Intramural
  Research of AHCPR, 157
Cesarean section, 84, 85t
CHAMPUS. *See* Civilian Health and Medical
  Programs of the Uniformed Services
CHAMPVA. *See* Civilian Health and Medical
  Programs of the VA
Children
  coverage of, 29
  insurance status of, 37–38, 40t
  physician visits by, 73
  use of preventive care by, 93–94, 94t
CHIP. *See* Comprehensive Health Insurance
  Program
Chronic disease as measure of health status,
  53–54
Chronically mentally ill, managed care
  programs for, 132
Civilian Health and Medical Programs of the
  Uniformed Services (CHAMPUS), 17, 18
Civilian Health and Medical Programs of the VA
  (CHAMPVA), 24, 25
Clinton, Bill, 137, 142, 146
COBRA. *See* Consolidated Omnibus Budget
  Reconciliation Act
Coinsurance, 45
  effects on access to care, 15
Community rating, 18, 145
Comparison groups in insurance status, 10–15,
  134–135
Comprehensive coverage, reform and,
  149–150
Comprehensive Health Insurance Program
  (CHIP), 139
Compulsory private systems for reform, 141–143
Consolidated Omnibus Budget Reconciliation
  Act (COBRA), 92
Continuation provision, 145
Continuity of coverage, Medicaid
  hospitalizations and, 77–78
  use of physicians and, 69–70
Convenience of care, 60–62, 61t

Cost control
  in managed care, 14
  in public insurance programs, 143
Cost-sharing
  effect on access to care, 113–124
    outcome indicators, 121–124, 122t, 123t
    process indicators, 114, 115t–119t, 116–121
  effects of reform on, 149
  insurance status and, 11–13, 13t
  United Mine Workers Health Plan study of,
    116t, 120
  See also RAND Health Insurance Experiment
"Cover sheet children," 29
Cover sheet questions, 29
CPS. *See* Current Population Survey
Current Population Survey (CPS), 10, 19–20,
  157
  March Supplement of, 26, 30

Deaths in hospitals, 100–101, 101t
Deductibles, 11, 45
Deficit Reduction Act (DEFRA), 38
DEFRA. *See* Deficit Reduction Act
Delays in seeking care
  by cancer patients, 90
  cost of care and, 91
Denial of care, factors in, 88
Denial of coverage
  by Omnibus Budget Reconciliation
    Act(OBRA), 124–125
  pre-existing conditions and, 22–23
  prohibited by Health Security Act (HSA),
    142
Department of Health, Education and Welfare
  (DHEW), 139
Department of Health and Human Services, 155
Department of Veterans Affairs, 17, 18
Dependents, employer-based coverage and,
  33–34, 35t
DHEW. *See* Department of Health, Education
  and Welfare
Disadvantaged groups, effects of reform on,
  148–149
Discretionary hospital admissions, 104
Disease(s)
  end-stage renal (ESRD), 17
  hospital admission rates by, 103
  managed care for mental illness, 132
  as measure of health status, 53–54
  sexually transmitted, effect of cost-sharing on
    treatment for, 124
Disease staging, 102
  cancer survival rates and, 108–109

Early and Periodic Screening, Diagnosis, and
  Treatment program (EPSDT), 93
EBRI. *See* Employee Benefit Research Institute
Economic models of demand for health care,
  3–6, 160n
Economic transfers. *See* Patient dumping
Education
  as barrier to care, 5
  insurance status and, 34–35, 38t
Elderly, insurance status of, 36
Eligibility
  industry-specific characteristics and, 21–22
  for Medicaid, 10–11, 24
  for outpatient care by VA Medical Centers,
    125–126
Emergency departments
  effects of cost-sharing on use of, 118
  effects of managed care on, 128–129, 163n
  overutilization of, 59–60
  as source of care, 56, 59
Emergency Medical Treatment and Active
  Labor Act, 92
Employee Benefit Research Institute (EBRI), 26
Employer(s)
  effects of reform on, 151–152
  proportion of premiums paid by, 22
  role in health insurance, 19
  small
    cost of insurance plans for, 20–21
    uninsured employees of, 33, 34t
Employer mandates, 141, 152
  drawbacks of, 141–142
Employment-based coverage, 17, 25–26
  problems with, 20–22, 21t
Employment characteristics of uninsured
  persons, 31–34, *32, 33*, 34t, 35t
Enabling characteristics of health system, 7, 160n
End-stage renal disease (ESRD), 17
EPSDT. *See* Early and Periodic Screening,
  Diagnosis, and Treatment program
ESRD. *See* End-stage renal disease
Ethnicity. *See* Race
Exclusion from coverage
  elimination of, 145
  of underinsured persons, 45
Expected payer. *See* Payment source
Experience rating, 15, 21

Family composition, insurance status and,
  40–41, 42t
Family Health Insurance Plan (FHIP), 139
Federal poverty guidelines, Medicaid and, 11,
  161n

FHIP. *See* Family Health Insurance Plan
Foregone care, studies of, 88, 89t–90t

GAO. *See* General Accounting Office
Gatekeeper systems, 131
Gender
  effect on physician visits, 70, 70t
  insurance status and, 38–39, 39t
  use of preventive care by adults and, 94–95,
    95t, 96t
  See also Women
General Accounting Office (GAO), 106
Geography
  as barrier to care, 5
  effect on physician visits, 70–71, 71t
  hospitalizations and, 78
  improvements in access and, 149
  insurance status and, 41, *43*
  physician utilization in South, 71, 71t
  rural areas, 149
Group Health Association of America, 19
  Library Reference Service, 159
Group plans, underinsurance and, 46–47

Harvard Malpractice Study, 86
HCFA. *See* Health Care Financing
  Administration
Health care
  characteristics of system, 7, 8t
  economic models of demand for, 3–6, 160n
  expenditures for, 64–66, 65t, 66t
    attributable to Medicaid, 23–24
    in United States, 1, 2t
  goals of, 3
  hospital care. *See* Hospital(s), care in
  outcomes of. *See* Outcomes of care
  physician visits. *See* Physician visits
  prescription drugs, 86–87, 118, 126–126
  preventive. *See* Preventive care
  quality of research on, 63
  reform in. *See* Health care reform
  regular source of, 55–58, 57t
  timeliness in obtaining, 87–92
  See also Access to care; Barriers to care;
    Quality of care
Health Care Financing Administration (HCFA),
  156
  Office of National Health Statistics of, 30, *31*
Health care reform
  access to care and, 133–137, 146–153
  effects on public, 152
  effects on research, 152–153
  history of, 137–140

Health care reform *(Continued)*
options for
all-government systems, 140–141
compulsory private systems, 141–143
incremental private strategies, 144–146
incremental public strategies, 143–144
Health insurance. *See* Insurance; Insurance
status
Health Insurance Plan of Greater New York, 19
Health maintenance organizations (HMOs),
11–13, 22
effects of reform on, 153
history of, 19
network model, 14
scandals involving Medicaid, 126–127
study of avoidable hospital admissions, 103
study of cost sharing in, 116t, 120
Health outcomes. *See* Outcomes of care
Health Planning and Administration database,
159
Health risk
race and, 39–40, 41t
self-selection of insurance plans and, 49
Health Security Act (HSA), 139, 142, 151, 152
Health status
cost sharing and, 122, 122t, 123t
hospitalizations and, 80
indicators of, 1, 2t
influences on, 99
measures of, 52–54
need for services and, 49–50, 161n
perceived, 50–53, 51t-53t, 109–110
physician visits and, 71–72, 73t, 74, 120
withdrawal of VA benefits and, 126
HealthPASS program of managed care, 131
Healthy Start Program for prenatal care, 98,
107–108
Heritage Foundation support for tax credits,
147
High-tech procedures, deficits in care to
uninsured and, 85
Hispanics
adverse patient outcomes for, 110
health risk of, 39–40, 41t
See also Race
HMOs. *See* Health maintenance organizations
Home care, cost-effectiveness of, 110
Hospital(s)
admissions to. *See* Hospital admissions
care in, 75–86
deaths, 100–101, 101t
length of stay, 76–80, 77t-80t
quality of, 85–86
resource use in, 80, 81t-82t, 83–85, 85t

as location of care, 58
municipal. *See* Municipal hospitals
See also Emergency departments;
Hospitalizations
Hospital admissions
avoidable, 102–106, 105t
rates of, 76–80, 77t-80t
severity of illness and, 101–102
Hospital Cost Containment Act, 139–140
Hospitalizations
age and, 76–77
avoidable, 102–106, 105t
patient health behaviors and, 104–105
effect of cost-sharing on, 118
effect of insurance status on, 78, 79t, 135
extent of Medicaid coverage and, 77, 78
factors affecting, 76–78, 78t, 79t, 80
severity of illness and, 101–102
HSA. *See* Health Security Act

Income
effect on physician visits, 71, 72t
hospitalizations and, 78, 78t, 79t
insurance status and, 34–35, 36, 37, 38t, 47
perceived health status and, 50–51, 52t, 54
Incremental strategies for reform
private
catastrophic coverage, 144
industry pooling mechanisms, 145
other options, 146
subsidized insurance for unemployed, 145
tax credits, 145–146
public, 143–144
Independent practice associations (IPAs), 14
Individual mandates, 141, 142
Industry pooling mechanisms, 145
Industry-specific characteristics
eligibility and, 21–22
of uninsured persons, 31–34, 32, 33, 34t, 35t
Institute of Medicine, 108
Insurance, 17–26
adequacy of, 12
changes in or loss of, 13, 113
outcome indicators, 126
process indicators, 124–126
deficiencies in system, 133
Medicaid. *See* Medicaid
Medicare. *See* Medicare
nongroup, 22–23, 25
private. *See* Private health insurance
public. *See* Medicaid; Medicare; Public
insurance programs
sources of coverage, 17–18
Insurance status

access to care and, 1–16, 2t, 134–137
age factors in, 36–37, 39t
of children, 37–38, 40t
comparisons in, 10–15
direct effects on health, 49
employment and industry characteristics,
    31–34, *32*, *33*, 34t, 35t
family composition and, 40–41, 42t
framework for study of, 3–9
gender and, 38–39, 39t
geography and, 41, *43*
hospitalizations and, 78, 79t, 135
income and education and, 34–35, *36*, *37*, 38t
patient satisfaction and, 111–112, 112t
race and ethnicity factors, 39–40, 41t
special cases in, 11–15
transitions in, 43–44
Intermediate process indicators
convenience, 60–62, 61t
location of care, 57t, 58–60, 59t
for measuring access to care, 7, 8t
use of municipal hospitals, 62
usual or regular source of care, 55–58, 57t
IPAs. *See* Independent practice associations

Kaiser Permanente program, 19
Kennedy, Edward, 139

Length of stay in hospital, 76–80, 77t–80t, 83
Life-saving measures, deficits in care to
    uninsured and, 85
Limitation of activity
as measure of health status, 52–53
physician visits and, 72
Location of care, 56, 57t, 58–60, 59t
effect of insurance status on, 135
hospital resource use and, 84
prenatal, 98, 98t
Longitudinal studies of insurance coverage,
    42–43, 44t, 45t

Managed care, 13–15
effects on service utilization, 128
limitations to study of, 14
Medicaid and, 15–16, 113–124, 126–128, 161n
outcome indicators, 130–132
process indicators, 128–130, 131t
programs for chronically mentally ill, 132
Mandatory renewal, 145
Medicaid, 23–24, 65, 139
Aid to Families with Dependent Children
    (AFDC) and, 41
application process for, 24
background of, 10–11, 160n–161n

costs and budgetary impact of, 2–3
funding levels, 148
spending attributable to, 23–24
effect on health care utilization, 74, 75t,
    162n
effectiveness of, 136–137
effects of loss on medically indigent adults
    (MIAs), 125
eligibility for, 10–11
expansion of, 143
extent of coverage, hospitalizations and,
    77–78
federal requirements, 23–24
income and, 34–35, *36*
managed care and, 15–16, 113–124, 126–128,
    161n
outcome indicators, 130–132
process indicators, 128–130, 131t
physician participation problems, 127
prevention of poor birth outcomes and,
    106–107, 107t, 163n
sporadic coverage, 69–70
use of preventive care by children and, 93–94,
    94t
Medicaid Competition Demonstrations,
    127–128
effect on perinatal outcomes, 130–131
major findings of, 128–129
satisfaction with care in, 130
Medicaid recipients
adequacy of prenatal care for, 96–98, 97t, 98t,
    162n
admission rates and hospital days of, 76–80,
    77t–80t
California "copayment experiment" for, 116t,
    121
emergency department as source of care for,
    59
limited activity of, 52–53
patient dumping and, 91–92, 93t
poor health status of, 54
use of physicians by, 67t, 67–69, 68t
use of prescription drugs by, 87
Medical Outcomes Study Short Form (MOS-SF),
    109
Medical underwriting, 21
Medically indigent adults (MIAs), 125
Medicare, 24–25, 139, 143, 152
funding levels for, 148
MEDLINE database, 159
MIAs. *See* Medically indigent adults
Military-related insurance programs, 17, 18, 24,
    25
Mills, Wilbur, 139

Models
economic, of demand for health care, 3–6, 160n
for measuring access to care, 6–7, 8t, 9
of Medicaid and health care utilization, 74, 75t, 162n
network, for HMOs, 14
Moral hazard, 4
MOS-SF. *See* Medical Outcomes Study Short Form
Municipal hospitals
closing of, 109
effects of reform on, 151
as source of care, 62, 162n

National Cancer Institute, 95
National Center for Health Services Research (NCHSR). *See* Agency for Health Care Policy and Research
National Center for Health Statistics (NCHS), 64, 156
National health insurance (NHI), history of reform efforts, 137–140
National Health Insurance Standards Act, 139
National Health Interview Survey (NHIS), 157
data on physician utilization, 70, 71
National Health Service (NHS [United Kingdom]), 140–141
National Medical Care Expenditure Survey (NMCES), 28, 64, 156–157
National Medical Care Utilization and Expenditure Survey (NMCUES), 11, 28, 53, 156, 162n
aggregate spending by uninsured, 64–65, 65t
physician utilization data, 70
National Medical Expenditure Survey (NMES), 23, 28, 64, 157
NCHS. *See* National Center for Health Statistics
NCHSR. *See* Agency for Health Care Policy and Research
Near-elderly, dynamics of insurance in, 44–45
Network model HMOs, 14
NHI. *See* National health insurance
NHS. *See* National Health Service
Nixon, Richard M., 139
NMCES. *See* National Medical Care Expenditure Survey
NMCUES. *See* National Medical Care Utilization and Expenditure Survey
NMES. *See* National Medical Expenditure Survey
Nongroup coverage, 22–23, 25
Nursing homes
discharge of insured patients to, 100–101
NMES survey of, 157

patient outcomes and, 110–111

OBRA. *See* Omnibus Budget Reconciliation Act
Obstetrical care
deficits in care to uninsured, 84, 85t
See also Prenatal care
Office of National Health Statistics of HCFA, 30, *31*
Office of Technology Assessment, 159
Omnibus Budget Reconciliation Act (OBRA), 38, 127
denial of Medicaid coverage by, 124–125
Out-of-pocket expenditures
per capita expenditures and, 64–66, 65t, 66t
for underinsured persons, 45–46
Outcome indicators
changes in or loss of health insurance, 126
cost-sharing and access to care, 121–124, 122t, 123t
measuring access to care, 7, 8t, 9
Medicaid and managed care, 130–132
Outcomes of care
for cancer, 108–109
effect of insurance status on, 135–136
hospital deaths, 100–101, 101t
hospitalizations
avoidable, 102–106, 105t
severity of illness and, 101–102
improved access and, 147–148
measures of health status and, 109–110
nursing homes and, 110–111
other factors affecting, 136
perinatal, 106–108, 107t, 130–131
satisfaction as, 111–112, 112t

Paperchase system (computerized records search), 159
"Pass-through" provisions, 151
Patient(s)
access to care and, 7, 8t, 160n
health behaviors of, 104–105
satisfaction with care, 111–112, 112t
Patient dumping, 91–92, 93t
Payment caps for insurance coverage, 143
Payment source
access to care and, 16, 152–153
connection with negligence, 86
for hospital care, 75–76
nursing home discharge status and, 111
Per capita expenditures, 64–66, 65t, 66t
Perceived health status, 50–52, 51t–53t, 109–110
Perinatal outcomes
effect of Medicaid managed care on, 130–131
prenatal care and, 106–108, 107t, 163n

Period-of-time estimates of uninsured, 28–29
Phase-in plans for reform, 150–151
Physician(s)
    effect on demand for health care, 4–5
    effects of reform on, 151
    NHIS data on utilization, 70, 71
    as regular source of care, 57–58
Physician visits, 66–75
    effects of cost-sharing on, 117–118
    factors affecting, 70–72
    by Medicaid recipients, 67t, 67–69, 68t
    multivariate analyses of, 72–74, 75t
    by uninsured persons, 67t, 69t, 69–70
"Play or pay" plan, 141
Point-in-time estimates of uninsured, 42–43
Policy characteristics of health system, 7
Policy implications of reform, 133–153
Poverty
    cost sharing and, 120–121
    perinatal outcomes and, 107, 163n
Pre-existing conditions
    denial of coverage and, 22–23, 142
    as measure of health status, 54
Prenatal care, 95–98, 97t, 98t
    adequacy of, for uninsured persons, 96–98,
        97t, 98t, 162n
    outcomes of, 106–108, 107t, 163n
    self-selection of insurance plans and, 49
Prescription drugs, 86–87
    effects of cost-sharing on use of, 118
    withdrawal of VA eligibility and, 125–126
Preventive care, 63–64
    demand for, 4
    prenatal, 95–98, 97t, 98t
    use by adults, 94–95, 95t, 96t
    use by children, 93–94, 94t
Price elasticity, 114
Private health insurance
    access to physicians and, 68t, 68–69
    admission rates, hospital days and, 76–80,
        77t–80t
    history of, 18–19
    out-of-pocket expenditures and, 65–66, 66t
    patient satisfaction with care and, 111–112,
        112t
    problems with, 20–22, 21t
    role of employers in, 19–20
    underinsured persons and, 45
Process indicators
    changes in or loss of insurance, 124–126
    cost-sharing and access to care, 114,
        115t–119t, 116–121
    intermediate, 55–62
    measuring access to care, 7, 8t

Medicaid and managed care, 128–130, 131t
    "ultimate," 63–98
Prospective Payment System, 83
Public health system
    infrastructure of, 147–148
    providers in, 153
    stigma associated with programs, 148
Public hospitals. *See* Municipal hospitals
Public insurance programs, 18
    cost-sharing in, 45
    Medicare, 24–25
    military-related, 25
    patient satisfaction with care and, 111–112,
        112t
    perceived health status and, 52

Quality of care
    effects of reform on, 150
    in hospitals, 85–86
        avoidable admissions and, 103
        mortality rates and, 101
    insurance status and, 135
    outcome-based criteria for, 123

Race
    adverse patient outcomes and, 110
    as barrier to care, 5
    effect on physician visits, 70–71, 71t
    hospital resource use and, 84
    hospitalizations and, 78
    insurance status and, 39–40, 41t
    use of preventive care by adults and, 94
    See also African-Americans; Hispanics
RAND Health Insurance Experiment (HIE), 13,
        80, 155–156, 161n
    categories of services, 117, 118t, 119t
    findings on utilization, 102, 116–117, 117t
    impact of cost-sharing, 114, 115t, 116,
        135–137
    Individual Deductible Plan, 117, 117t
    outcomes of care, 135–136
    indicators of, 121–124, 122t, 123t
    sampling and methodological issues, 118–119
Reagan, Ronald, 126, 140
Risk adjustment, 148–149
"Risk and profit" charges for small group plans,
        20–21
Risk factors, insurance status and, 30, 88
Risk pools for individuals, 145
Robert Wood Johnson Foundation (RWJF)
    surveys, 53, 86, 155, 161n
    of foregone care, 88, 89t
    on use of preventive care by children, 93–94
Roosevelt, Theodore, 137

Rural areas. *See* Geography
RWJF surveys. *See* Robert Wood Johnson
Foundation surveys

Self-selection of insurance plans, 49
Sentinel events, 104
"Set asides," 151
Sexually transmitted diseases, effect of
cost-sharing on treatment for, 124
Single-payer insurance approach, 141, 147
SIPP. *See* Survey of Income and Program
Participation (SIPP)
"Skimming," 148, 161n
Social distance as barrier to care, 5–6
Social Security Act, 36, 138
Title XIX of, 10
Sources of coverage for uninsured persons,
17–26
Southern states, physician utilization in, 71, 71t
SSI. *See* Supplemental Security Income
Subsidized insurance for unemployed persons,
145
Supplemental Security Income (SSI), 23
Supply-side approach to health insurance,
143–144
Survey of Income and Program Participation
(SIPP), 28, 157–158

Tax credits, 145–146
Timeliness of care
patient dumping, 91–92, 93t
problems getting care, 87–88, 89t–90t, 90–91
Transitions in insurance status, 43–44
Travel time, convenience of care and, 61, 61t
Truman, Harry S, 137–139
"20 percent share," 142
Two-tiered health care system, reform and, 148

Ultimate process indicators, 63–98
Underinsurance, 12, 45–47
catastrophic expenses and, 45
defined, 46
Unemployed persons, insurance subsidy for,
142, 145

Uninsured persons, 17–48
adequacy of prenatal care for, 96–98, 97t, 98t,
162n
admission rates and hospital days of, 76–80,
77t–80t
characteristics of, 30–41
dynamics of insurance coverage and, 42–45,
44t, 45t
emergency department use, 59
free or subsidized care for, 5
in-hospital mortality rates for, 100–101, 101t
in-hospital resource use, 80, 81t–82t, 83–85,
85t
issues in measuring, 28–29
lack of regular source of care, 56–57, 57t
numbers of, 29–30, *31*, 31t
increase in, 2–3, 47–48, 133, 160n
physician use, 67t, 69t, 69–70, 73
access and, 68t, 68–69
satisfaction with care and, 111–112, 112t
sources of coverage and, 17–26
survey data on, 26, 28
United Mine Workers Health Plan, 116t, 120
United States
health care costs in, 1, 2t, 133–134
insurance programs contrasted with Canadian
system, 26, 27t
Universal coverage, 146–147
Use-disability ratio, 72
Utilization shortfalls, 73, 80

VA Medical Centers, eligibility for outpatient
care by, 125–126

Waiting times
adverse patient outcomes and, 109–110
convenience of care and, 61–62, 162n
Welfare safety net, 1
Women
prenatal care for, 95–98, 97t, 98t
adequacy of, 96–98, 97t, 98t, 162n
outcomes of, 106–108, 107t, 163n
self-selection of insurance plans and, 49
use of preventive care by, 94–95, 95t, 96t